Intelligence, Espionage, Counterespionage, and Covert Operations

INTERNATIONAL RELATIONS INFORMATION GUIDE SERIES

Series Editor: Garold W. Thumm, Professor of Government and Chairman of the Department, Bates College, Lewiston, Maine

Also in this series:

ARMS CONTROL AND MILITARY POLICY—*Edited by Donald F. Bletz**

THE INTERNATIONAL RELATIONS OF EASTERN EUROPE—*Edited by Robin Remington**

THE EUROPEAN COMMUNITIES—*Edited by J. Bryan Collester**

INTERNATIONAL AND REGIONAL POLITICS IN THE MIDDLE EAST AND NORTH AFRICA—*Edited by Ann Schulz*

INTERNATIONAL ORGANIZATIONS—*Edited by Alexine Atherton*

LATIN AMERICA—*Edited by John J. Finan**

THE MULTINATIONAL CORPORATION—*Edited by Helga Hernes*

POLITICAL DEVELOPMENT—*Edited by Arpad von Lazar and Bruce Magid**

SOUTH ASIA—*Edited by Richard J. Kozicki**

SOUTHEAST ASIA—*Edited by Richard Butwell**

THE STUDY OF INTERNATIONAL RELATIONS—*Edited by Robert L. Pfaltzgraff, J*

SUB-SAHARAN AFRICA—*Edited by W.A.E. Skurnik*

U.S.S.R.—*Edited by David Williams and Karen Williams**

U.S. INVOLVEMENT IN VIETNAM—*Edited by Allan W. Cameron*

*in preparation

The above series is part of the
GALE INFORMATION GUIDE LIBRARY

The Library consists of a number of separate series of guides covering major areas in the social sciences, humanities, and current affairs.

General Editor: Paul Wasserman, Professor and former Dean, School of Library and Information Services, University of Maryland

Managing Editor: Denise Allard Adzigian, Gale Research Company

Intelligence, Espionage, Counterespionage, and Covert Operations

A GUIDE TO INFORMATION SOURCES

Volume 2 in the International Relations Information Guide Series

Paul W. Blackstock

Professor of International Relations
University of South Carolina
Columbia

Frank L. Schaf, Jr.

U.S. Army Colonel (Ret.)
Presently affiliated with Westinghouse
Corporation

Gale Research Company
Book Tower, Detroit, Michigan 48226

Library of Congress Cataloging in Publication Data

Blackstock, Paul W
   Intelligence, espionage, counterespionage, and covert operations.

   (International relations information guide series; v.2)
   Bibliography: p. 255
   Includes index.
   1. Intelligence service—Bibliography. 2. Espionage—Bibli-
ography. 3. Subversive activities—Bibliography. I. Schaf,
Frank L., joint author. II. Title.
Z6724.17B55   [UB250]   016.327′12   74-11567
ISBN 0-8103-1323-5

VITAE

Paul W. Blackstock is a professor of international relations in the department of government and international studies at the University of South Carolina in Columbia. He attained his Ph.D. magna cum laude in international relations from American University. He served in army intelligence during World War II; was an intelligence specialist on Western Europe and North Africa for Army G-2, 1945-51; and was a psychological warfare specialist in the office of the chief of psychological warfare, specializing in Russian and Eastern European satellite affairs, 1951-60. Blackstock is the author of THE STRATEGY OF SUBVERSION: MANIPULATING THE POLITICS OF OTHER NATIONS; AGENTS OF DECEIT: FRAUDS, FORGERIES AND POLITICAL INTRIGUE AMONG NATIONS; THE SECRET ROAD TO WORLD WAR II, SOVIET VERSUS WESTERN INTELLIGENCE, 1921-39; as well as numerous scholarly articles and monographs.

Frank L. Schaf, Jr., is a retired U.S. Army colonel presently working with Westinghouse Corporation in intelligence subject matter; he has also served as a consultant and advisor to various government agencies since his retirement. He attended the University of Cincinnati in 1940 and has also attended U.S. Air Force Command and Staff College, U.S. Army War College, Lacaze Academy of Language, specializing in French, and the University of Utah, specializing in Russian. During his military career he served as senior intelligence advisor to the South Vietnamese assistant chief of staff; worked for the Defense Intelligence Agency; was chief of intelligence and security of an Army Technical Service; a military technical intelligence officer in the office of the assistant chief of staff (intelligence), Department of Army Headquarters during the Korean War; and technical intelligence officer in the Philippines during World War II.

CONTENTS

Contents

Contents

ACKNOWLEDGMENTS

The authors wish to express their appreciation for the helpful cooperation of the interlibrary loan staff of the University of South Carolina's McKissick Memorial Library in the preparation of this volume. The patient, unflagging aid of two graduate assistants, Michael Janas and Theodore Bucholz, in the early compilation stages is also acknowledged. Professor Blackstock also thanks the Department of Government and International Studies for released research time during the summer of 1974, and for assistance in the typing and preparation of the manuscript. In this regard the work of Annie J. Mobley was outstanding. Colonel Schaf wishes to thank his wife, Leva S. Schaf, for her encouragement and assistance. He also thanks Denise Allard Adzigian, the editor from Gale Research Company, for her assistance over and above the usual.

Department of Government and International Studies,
University of South Carolina

Paul W. Blackstock
Frank L. Schaf, Jr.

Introduction

A GENERAL CRITIQUE OF THE LITERATURE

The importance of intelligence, espionage, and covert political operations can hardly be overemphasized in a world which lives under the shadow of thermonuclear holocaust. Each of the nuclear powers regards intelligence as essential to its security, makes use of espionage to collect information, and employs covert operations as a substitute for the open use of military force. All states make use of counterespionage agencies or techniques to thwart the positive intelligence efforts directed at themselves by their neighbors and, if possible, to abort any covert operations of which they may be the targets.

Given the importance of intelligence, the lack of a selected, annotated bibliography on the subject is surprising, and it is hoped that this reference guide will help meet the need. However, there are reasons for the gap. Not only does the subject have many politically sensitive ramifications, but even the terms used are confused and confusing. Expressions such as "Soviet (or U.S.) intelligence" are used as a kind of shorthand for all the intelligence and security agencies of the state concerned. The primary function of such agencies is the collection, evaluation, and dissemination of information for decision-making purposes. Only a fraction of such information is collected by espionage agents using clandestine techniques and methods. Nevertheless, popular usage confuses espionage, which is only one means of collecting information, with the entire intelligence function. Melodramatic spy novels and motion pictures reinforce this mistaken notion.

Because there is so much confusion in terminology, the student or businessman seeking a comprehensive view of the subject must look through the card index files of whatever library he uses under a variety of headings such as "Intelligence," "Espionage and Counterespionage," and "Secret Service."

Roughly nine tenths of the serious literature on intelligence has been written in English or German. But the scholar using German libraries and sources will find a similar confusion of terms such as Nachrichtendienst ("Intelligence Service"), Geheimdienst ("Secret Service"), and Spionage ("espionage").

Whatever library he uses, the inquirer will find its holdings heavily weighted in favor of espionage and espionage fiction in the "great, true spy stories" tradition. The serious literature dealing with intelligence, its production and use, as a basis for foreign policy decision making tends to be lost in the flood of glamorized memoirs or historical accounts of the "now it can be told" variety. The serious student will quickly discover that the relevant literature is based almost entirely on secondary sources, since governments classify their official intelligence records as secret and attempt to prevent any unauthorized disclosure of intelligence methods or sources. Unlike diplomatic archives and similar official papers, intelligence records are rarely made available to scholars; and intelligence aides leaving government service are sworn to secrecy for a period of several years. In one case a former intelligence aide, who had written a second novel based on his experiences inside the American intelligence community, was required by court order to submit that novel to the CIA for security clearance.

Unfortunately, authorized disclosures by intelligence agencies themselves must also be used with caution since they are usually made for mixed security or political warfare purposes. Official revelations about the extent and menace of enemy espionage serve to heighten vigilance and bolster or tighten internal security. Such disclosures were extensively used by both sides during the cold war; they have continued during the detente which followed. For example, between 1964 and 1970 the USSR published roughly 190 articles extolling the exploits and virtues of Soviet intelligence, and some 490 articles warning against Western intelligence. In all fairness it should be noted that many of the publications by the U.S. Senate Judiciary Internal Security Subcommittee serve a similar warning function in the United States.

Since intelligence agencies try to improve their respective images and blacken those of their rivals, the reader would do well to treat all official and semi-official disclosures with caution and a large dose of skepticism. After all, one should always bear in mind that part of the mission of any intelligence agency is to confuse and mislead its rivals or opponents. This political warfare function has assumed such importance in the post-World War II period that some intelligence agencies have departments which specialize in the subtle spread of misinformation by spurious or forged documents, memoirs, and so forth. Some of the outstanding products of such disinformation departments are noted in the section of this bibliography which deals with covert operations.

But there are other factors which make for bias or slanting even in the serious literature of this obviously controversial field. Intelligence agencies are tightly closed societies which produce intense parochial institutional loyalties. Officials who retire or leave this field and later write about it naturally reflect a favorable bias toward their craft, and toward the particular agency in which they have served, especially if their careers have been highly rewarding both personally and professionally. In such cases their memoirs tend to read like institutional advertising. Allen Dulles's THE CRAFT OF INTELLIGENCE (1963), Lyman Kirkpatrick's THE REAL CIA (1968), and Roger Hilsman's TO MOVE A NATION (1967), clearly manifest this tendency. On the other hand, there is a growing body of literature produced by former intelligence aides who have become disillusioned with the profession, and especially with the way intelligence has been organized or has functioned. Books written by such authors tend to be highly critical and to reflect a negative bias. Even when the purpose of such criticism is to call attention to the need for organizational and functional reforms, the memoirs of former working-level aides are likely to be dismissed as inconsequential by reviews in the press. For example, Patrick McGarvey's CIA: THE MYTH AND THE MADNESS (1972) was tersely dismissed as "a useful book as far as it goes" in an anonymous twenty-line review in the NEW YORK TIMES BOOK REVIEW (23 March 1973).

Finally, on the other end of the spectrum from institutional advertising, there is a class of popular, journalistic literature which specializes in sensational revelations concerning covert operations such as the CIA-conducted Bay of Pigs episode. Clearly such works must be treated with caution in spite of their transient popularity. Wherever possible the annotations to the items listed in this bibliography attempt to indicate whatever bias or slanting is apparent.

SCOPE AND ORGANIZATION OF THIS BIBLIOGRAPHY

Two comprehensive bibliographies dealing with intelligence are discussed in the section on bibliography resources below. By contrast, this bibliography is highly selective. Since it is designed primarily for the general American public, it is limited mainly to books and articles in the English language. Only the most important foreign language titles are noted. Foreign language works of lesser significance are accessible through the comprehensive bibliographies listed. For each entry an attempt has been made to provide as much publication data as is available. Unfortunately, it is not possible to supply complete publication data for each work cited, since many publications appeared originally in classified form or have classified annexes to which public access is denied. The information given about the plethora of paperback editions, often in foreign languages, is also strictly limited. Most libraries do not acquire such editions, and information about them can be sought in either comprehensive bibliographies or in publishers' guides. The primary emphasis here is on hardcover editions of important books. However, important journal or magazine articles as well as key articles from major newspapers such as the NEW YORK TIMES are also included.

The bibliography is intended as a guide for the layman but may also be found useful by political analysts and students of international relations and foreign affairs.

Part I
GENERAL BIBLIOGRAPHIC RESOURCES

Due to the confusion of terms, books and articles on intelligence, espionage, and covert operations are listed under a wide variety of headings in the subject index of the U.S. Library of Congress and in the corresponding catalogs of other libraries. However, there are two comprehensive bibliographies which may be consulted to identify books on these subjects. Each of these bibliographies has an extended critique of the literature. In addition there are certain specialized bibliographies which are useful to the person interested in researching a specific aspect of intelligence, espionage, or covert operations. These comprehensive and specialized bibliographies are cited in the following pages.

Chapter 1

COMPREHENSIVE BIBLIOGRAPHIES

Gunzenhauser, Max. GESCHICHTE DER GEHEIMEN NACHRICHTENDIENST: (SPIONAGE, SABOTAGE UND ABWEHR): LITERATUR BERICHTE UND BIBLIOGRAPHIE. Frankfurt: Bernard und Graefe, 1968. xiv, 434 p. Name, author, and geographic indexes.

"The second comprehensive bibliography of secret intelligence. An 80-page introductory essay precedes some 400 pages of bibliography. Although a smaller effort than Harris (1968), it includes many items, particularly German ones, missed by the earlier work. Moreover, the two bibliographies complement one another as the Gunzenhauser bibliography is organized chronologically and geographically while the Harris one is organized under 27 topics." Barton Whaley, CODEWORD BARBAROSSA (Cambridge, Mass.: M.I.T. Press, 1973, pp. 329-30).

The 4,000 entries cover titles in English and several European languages, without annotation, although the most important works are discussed in the introductory critique of the literature. The discussion of strategic intelligence is relatively weak; nevertheless, this work is an indispensable guide for the scholar and researcher, and has been used extensively in compiling the present bibliography.

Harris, William R. INTELLIGENCE AND NATIONAL SECURITY: A BIBLIOGRAPHY WITH SELECTED ANNOTATIONS. Rev. ed. Cambridge, Mass.: Harvard University, Center for International Affairs, 1968. xcii, 838 p. Multilithed.

"With 838 pages covering several thousand books, articles, and papers, this is the most comprehensive bibliography of the subject publicly available. The author's 92-page introductory bibliographic essay is the only such guide into the labyrinthine literature of intelligence." Barton Whaley, CODEWORD BARBAROSSA (Cambridge, Mass.: M.I.T. Press, 1973, p. 330).

The work is divided into three volumes: a 92-page volume which contains a critique of the literature, and two supplements in which the titles are listed--an extremely awkward arrangement described by the author as "unwieldy and unplanned."

Chapter 2

SELECTIVE BIBLIOGRAPHIES

As a result of the interest in intelligence stimulated by World War II, three bibliographies on intelligence and espionage were prepared by U.S. agencies. A fourth bibliography was authored by Joseph S. Galland. All suffer from being out of date. Additionally, the majority of the items in the three government bibliographies are mainly personal memoirs by individual espionage or counterespionage agents, and illustrate the limitations for serious study of all such works.

Galland, Joseph Stanislaus. AN HISTORICAL AND ANALYTICAL BIBLIOGRA-PHY OF THE LITERATURE OF CRYPTOLOGY. Northwestern University Studies in the Humanities Series, no. 10. Evanston, III.: Northwestern University Press, 1945. viii, 209 p. Reprint. New York: AMS Press, 1970. 209 p.

> A solid work. An adequate substitute may be found in David Kahn's THE CODE BREAKERS (cited in chapter 11, section A), which in effect represents a sort of classified bibliography on communications intelligence.

Haven, Violet S., comp. "Espionage: Bibliography--1942." Washington, D.C.: U.S. Department of Justice Library, 1942. Unpaged. Typescript, mimeographed.

> This list consists of sixteen typewritten pages containing about 250 entries, with emphasis on counterespionage.

U.S. Department of State. "Intelligence, a Bibliography of its Functions, Methods and Techniques, Part I, Bibliography No. 33." Washington, D.C.: December 20, 1948. Mimeographed, unbound.

> See next item.

_____. "Intelligence, a Bibliography of Its Functions, Methods, and Techniques, Part II: Periodical and Newspaper Articles, Bibliography No. 331." Washington, D.C.: April 11, 1949. Mimeographed, unbound.

Selective Bibliographies

The two-part State Department bibliography of more than 700 items was compiled from an unpublished bibliography developed by the Office of Strategic Services (OSS), and from entries in the Library of Congress card index.

Chapter 3
ENCYCLOPEDIA ARTICLES

The concept of covert operations is so new that there are no encyclopedia articles on the subject in spite of the fact that the United States and Great Britain developed special agencies (the American Office of Strategic Services and the British Special Operations Executive) to carry out such operations during World War II.

The first encyclopedia article on espionage appears in Diderot's classic ENCYCLOPEDIE (Paris, 1751, V, 971) under the rubric espion. The spy is defined as "a person paid to examine the actions, movements, etc. of another, and especially to discover the state of military affairs." This brief article also contains the famous observation that "an ambassador is sometimes a distinguished spy who is protected by the law of nations."

Most encyclopedia articles on either espionage or intelligence reflect the fact that intelligence agencies regard any disclosure of sources or methods as a breach of security. Hence the articles tend to be historical summaries rather than substantive or analytical treatments of either espionage or intelligence. With a few recent exceptions most articles also omit consideration of modern scientific and technological advances such as technical sensors, which have produced important new means of collecting information. Representative articles are annotated below.

BOL'SHAIA SOVETSKAIA ENTSIKLOPEDIIA. 2d ed. Moscow: 1955. Vol. 35, pp. 591-92.

> Although the USSR has one of the most formidable combined espionageintelligence-security police organizations of modern times, the Soviet encyclopedia has only one article under the heading "intelligence" (razvedka) which deals exclusively with military reconnaissance. There is nothing under the rubrics "espionage" or "security services."

Encyclopedia Articles

ENCYCLOPEDIA AMERICANA

Blackstock, Paul W. "Espionage." International ed. New York: Americana Corp., 1973. Vol. 10, pp. 584-87.

> The article discusses and evaluates espionage as one of the means by which intelligence agencies collect information through their clandestine services, and notes the relative decline of its importance as new technological means of surveillance have been developed (technical sensors). Summarizes principles and techniques of recruitment, cover, communications, agent handling, and organization of clandestine services.

Hoover, John Edgar. "Espionage and Counterespionage." New York: Americana Corp., 1965. Vol. 10, pp. 504-6.

> The article by the former director of the Federal Bureau of Investigation begins with a definition of terms, followed by a historical summary of famous espionage cases from ancient times through the post-World War II period. There is a section on the espionage agent and his training, another on techniques, and a final section on "security and democracy," which reflects the familiar cold war orientation of the author of MASTERS OF DECEIT (cited in chapter 7, section A).

Ransom, Harry Howe. "Intelligence, Strategic." International ed. New York: Americana Corp., 1973. Vol. 15, pp. 246-48.

> This substantive article by the author of THE INTELLIGENCE ESTABLISHMENT (see chapter 4, section A), stresses basic definitions and concepts, the intelligence process (collection, evaluation, and dissemination to decision makers), and describes briefly the intelligence organizations of the United States, Great Britain, and the Soviet Union.

ENCYCLOPAEDIA BRITANNICA

Don, W.J. [pseud.]. "Espionage." Chicago: Encyclopaedia Britannica, 1954. Vol. 12, pp 459-62.

> The author is presumably William Joseph Donovan, head of the U.S. Office of Strategic Services during World War II. The article is a general survey which discusses the necessity, scope, types of intelligence, and organization, stressing the argument: "It is only when intelligence collection, analysis, evaluation, synthesis and dissemination are in one place and under one direc-

tion that the optimum value can be obtained."

Ransom, Harry Howe. "Intelligence and Counterintelligence."
15th ed. Chicago: Encyclopaedia Britannica, 1974. Vol. 9,
pp. 679-86.

> The author of this excellent, substantive article also
> wrote the article on the same subject for the ENCY-
> CLOPEDIA AMERICANA (above). It discusses defini-
> tions, concepts, the intelligence process itself, and
> describes briefly the intelligence organizations of the
> great world powers. Brief bibliography included.

Stessin, Lawrence. "Intelligence, Military, Political and Industrial." Chicago: Encyclopaedia Britannica, 1972. Vol. 12,
pp. 347-50.

> The article is for the most part a general historical sur-
> vey with brief descriptions of the modern intelligence
> organizations of the United States, the USSR, Great
> Britain, and France, followed by a section on industrial
> espionage.

ENCYCLOPEDIA OF THE SOCIAL SCIENCES

Rowan, Richard Wilmer. "Espionage." New York: Macmillan,
1931. Vol. 5, pp. 594-96.

> This three-page article by a prolific writer and historian
> in the espionage field is devoted almost entirely to a
> history of espionage since ancient times, with an added
> paragraph on industrial espionage and a generalized dis-
> cussion of countermeasures.

INTERNATIONAL ENCYCLOPEDIA OF THE SOCIAL SCIENCES

Ransom, Harry Howe. "Intelligence, Political and Military."
New York: Macmillan and the Free Press, 1968. Pp. 415-21.

> The article is a general survey which stresses definitions,
> reviews the basic literature, and gives suggestions for
> further social science research.

Seth, Ronald. ENCYCLOPEDIA OF ESPIONAGE. Garden City, N.Y.:
Doubleday, 1974. 718 p. Index. British ed. London: New English Library,
1975. 683 p. Bibliography.

> A remarkable compilation of information on espionage by a very
> prolific author on intelligence subject matter and a World War II

British agent. Easy to use, the encyclopedia arranges entries by names of spies (the first entry is ex-Soviet agent Colonel Rudolph Abel), intelligence organizations, espionage networks, and well-known espionage incidents. Each entry is followed by bibliographic references for additional reading or research. The author notes that "where no such bibliography is provided, in most cases the information has come only from my notebooks."

Although this work is billed on the cover of the English edition as "the Spy's Who's Who," its coverage is almost entirely historical. It is useful as a biographical reference and also because it describes various networks and operations such as the Red Orchestra or Gieske's Englandspiel. However, there are many curious gaps in the biographical coverage. For example, there are almost three pages on Sir Paul Dukes who directed British espionage in the USSR during the revolutionary period, but nothing at all on Sir Bruce Lockhart, Sidney Reilly, Boris Savinkov, Captain George Hill, and other British agents active during the same period. Moreover, the lack of an index makes the work more suitable for bedside reading than for reference purposes.

U.S. Department of Defense. DICTIONARY OF MILITARY AND ASSOCIATED TERMS. Joint Chiefs of Staff Publication, no. 1. Washington, D.C.: Government Printing Office, January 3, 1972. vii, 350 p.

An important reference for definitions of terms used in intelligence. Contains more than 200 definitions of terms used in intelligence, counterintelligence, and security. Appendix D contains a list of terms used in intelligence handling, and Appendix E a list of terms used in reconnaissance and surveillance. Also listed are definitions of intelligence terms agreed to by the North Atlantic Treaty Organization (NATO), Southeast Asia Treaty Organization (SEATO), Central Treaty Organization (CENTO), and the Inter-American Defense Board (IADB) through international standardization agreements.

Part II
STRATEGIC INTELLIGENCE

In modern American usage "intelligence" or "strategic intelligence" means "evaluated or processed information about the power and intentions of foreign nations or other external phenomenon of significance in decision-making councils. Most generally the term refers to the informational needs of national government officials, particularly foreign and defense policy makers. Harry Howe Ransom, STRATEGIC INTELLIGENCE (Morristown, N.J.: General Learning Press, 1973, p. 1). The term is thus roughly equivalent to "foreign intelligence" as in the German, Feindnachrichtendienst. Since intelligence information is processed by bureaucracies, most general works on the subject discuss organizational needs as well as methods of collecting, processing, and disseminating information to policy makers for their use in decision making. In addition to their reporting and analytic functions, intelligence agencies also provide the policy maker with political, economic, and military estimates or assessments. In American practice these estimates include short- and long-range appraisals of the political-economic-military capabilities, vulnerabilities, intentions, and probable courses of action of other states, and are called National Intelligence Estimates. In addition to such traditional areas of appraisal, estimates concerning foreign scientific and technological developments have recently been added, and have increased in importance since World War II.

Of special interest and importance to both the general reader and the policy or decision maker are the intelligence-based studies and estimates produced by such established organizations as the International Institute for Strategic Studies in London and the Stockholm International Peace Research Institute (SIPRI). The London institute is international in its membership, staff, and governing council, and is independent of governments. (For a description of the work of the London institute see the article by Drew Middleton, "London Group Provides Army Intelligence to All," New York Times, 27 December 1972.)

Much of the serious literature on intelligence has been written by American or British authors and is based on the experience of the agencies of their respective countries. However, the conclusions reached may well apply to the intelligence process and agencies of other states as well, after due allowances have been made for significant differences in the culture patterns concerned.

Part II

STRATEGIC INTELLIGENCE

Chapter 4

THEORY, DOCTRINE, AND ORGANIZATION

A. UNITED STATES (GENERAL WORKS AND SURVEYS)

Alsop, Stewart. THE CENTER: PEOPLE AND POWER IN POLITICAL WASHING-
TON. New York: Harper & Row, 1968. xiv, 365 p. Index.

> The author, the late Washington columnist and political journalist,
> provides a vivid portrait of political Washington, D.C., and the
> people who inhabit it. This is not a book about intelligence, but
> in it there are some excellent descriptions of the people who were
> important in the CIA at the time the book was written. Described
> in detail are the various directors of Central Intelligence and their
> senior directorate chiefs: the deputy director for plans (now deputy
> director of operations and head of the Clandestine Services), the
> deputy director for intelligence, the deputy director for research,
> and the head of the Board of National Estimates. Also described
> are the origin of the U-2 project and the Bay of Pigs operation.
> The descriptions are always in terms of the political atmosphere
> of the Washington scene.

Blackstock, Paul W. "Intelligence and Covert Operations: Changing Doctrine
and Practice." Columbia: University of South Carolina, Department of Government and International Studies, December 1973. 125 p. Mimeographed.

> "Another example of imaginative and rewarding work on the re-
> search frontier is the project undertaken by Paul W. Blackstock
> of the Institute of International Studies, University of South Caro-
> lina. Professor Blackstock circulated a 'Confidential Intelligence
> Questionnaire' among a group of intelligence aides experienced in
> key posts 'at the working level' within the intelligence system.
> In his questionnaire, Blackstock set forth a number of published
> observations by scholars relating to a broad range of topics re-
> lated to the intelligence system, requesting detailed comments
> on such observations from his respondents." Harry Howe Ransom,
> STRATEGIC INTELLIGENCE (Morristown, N.J.: General Learning
> Press, 1973, p. 19).

A second such questionnaire was sent out following President Richard M. Nixon's reorganization of U.S. intelligence in the fall of 1971. Questionnaires were also sent to Major General Sir Kenneth Strong, former head of the British joint intelligence bureau and author of MEN OF INTELLIGENCE (cited in chapter 5, section A). With his permission, perceptive judgments from this work were added where pertinent.

Although the sample was limited, this is the first survey research of its kind outside the restricted studies made within the intelligence community itself. Part 1 deals with major continuing problems of intelligence doctrine and practice, part 2 with covert political operations, and part 3 with intelligence estimates and decision making. The appendix is a case study of intelligence and decision making in the Gulf of Tonkin incident.

Cline, Ray S. SECRETS, SPIES AND SCHOLARS: BLUEPRINT OF THE ESSENTIAL CIA. Washington, D.C.: Acropolis Books, 1976. 294 p. Index, notes, glossary of terms, illustrations, organization charts.

An authoritative description and explanation of the evolution of central intelligence organization and functions in the United States from 1939 to the present. The author, presently director of studies at the Georgetown University Center for Strategic and International Studies, was a member of OSS, an official of the CIA from 1949 to 1969, deputy director of CIA for intelligence production from 1962 to 1966, and director of the Intelligence and Research Division of the Department of State from 1969 through 1973, uses this extensive background and experience to authenticate and explain how the CIA evolved as it did. He covers how it conducted its purely intelligence functions of information collection, analysis, and estimation, and how it became involved extensively in covert political actions. Cline evaluates the last two years of intense publicity and investigation of intelligence activities and explains the right and wrong actions performed by the CIA. Recommendations are made regarding the separation of intelligence and covert action functions through organizational rearrangement. The author describes his work as one third intelligence history, one third personal memoir, and one third political explanation and evaluation. A unique and important contribution to intelligence literature.

Dulles, Allen Welsh. THE CRAFT OF INTELLIGENCE. New York: Harper & Row, 1963. 277 p. Bibliography, index, photographs.

For its time a rare insight into the philosophy and doctrine of strategic intelligence by the director of the CIA during the period 1953-61. The process of intelligence is described from the development of the requirements of U.S. decision makers through information collection and analysis. The useful bibliography of twenty-one titles is devoted mainly to books on espionage and covert political operations. Dulles was one of the first officials of the intelligence community to expose details of the collection of foreign intelligence information by means of technical sensors. A solid contribution to the basic literature on intelligence and its contribution to national security.

Farago, Ladislas. WAR OF WITS, THE ANATOMY OF ESPIONAGE AND IN-TELLIGENCE. New York: Funk & Wagnalls, 1954. ix, 379 p. Notes, index of names, illustrations.

A more or less journalistic treatment of the complete panorama of intelligence and its allied subjects--counterintelligence, espionage, sabotage, and psychological warfare. The author was affiliated with naval intelligence during World War II. Twenty-four pages of notes and references present useful bibliographic source material.

Kellis, James G. "The Development of U.S. National Intelligence, 1941-1961." Doctoral dissertation, Georgetown University, 1963. 352 p. Appendix, bibliography, organization charts, no index.

The preface states that the author "has limited his effort to the history of the U.S. Intelligence for the past twenty years. He has emphasized the causes which led to the acceleration of our effort in intelligence, traced the history of the various organizations which constitute the U.S. intelligence community, reviewed some of their accomplishments and failures, and discussed their organization. . . . The establishment, development, organization, and accomplishments of the OSS are discussed at considerable length. This is partly due to the fact that . . . a substantial source of original material on the OSS was made available to the author by the late Major General William J. Donovan, the Director of OSS from 1941 to 1945."

The author served in the OSS, and in the Far East with the CIA until 1954. In addition to certain of the Donovan papers, the bibliography lists a number of State and Defense Department mimeographed papers on various aspects of intelligence.

Kent, Sherman. STRATEGIC INTELLIGENCE FOR AMERICAN WORLD POLICY. 3d ed. Hamden, Conn.: Archon Books, 1965. 226 p. Index, appendix, illustrations.

The first edition was published by Princeton University Press in 1949 and thus was one of the early basic texts on the development of postwar strategic intelligence doctrine. A basic primer on the intelligence analytical process as opposed to collection or espionage. The author, one-time Yale history professor, was a wartime member of the Research and Analysis Branch of OSS, and transferred to State Department intelligence when the branch of OSS was transferred. After the formation of the CIA he became the leading theoretician on the Board of National Estimates, and helped evolve the methodologies for producing the family of National Intelligence Estimates supporting security policy development in the United States. The 1965 edition has a new preface in which Kent defends U.S. emphasis on research and analysis of open sources as a main thrust of intelligence production. This is contrasted to Soviet emphasis on espionage as an information source, which was set forth in Alexander Orlov's HANDBOOK OF INTELLIGENCE AND GUERRILLA WARFARE (cited in chapter 4, section B2).

Knorr, Klaus, FOREIGN INTELLIGENCE AND THE SOCIAL SCIENCES. Research Monograph, no. 17. Princeton, N.J.: Princeton University Press, 1964. 58 p. Bibliography.

In this work Knorr sets forth the need for a comprehensive theory to support the predictive function of intelligence production, as opposed to the traditional acceptance of the wisdom of the estimator, or acceptance of traditional doctrine that does not make use of the lessons to be derived from social science analysts and methodologies. He argues that in the absence of theories "we have no criteria for measuring or judging whether intelligence production in the United States is done well or badly, or for specifying ways of improving it."

Pettee, George S. THE FUTURE OF AMERICAN SECRET INTELLIGENCE. Washington, D.C.: Infantry Journal Press, 1946. ix, 120 p. Index.

Written by a World War II intelligence analyst and professor of political science at Amherst, this is the first published comprehensive critique of wartime strategic intelligence. Pettee summarizes the shortcomings of wartime strategic intelligence production, sets down the essential lessons to be learned from the wartime experience, and forecasts the steps necessary to ensure proper intelligence support of the nation's decision process in both war and peace. He was one of the very first authors to set down the requirements for the management of big postwar strategic intelligence. Despite its date of publication the book remains valuable.

Platt, Washington. STRATEGIC INTELLIGENCE PRODUCTION: BASIC PRINCIPLES. New York: Praeger, 1957. xv, 302 p. Appendix, index, bibliography for each chapter, charts.

A retired brigadier general of the U.S. Army Reserve, experienced in two wars in the field of combat intelligence, provides a definitive analysis of the job of an intelligence officer. He distinguishes between traditional combat intelligence and the newer (at that time) strategic intelligence. He explains the basic principles and doctrine of intelligence production and examines the application of the social sciences and related fields to intelligence production. Platt suggests that business management specialists may also find applications for some of the concepts developed by the strategic intelligence analyst. This has been the case and users of modern systems analysis have borrowed some of the concepts developed in intelligence.

Ransom, Harry Howe. CAN AMERICAN DEMOCRACY SURVIVE COLD WAR. Garden City, N.Y.: Doubleday, 1963. Paperback ed. Garden City, N.Y.: Doubleday, Anchor, 1964. xvi, 262 p.

In chapters 6 and 7 Ransom deals with strategic intelligence and some of the basic problems of an intelligence system in a democratic society. He also gives a case history of intelligence in the Korean War.

_____. CENTRAL INTELLIGENCE AND NATIONAL SECURITY. Cambridge, Mass.: Harvard University Press, 1959. xiv, 287 p. Appendix, index, bibliography, notes, chart.

One of the best texts published in the late '50s on the nature of intelligence. The author prepared the book from materials prepared for use in the defense policy seminar conducted by the Defense Studies Program of Harvard University. The book is an early edition of THE INTELLIGENCE ESTABLISHMENT (see below).

_____. THE INTELLIGENCE ESTABLISHMENT. Cambridge, Mass.: Harvard University Press, 1970. 309 p. Bibliography, notes, index.

The best single scholarly work on the subject. Ransom's goal was "to describe objectively contemporary central intelligence insofar as this can be done from non-secret sources." He summarizes the contents of his work as "a descriptive analysis of the nature of intelligence, the development of the central intelligence structure, an overview of the national intelligence community, intelligence in the military services and other major government agencies, top-level coordination of intelligence, the issue of secrecy and congressional surveillance, a description of how the British have managed similar problems and functions, and a discussion of some major problems of organization, procedure, and performance."

_____. STRATEGIC INTELLIGENCE. Morristown, N.J.: General Learning Press, 1973. 20 p. Bibliography.

An excellent, tightly written "learning module" designed for both students and the general public, similar in scope and content to an encyclopedia article. The second half of the article, "Strategic Intelligence as a Research Frontier," incorporates the results of an interview survey made in 1971-72.

Roberts, John W., Jr. "Toward a Theory of Intelligence: Testing for Correlates of Forecasting." Master's thesis, University of Georgia, 1973. 228 p. Mimeographed.

Roberts applies a nomothetic or "behavioral" approach to intelligence estimates. He states, "In the light of the important contribution intelligence carries into the policy-making process, and the problems associated with forecasting, this paper proposes to investigate the process and limitations of intelligence forecasting and the role it plays in policy decision-making." Under "Findings and Implications" he summarizes the work as follows: "This study has attempted to contribute to the development of a theory of intelligence by: (1) exploring the present state of intelligence theory; (2) discussing basic concepts and assumptions of the intelligence function; and (3) testing the relationships between analytically operationalized concepts believed to be operating in the intelligence forecasting process. Based upon the test applied to these correlates of forecasting, this final section will include a discussion of: the results of the test; the validity of the data; the theoretical implications of the results; and the limitations of the investigation." The first section, "A Perspective on Intelligence Theory," is an excellent summary of general intelligence doctrine.

Schaf, Frank L., Jr. "The Evolution of Modern Strategic Intelligence." Carlisle Barracks, Pa.: U.S. Army War College, 1965. 698 p. Mimeographed. Bibliography, organization charts.

The author, an army officer (now retired) with extensive experience in strategic intelligence, examines the intelligence organizations of England, France, Germany, USSR, and the United States that evolved during World War II, and points up the differences and similarities. He provides comparative analysis of the organizational and doctrinal responses in each country as warfare changed and as requirements for intelligence changed. Emphasis is placed on analysis of the advent of long-range missiles, radar, atomic weapons, and other technological innovations into strategic warfare, and the effects these innovations had on intelligence. The effects of the World War II experience on U.S. strategic intelligence are analyzed for the period 1945 through 1964.

U.S. Congress. Senate. Select Committee to Study Governmental Operations with Respect to Intelligence Activities. FOREIGN AND MILITARY INTELLIGENCE, Book I, and INTELLIGENCE ACTIVITIES AND THE RIGHTS OF AMERICANS, Book II. 94th Cong., 2d sess., April 26, 1976. Rept. no. 94-755. Book I: 651 p. Glossary, organization charts, appendices, footnotes. Book II: 396 p. Appendices, footnotes with bibliographic references.

The result of fifteen months of investigation into the activities of the CIA, FBI, the defense intelligence community, National Security Agency, National Security Council, and the Office of the Director of Central Intelligence, this final report of the committee chaired by Senator Frank Church of Idaho contains a wealth of information, not previously published, on the scope, activities, and evolution of the Washington-based national (or strategic) intelligence community. The report also contains the recommendations of the Select Committee for reforms in the intelligence community.

Book I contains an abundance of details on the evolution of the organizations of U.S. strategic intelligence, primarily the CIA. Included also is a windfall of information and analyses on the production of intelligence estimates in support of national decision making, on counterintelligence, and on covert action or political warfare activities of the CIA. There are good analyses of the relationships between intelligence producers and intelligence consumers and of the process of generating intelligence requirements. Details are also available on the intelligence budget process, and a constitutional framework for intelligence activities is presented.

Book II contains a remarkably detailed history of the development and growth of domestic intelligence from 1936, through the cold war period, to the present. Activities of the FBI and the CIA are emphasized, including their illegal activities of mail opening, electronic surveillance, political harrassment, and surreptitious entries. Information is also included regarding the overseas activities of the FBI and CIA to the extent that these activities affect the constitutional rights of Americans.

An absolutely unique source of data on intelligence activities, regardless of whether or not the researcher agrees with the findings and recommendations of the Select Committee.

_____. SUPPLEMENTARY REPORTS ON INTELLIGENCE ACTIVITIES, Book VI of Final Report. 94th Cong., 2d sess., April 23, 1976. Rept. no. 94-755. vi, 368 p. Bibliography, appendices, footnotes.

The staff of the Select Committee of the Senate (chaired by Senator Frank Church of Idaho) published, in this supplementary report to the final committee report, a brief history of the evolution and organization of the U.S. federal intelligence function from 1776 through 1975. Part one of the history deals with the period 1776-1914, part two the period 1914-39, while part three describes the period of the national security colossus, 1939-75. An excellent bibliography is included which provides references to numerous magazine articles. The report also provides a general history of the development of government information security classification policy, again with a substantial bibliography.

WHO'S WHO IN THE CIA. Berlin: Julius Mader, 1968. 605 p. Index.

A biographical register of 3,000 officers of the civil and military branches of American intelligence agencies who have operated in 120 countries. Actually, "CIA" in the title is misleading, since the compilation includes names and biographies of present and former officers of all the intelligence agencies of the United States. Many of the former OSS (Office of Strategic Services) personnel listed eventually found their way after World War II into postwar intelligence, especially the CIA. However, many of the foreign service and other officers listed have not been connected with intelligence for years. The biographical sketches include date and place of birth, past military or intelligence affiliations, education, languages, and present operating areas (as of 1968).

Wilensky, Harold L. ORGANIZATIONAL INTELLIGENCE: KNOWLEDGE AND POLICY IN GOVERNMENT AND INDUSTRY. New York: Basic Books, 1967. 226 p. Bibliography, index, charts.

An important work by a sociologist who examines the use and misuse of intelligence in both government and business organizations. Wilensky uses the case of strategic bombing to illustrate two kinds of "information pathology": (1) "intelligence agencies tend to report what they think their leaders want to hear or see," and (2) "leaders see or hear what they want, no matter what intelligence is reported."

Zlotnick, Jack. NATIONAL INTELLIGENCE. Rev. ed. Washington, D.C.: Industrial College of the Armed Forces, 1964. 75 p. Index, chart, bibliography.

A textbook of the Industrial College of the Armed Forces, the 1960 edition of which was written by former CIA officer Zlotnick while a student at the college. Contains concise descriptions of the makeup of the national intelligence community along with some of its operating principles. There are useful categorizations of the specialized production divisions of intelligence such as estimates, basic intelligence, and current intelligence. Also described are the various categories of subject matter such as political, economic, military, and scientific and technical intelligence.

B. THE SOVIET UNION

Although the comprehensive Gunzenhauser bibliography (cited in chapter 1) lists some 200 titles dealing with the subject, there is no single work on Soviet intelligence comparable to Harry Howe Ransom's THE INTELLIGENCE ESTABLISHMENT (cited in section A, above), which deals with the U.S. intelligence community. Soviet intelligence agencies, both civilian and military, are closely integrated and it is difficult to draw a fixed line between internal security police functions (such as those performed by the FBI in the United States) and foreign or strategic intelligence proper. Moreover, most works on the subject are slanted, pro or con, for political warfare purposes, and are heavily laden with cold war propaganda. This observation applies equally to Soviet works praising the exploits of the Soviet security organs and to Western works warning of the dangers of Soviet espionage. Most of the literature thus falls into the espionage/counterespionage category, or the covert operations category, and is so listed in this bibliography. Books dealing specifically with counterintelligence and internal security are listed in chapter 7 for the United States and in chapter 9 for the Soviet Union. A separate subsection dealing with a special comprehensive bibliography of Soviet publications on intelligence and related topics precedes the listing of general works below.

1. Special Bibliography of Soviet Sources

U.S. Congress. Senate. Committee on the Judiciary. Internal Security Subcommittee. SOVIET INTELLIGENCE AND SECURITY SERVICES, 1964-70: A SELECTED BIBLIOGRAPHY OF SOVIET PUBLICATIONS. WITH SOME ADDITIONAL TITLES FROM OTHER SOURCES. 92d Cong., 1st sess., 1972. 289 p. Author index.

> A comprehensive, briefly annotated bibliography of 2,507 listings "prepared by the Foreign Affairs Divisions." The first three parts present annotated sources under the headings Soviet State Security (items 1-714), Soviet Military Intelligence (items 715-927), and Partisans and Underground Activity (items 928-1657). Part 4, also annotated, contains listings under the title, "Articles on the 50th Anniversary of the State Security Service" (items 1658-851). Part 5 lists, without annotations, articles described as "Warnings Against Western Intelligence" (items 1852-2443). Part 6, "Soviet Intelligence Activities: A View from Other Sources" (items 2444-507) is an annotated, substandard potpourri of primarily English books and articles apparently put together as an afterthought for political warfare purposes.

> According to the introduction, beginning in September 1964 "there has been a spate of articles and books extolling the Soviet intelligence and security services and creating a new pantheon of heroes . . . . The more than 2400 items in this bibliography from Soviet sources reflect the new trend. . . .

> "No attempt has been made in this compilation to comment on the accuracy of the Soviet materials, although frequently the claims made in them are at variance with other information available in various sources published outside the Soviet Bloc. . . . Despite the problems of credibility . . . the publications of the Soviet regime about its intelligence services, taken as a whole, are a valuable tool for students and specialists in the Western world who know how to use it. . . ."

> A curious omission in part 5 of this bibliography is the two-part article by F. Sergeyev, "The Secrets of Secret Services" published in NEDELYA, the IZVESTIA Sunday Supplement, no. 46, 9-15 November 1970, and no. 47, 16-22 November 1970. The article stresses the importance attached by the U.S. intelligence community to the research and analysis of a wide range of open source materials. In addition to the "warning against Western Intelligence function," the essay makes a convincing case that "it is no longer possible to solve such a complex riddle as the military-economic potential of another state by the use of old traditional espionage

methods alone and this is one of the chief goals of the intelligence services." The omission is interesting since the article was translated and circulated within the U.S. intelligence community.

A more important omission is the anonymous article (written by Soviet intelligence) entitled "Soviet State Security Organs in the Years of the Great Patriotic War," which was also translated into English and circulated in the U.S. intelligence community. This is an authoritative essay on the role of Soviet intelligence and counterintelligence during World War II, and was published in the leading Soviet historical journal, VOPROSY ISTORII [Historical questions], May 1965. (For an evaluation of this article see the bibliography section of Barton Whaley's CODEWORD BARBAROSSA, chapter 5, section A, below.)

About thirty-five of the books and articles listed in this bibliography have been translated into English by the Joint Publications Research Service (JPRS) of the Department of Commerce. Such items are denoted by an asterisk and may be purchased from the National Technical Information Service, Springfield, Virginia 22151. Since most requests for these translations originate with government analysts, the subject categories are themselves of interest. In rough historical sequence, three concern the so-called Lockhart conspiracy and related anti-Bolshevist activities of British intelligence in Russia during the fall of 1918. Five of them concern the "Trust," a Soviet counterintelligence ruse which lured British agents Sidney Reilly and Boris Savinkov back into the USSR in the mid-1920s. (For an authentic, documented account of this operation, see Paul W. Blackstock's THE SECRET ROAD TO WORLD WAR II, cited in chapter 16.) Three concern Artuzov and Pilyar, two rehabilitated Chekists who were involved in the Trust. One concerns a group of eighteen women who worked for Soviet intelligence during the Spanish Civil War. Eight concern Soviet intelligence during World War II, including one article each on the Red Orchestra and on the German intelligence operation Zeppelin. Two concern the work of the Soviet "master spy," Colonel Rudolf Abel and two concern his assistant Gordon Lonsdale. Five concern Richard Sorge, the outstanding Soviet military intelligence agent caught and executed by the Japanese during World War II. Four concern the activities of miscellaneous Soviet intelligence agents, some of them "old Chekists." Two concern the "machinations" of U.S. intelligence and sociological research, and finally, one is a translation of a typical counterespionage spy thriller.

2.   Books and Articles (Western Sources)

Deacon, Richard [pseud.]. A HISTORY OF THE RUSSIAN SECRET SERVICE. New York: Taplinger, 1972. 568 p. Notes, bibliography, index. London: Muller, 1972. viii. 568 p. Index, bibliography, illustrations.

A history of the Russian secret services from earliest times to present by a British author experienced in intelligence matters. See the main entry in chapter 14, section D.

Garthoff, Raymond L. "Prediction, Intelligence, and Reconnaissance." In SOVIET MILITARY DOCTRINE, pp. 253-64. Glencoe, Ill.: Free Press, 1953.

An authoritative review of the place of intelligence in Soviet doctrine by the author of the definitive work on the subject (see below). Garthoff was a member of the RAND Corporation when he wrote this work.

_____. "The Soviet Intelligence Services." In THE SOVIET ARMY, edited by B.H. Liddell Hart, pp. 265-75. London: Weidenfeld and Nicolson, 1956. American ed. THE RED ARMY, pp. 265-74. New York: Harcourt, Brace, 1956.

An expansion of material in the author's SOVIET MILITARY DOC-TRINE (see above). Although somewhat dated it remains one of the most authoritative brief reviews of the complex of Soviet intelligence services.

Hingley, Ronald. THE RUSSIAN SECRET POLICE, MUSCOVITE, IMPERIAL RUSSIAN AND SOVIET POLITICAL SECURITY OPERATIONS. New York: Simon & Schuster, 1970. xiii, 313 p. Bibliography, index, notes.

Hingley, one of England's most eminent Russian scholars and a member of the Royal Army Intelligence Corps during World War II, provides a careful history of the role played by intelligence and security forces in internal Russian political life. He discusses the techniques of intrigue, provocation, and infiltration practiced by the Cheka, NKVD, MGB, and KGB within Russia.

Orlov, Alexander. HANDBOOK OF INTELLIGENCE AND GUERRILLA WAR-FARE. Ann Arbor: University of Michigan Press, 1963. 187 p. No index.

The author, a Soviet defector, writes: "Before World War II, when I was one of the chiefs of the Soviet intelligence, I lectured at the Central Military School in Moscow on the tactics and strategy of intelligence and counterintelligence. In 1936 I wrote down the basic rules and principles of Soviet intelligence in the form of a manual which was approved as the only textbook for the newly created NKVD schools for undercover intelligence officers and for the Central Military School in Moscow."

This book is the American equivalent of the manual. Orlov argues that Soviet intelligence relies heavily on classical espionage as a means of collecting strategic intelligence, in contrast to the emphasis placed by Western powers on research and analysis of information from open sources.

C. GREAT BRITAIN

There is no work on British intelligence comparable to Harry Howe Ransom's work on American intelligence, THE INTELLIGENCE ESTABLISHMENT, which includes a chapter on "The British Intelligence System" (see below). However, information on the working of various agencies within the British intelligence community is scattered throughout books dealing with espionage, counterespionage, the operations of the wartime Special Operations Executive (see chapter 17), and so on. For an extensive listing of both English and foreign language titles the comprehensive Gunzenhauser bibliography should be consulted (see chapter 1).

Bulloch, John. M.I.5: THE ORIGIN AND HISTORY OF THE BRITISH COUNTER-ESPIONAGE SERVICE. London: A. Baker, 1963. 206 p. Illustrated.

See main entry and annotation in chapter 15, section A.

Deacon, Richard [pseud.]. A HISTORY OF THE BRITISH SECRET SERVICE. New York and London: Taplinger, 1970. 440 p. Index, notes, illustrations.

See main entry and annotation in chapter 14, section E.

Ransom, Harry Howe. "The British Intelligence System." In his THE INTELLIGENCE ESTABLISHMENT, pp. 180-207. Cambridge, Mass.: Harvard University Press, 1970.

_____. "Great Britain's Secret, Secret Service." MIDWAY 8 (June 1967): 19-35.

A general survey of the British system and a look at how secrecy is maintained in England.

Strong, Sir Kenneth. INTELLIGENCE AT THE TOP: THE RECOLLECTIONS OF AN INTELLIGENCE OFFICER. Garden City, N.Y.: Doubleday, 1969. xiv, 366 p. Index, bibliography, appendix, illustrations, maps. British ed. London: Cassell, 1968. xv, 366 p. Index, bibliography.

The author, who spent forty years in British military intelligence work, writes in considerable detail about the British system. He stresses intelligence in the World War II period; see also the annotation for this work in chapter 6, section A. The bibliography of seventeen items is confined to his historical sources.

Wise, David, and Ross, Thomas B. "Great Britain." In their THE ESPIONAGE ESTABLISHMENT, pp. 78-131. New York: Random House, 1967.

A popular journalistic account by the authors of THE INVISIBLE GOVERNMENT (cited in chapter 5, section A). Concentrates on a number of security and espionage scandals of the 1960s. See also the main entry for THE ESPIONAGE ESTABLISHMENT in chapter 14, section A.

D. GERMANY

The comprehensive Gunzenhauser bibliography (see chapter 1) lists more than 250 titles dealing with German intelligence, espionage, and counterespionage activities. Most of these works are concerned with intelligence in World Wars I and II. In this section are listed the few works dealing with the German intelligence services.

Bartz, Karl. DIE TRAGODIE DER DEUTSCHEN ABWEHR. Oldendorf, Germany: Verlag K.W. Schutz K.G., 1972. 274 p.

> Based on new material, a revisionist "study of the fall of the head of German military intelligence (the Abwehr), Admiral Canaris, and the take-over by the Nazi Party intelligence organization (Sicherheitsdienst [SD]) under Himmler."

Brissaud, Andre. THE NAZI SECRET SERVICE. Translated from the French by Milton Waldman. New York: Norton, 1974. French ed. HISTOIRE DU SECRET SERVICE NAZI. Paris: Plon, 1972. 320 p. Index, bibliography, organization charts, illustrations.

> Andre Brissaud, free-lance French journalist, recounts the activities of the Nazi party intelligence, counterintelligence, and covert operations organization, the Sicherheitsdienst (SD) of the SS. The author has limited himself to the first period of the SD--from its creation in 1931 through 1939. Brissaud has based his work on available written and spoken evidence, including personal conversations with Walter Schellenberg and Heinz Jost. A comprehensive bibliography is provided. Extensive insights into the in-fighting and rivalries of the various intelligence and political leaders are detailed as well as descriptions of the part the SD played in the Tukhachevsky affair and the Gleiwitz deception. Some details on the organizational evolution of the SD are included.

Hagen, Walter [Wilhelm Hoettl]. THE SECRET FRONT. THE STORY OF NAZI POLITICAL ESPIONAGE. Translated by R.H. Stevens. Edited, with an introduction, by Ian Colvin. New York: Praeger, 1954. 327 p. Index, illustrations. British ed. London: Weidenfeld and Nicolson, 1953. 327 p.

> The original German edition, DIE GEHEIME FRONT: ORGANISATION, PERSONEN, UND AKTIONEN DES DEUTSCHEN GEHEIMDIENSTES. (Zurich: Europa-Verlag, 1950), was published under the pseudonym Walter Hagen. The book contains an account of the organization and evolution of the Foreign Intelligence Service (Sicherheitsdienst [SD]) of the Nazi party. Emphasized is the work

of the SD in Czechoslovakia, Yugoslavia, Rumania, Bulgaria, and Hungary during World War II. The author was an Austrian intelligence officer who, after 1938, joined the SD and worked in the Berlin headquarters and in Italy and the Balkans.

Hohne, Heinz. THE ORDER OF THE DEATH'S HEAD: THE STORY OF HITLER'S SS. Translated by Richard Barry. New York: Coward, McCann & Geoghegan, 1969. xiii, 786 p. Index, bibliography, notes, appendices, maps, organization charts, illustrations, glossary.

A completely documented history of the SS with a separate chapter on the Nazi party intelligence service under Himmler, the Sicherheitsdienst (SD). Unusual detail on organization. Describes the evolution of the party intelligence service from its original role of imposing party security to a foreign intelligence mission directly competing with the military intelligence service (the Abwehr).

Krausnick, H., et al. ANATOMY OF THE SS STATE. Introduction by Elizabeth Wiskemann. Translated by Richard Barry, Marian Jackson, and Dorothy Long. New York: Walker & Co., 1968. 614 p.

Contains chapters on all of the SS activities. Especially good detail on the organization and evolution of the Nazi party intelligence apparatus--the Sicherheitsdienst (SD).

Leverkuehn, Paul. GERMAN MILITARY INTELLIGENCE. Translated by R.H. Stevens and Constantine Fitzgibbon. London: Weidenfeld and Nicolson; New York: Praeger, 1954. vii, 209 p. Illustrations, organization chart.

A useful account of the methods, procedures, and techniques of the Abwehr--the Wehrmacht intelligence service, composed of army, navy, air force, and civilian personnel. Largely a collection of brief stories of espionage and intrigue, authored by a reserve officer who served with the Abwehr in Iran and Turkey. See also the entry for this book in chapter 6.

E. FRANCE AND OTHER COUNTRIES (CANADA, ISRAEL, SWITZERLAND, CHINA, AND JAPAN)

Collier, Richard. TEN THOUSAND EYES. New York: Dutton, 1958. 320 p. Illustrations, appendix ("Cast of Principal Characters"), maps.

An excellent account of intelligence collection operations against the defenses of Hitler's Atlantic Wall before D-Day by French resistance personnel. For main entry see chapter 6, section A.

de Vosjoli, Pierre L. Thyraud. THE COMMITTEE. Forthcoming.

Ex-agent de Vosjoli's book contains a number of alleged revelations of the operations of the French intelligence services including assassinations and the opening of diplomatic mail of foreign embassies, including the U.S. mail. The author describes the activities of a secret committee consisting of high-level intelligence officials and civil servants, which was presided over at times by Georges Pompidou. During the 1960s the committee gave instructions for covert operations. The book is also a defense of a former colleague of the author, ex-intelligence agent Leroy-Finville, who was imprisoned for alleged involvement in the kidnapping of Moroccan political leader Mehdi Ben Barka.

_____. LAMIA. Boston: Little, Brown and Co., 1970. 344 p.

De Vosjoli, code name Lamia, was at age nineteen an underground intelligence specialist during World War II. Later he was chief intelligence representative of General de Gaulle in Washington, and coordinator and liaison agent between French intelligence and the intelligence agencies of the NATO nations. He specialized in intelligence on Cuba, and passed information to the CIA confirming events which led to the Cuban missile crisis. A valuable book for its insights into intelligence operations, how information is procured by field agents, and actions taken by the opposition to frustrate information collection (counterespionage). De Vosjoli apparently furnished information to novelist Leon Uris who, on the basis of the information, wrote the best seller TOPAZ (cited in chapter 14, section H).

Stead, Philip John. SECOND BUREAU. London: Evans Brothers, 1959. 212 p. French ed. LE DEUXIEME BUREAU. Paris: Fayard, 1966. 240 p.

First comprehensive book in English on the subject of the history of the regular French military intelligence service. Stead is a British author of several books on French subject matter, one being a history of the police of Paris. See also the annotation in chapter 6, section A.

Canada

Elliot, S.R. "The Canadian Intelligence Corps." CANADIAN ARMY JOURNAL 17 (April 1963): 122-27.

A brief summary article.

Hahn, James E. THE INTELLIGENCE SERVICE WITHIN THE CANADIAN CORPS. 1914-1918. HISTORICAL RESUME BY GENERAL SIR ARTHUR CURRIE. Toronto: Macmillan, 1930. xxii, 263 p. Maps, illustrations, aerial photographs.

Israel

Aldouby, Zwy, and Ballinger, Jerrold. THE SHATTERED SILENCE; THE ELI COHEN AFFAIR. New York: Coward, McCann and Geoghegan, 1971. 453 p.

Israeli journalist Zwy Aldouby and American writer Jerrold Ballinger collaborated to reconstruct the fantastic life and death of Israeli master spy Eliahu ben Shaul Cohen. For nearly three years Cohen sent coded intelligence reports to Tel Aviv by radio from Damascus until his radio signal was traced and he was captured, tortured, tried for espionage in a military court, and finally hanged in May 1965.

Bar-Zohar, Michael. SPIES IN THE PROMISED LAND. ISER HAREL AND THE ISRAELI SECRET SERVICE. Translated from French by Monroe Stearns. Boston: Houghton Mifflin, 1972. 292 p.

An account of the Israeli secret service from its founding in 1948 to the resignation of Iser Harel in 1963.

Dayan, Moshe. DIARY OF THE SINAI COMPAIGN. New York: Harper, 1966. 236 p. Maps, illustrations, portraits.

Includes interesting assessments of intelligence acquired by both sides in the Sinai conflict.

Dekel, E. Shai. SHAI; THE EXPLOITS OF HAGANA INTELLIGENCE. New York: Yoseloff, 1959. 369 p.

Lotz, Wolfgang. THE CHAMPAGNE SPY; ISRAEL'S MASTER SPY TELLS HIS STORY. New York: St. Martin's Press, 1972. 240 p. Illustrations.

The autobiography of Israel's intelligence agent in Egypt during a five-year period beginning in 1960. Lotz, who posed as a rich ex-Nazi in Egypt, tells his story from his training in Tel Aviv to his capture, imprisonment, and eventual release.

Switzerland

Kimche, Jon. SPYING FOR PEACE: GENERAL GUISAN AND SWISS NEUTRALITY. 2d ed. London: Weidenfeld and Nicolson, 1961. 168 p. Illustrations.

A complete journalistic account of the presumed interrelationship of Swiss, Russian, German, British, and American intelligence services during World War II. All of these services actively operated in Switzerland, and Swiss intelligence had the declicate job of using its knowledge of all of them as a means of preserving neutrality and warning of possible attack. Kimche was military correspondent for the LONDON EVENING STANDARD during World War II.

China

Deacon, Richard [pseud.]. THE CHINESE SECRET SERVICE. New York: Taplinger, 1974. 523 p. Index, notes, bibliography, illustrations.

Deacon, retired foreign manager of the London SUNDAY TIMES and prolific author of histories of secret services, has compiled from numerous reports and from information obtained from his own private sources the only comprehensive account of the Chinese secret service. The author traces the beginnings of the Chinese service and then goes on to describe its evolution and operations down to 1974. After the period of World War II the chronicle tells of the Chinese Communist secret service and its operations in Korea, Taiwan, Europe, Africa, and the Middle East. The bibliography is excellent and contains references to accessible sources.

Japan

Seth, Ronald. SECRET SERVANTS. A HISTORY OF JAPANESE ESPIONAGE. New York: Farrar, Straus and Cudahy, 1957. x, 278 p. Bibliography, no index.

The author, member of British intelligence during World War II and a teacher, consulted hundreds of original Japanese documents captured at the end of World War II in order to compile this detailed and dramatic history of Japanese espionage. He describes Japanese infiltration of Hawaii as early as 1876, the role of Japanese intelligence in the Russo-Japanese War of 1904-5, and the penetration of the United States as well as Central and South America. Most sources listed in the bibliography are accessible only with difficulty, but a few are available books of the early 1940s.

Chapter 5

UTILIZATION OF INTELLIGENCE

A. BOOKS, MONOGRAPHS, DISSERTATIONS

Most of the books and articles on the utilization of intelligence are written by active or retired military personnel, and concern the use of intelligence for military purposes ranging from tactical combat to strategic estimates and decision making. A second and much smaller group consists of articles or chapters by scholars concerning the role of intelligence in foreign policy decision making or grand strategy, such as the role of intelligence during World War II. Such articles are listed here rather than under the historical section dealing with espionage in World War II because of their general interest. The main areas of concern of most of these articles are indicated by their titles so that annotations are for the most part unnecessary. However, certain important articles which have attracted much interest and have had considerable effect are annotated more extensively. A third group consists of certain series of newspaper or other periodical articles which have also been important either as sources of information or as quasi-official "leaks" of either information or comment.

Bryan, George S. THE SPY IN AMERICA. Philadelphia: Lippincott, 1943. 256 p.

A brief, popular history of American intelligence from the Revolutionary War through the First World War.

COMMISSION ON THE ORGANIZATION OF THE GOVERNMENT FOR THE CONDUCT OF FOREIGN POLICY. Washington, D.C.: Government Printing Office, June 1975. 278 p.

This publication presents the findings and recommendations of a joint congressional and presidential study commission established by Public Law 92-352 for the purpose of providing a more effective system for the formulation and implementation of the nation's foreign policy. The commission, known also as the Murphy Commission, after its chairman Ambassador Robert Murphy, spent two years in research and analysis; intelligence played an important part in the work. A special panel of investigators developed research papers on intelligence. Their findings are summarized in chapter 7 of the report. Detailed organization charts of the national intelligence community structure and the National Security Council intelligence structure are a valuable and authoritative addition. Research papers of scholars and expert practitioners developed during the course of the work are set forth in seven volumes of appendixes. Appendix U of volume 7 contains eight intelligence papers. Senator Mike Mansfield, member of the commission, records his differences with portions of the report. Pages 228-33 of the report contain his comments. He starts off--"With regret I must record my differences with some segments of the report . . ."

Deaver, William C. II. "The History of the Intelligence Division of the British War Office and Its Role in Imperial Affairs 1854-1901." Doctoral dissertation, University of Oxford. In progress.

Dulles, Allen Welsh. THE CRAFT OF INTELLIGENCE. New York: Harper & Row, 1963. 277 p. Index, bibliography, photographs.

See main entry in chapter 4, section A.

Freedman, Larry. "Definition of the Soviet Threat in Strategic Arms Decisions of the United States, 1961-1974." Doctoral dissertation, University of Oxford. In progress.

Goulden, Joseph C. TRUTH IS THE FIRST CASUALTY; THE GULF OF TONKIN AFFAIR: ILLUSION AND REALITY. Chicago: Rand McNally, 1969. 285 p. Maps, bibliography.

An excellent journalistic account of the Gulf of Tonkin incident with special emphasis on the problems involved in the use of intelligence information collected by such technical sensors as sonar and radar.

Hilsman, Roger. STRATEGIC INTELLIGENCE AND NATIONAL DECISIONS. Glencoe, Ill.: Free Press, 1956. 187 p. Index, footnotes with some bibliographic references.

Hilsman, wartime member of OSS in the Far East, former CIA officer, and director of the State Department's Bureau of Intelligence and Research in the Kennedy administration, based his book on materials gathered from interviews of Washington intelligence officials and departmental policy-making officials--the users of strategic intelligence. A valuable account of the relationship between intelligence and the policy-making and decision-making processes of the federal government. In the preface Hilsman describes his book as "an attempt to identify the doctrines that have grown up in the intelligence agencies, to examine the doctrines discovered critically, and to compare them with various alternatives." Although Hilsman's personal views were later modified in favor of more "policy-oriented" intelligence, this work gives an excellent summary of American strategic intelligence doctrine vis-a-vis intelligence users' requirements in the first postwar decade.

TO MOVE A NATION. THE POLITICS OF FOREIGN POLICY IN THE ADMINISTRATION OF JOHN F. KENNEDY. Garden City, N.Y.: Doubleday, 1967. xxii, 602 p. Index, notes, maps.

A very valuable analysis of the relationships between policy and intelligence during the Kennedy administration. Hilsman was first the director of State Department's Bureau of Intelligence and Research and in 1963 became a policy maker as assistant secretary of state for Far Eastern affairs. Part 3 of the book deals with President Kennedy and his relationships with the CIA. Hilsman's main theme here is that while the CIA was under the directorship of Allen Dulles, covert action (the Bay of Pigs for example) was overused as an instrument of foreign policy, and the reputation of the United States suffered more and more. In part 5 the intelligence aspects of the Cuban missile crisis are discussed and analyzed.

Johnson, Haynes, et al. THE BAY OF PIGS; THE LEADER'S STORY OF BRIGADE 2506. New York: Norton, 1964. 368 p. Index, maps, bibliographic notes, photographs, portraits.

Johnson, worked from recorded interviews of Cuban leaders of Brigade 2506, selected by the CIA to lead the landing in Cuba in 1961, to prepare this best-known of the accounts of the Bay of Pigs operation. He has used his own sources of information to provide insights into the White House, Pentagon, and CIA policy-making aspects of the incident.

Kim, Young Hum, ed. THE CENTRAL INTELLIGENCE AGENCY: PROBLEMS OF SECRECY IN A DEMOCRACY. University of Wisconsin, Problems in Political Science series, edited by Neal Riemer. Lexington, Mass.: D.C. Heath, 1968. 113 p. Paperbound.

This collection of twelve articles is part of a series intended to provide students of politics with texts concerning the problems of secrecy in a democratic society. Provocative essays of interest to the general reader.

Kirkpatrick, Lyman B., Jr. CAPTAINS WITHOUT EYES: INTELLIGENCE FAILURES IN WORLD WAR II. Toronto: Macmillan, 1969. xiv, 303 p. Bibliography, index, illustrations.

Kirkpatrick, former executive director of the CIA, attempts to explore the real issues of the role of intelligence in decision making.

As a means to this end he discusses the intelligence role played in five specific battles of World War II. The section on Pearl Harbor adds little to that which has already been written. The sections on the battles of Arnhem and Dieppe are well developed. The author analyzes the difficulties of collecting the specific information required for decision making, and here his insights are useful.

_____. THE REAL CIA. New York: Macmillan, 1968. 312 p. Index.

This memoir provides a behind-the-scenes view of the CIA's efforts in the sphere of foreign policy. The author began his more than twenty-two years in the intelligence services of the United States with the OSS and as an intelligence staff officer at the headquarters of Omar Bradley's Twelfth Army Group. He later joined the CIA, rose to executive assistant to the director, and finally was appointed to the number three position, executive director. He recounts various incidents in which the CIA played an integral part: Batista and Cuba, the Bay of Pigs, the Suez of 1956, and the U-2 incident.

_____. THE U.S. INTELLIGENCE COMMUNITY: FOREIGN POLICY AND DOMESTIC ACTIVITIES. New York: Hill and Wang, 1973. ix, 212 p. Selective bibliography, index.

A valuable contribution to the history and development of the U.S. intelligence community, including the CIA, FBI, Defense Intelligence Agency, Atomic Energy Commission, Department of State, Treasury, and the intelligence organizations of the military services. The author also relates intelligence to policy formulation and contrasts the Cuban missile crisis, as an example where the intelligence community and decision makers worked well together, to the Vietnam War where they did not. The author lists many of the criticisms of the domestic role of the CIA that have appeared in the press. He does not list any that have subsequently been brought to light during congressional investigations, although he must have been aware of them when he was executive director of the CIA. His evaluation of the role of intelligence in policy making is good; his evaluation of the role of intelligence in a free society, the controls Congress should have, and the domestic activities of intelligence organizations is disappointing.

McCoy, Alfred W. THE POLITICS OF HEROIN IN SOUTHEAST ASIA. New York: Harper & Row, 1972. 464 p. Notes, index.

A carefully documented but controversial book, since it was attacked by the CIA in its prepublication stages. According to a lead review by James M. Markham in the NEW YORK TIMES BOOK REVIEW (3 September 1972), what the author, a Yale graduate student, "has given is not--as advertised--an expose of the 'CIA involvement in the drug traffic' but rather a fascinating, often meticulous unraveling of the byzantine complexities of the Southeast Asian opium and heroin trade. . . . The book's theme . . . is that when the United States moved into the Indochinese vacuum left by the French, it picked up, and struck alliances with shaky governments, politocos and mercenaries (like the Kuomintang remnants in Burma) that earned a good deal of money from opium smuggling. And . . . for a long time American diplomats and C.I.A. agents had considered opium trafficking by their client allies a quaint local custom that didn't interfere with the war against Communists. Thus for example, it was natural that Air America (a CIA-affiliated air line) would carry Meo opium in Laos."

McGarvey, Patrick J. CIA: THE MYTH AND THE MADNESS. New York: Saturday Review Press, 1972. 240 p. No index.

The author served for fourteen years at the working level in the DIA, the NSA, and the CIA. His book was cleared for publication (after certain deletions and changes for security reasons) by the CIA, and gives a popular account of the human side of intelligence work, with special attention to a number of blunders and shortcomings. In spite of such negative aspects McGarvey, like other professionals, regards the intelligence system as the first line of national defense, but one in need of a major overhaul rather than periodic "cosmetic changes." He advocates a total functional reorganization around the basic steps involved-- collection, processing, reporting, and clandestine operation. He argues that Congress has lost effective control over the intelligence community and that what is needed for this purpose is a joint committee of both houses modeled after the Joint Atomic Energy Committee. In order to restore public confidence in intelligence he recommends that the president, through his Foreign Intelligence Advisory Board, make public an annual report on the activities of the community, a suggestion which was later taken up by Lyman Kirkpatrick.

Marchetti, Victor, and Marks, John D. THE CIA AND THE CULT OF INTELLIGENCE. New York: Knopf, 1974. 398 p. Index.

For main entry see chapter 16; also cited in chapter 8, section A.

Meyer, Karl E., and Szulc, Tad. THE CUBAN INVASION. New York: Praeger, 1962. 160 p.

A competent journalistic account of the Bay of Pigs fiasco in April 1961. Tad Szulc covered the story for the NEW YORK TIMES.

Strong, Sir Kenneth. MEN OF INTELLIGENCE: A STUDY OF THE ROLES AND DECISIONS OF CHIEFS OF INTELLIGENCE FROM WORLD WAR I TO THE PRESENT DAY. New York: St. Martin's Press, 1971. 183 p. Bibliography, index.

> Primarily a study of the military estimates of the major powers in World Wars I and II. Scattered throughout are highly perceptive observations and judgments on the relationship of intelligence estimates to military and foreign policy decision making. In addition, Major General Strong has added an important chapter on the limitations of espionage in which he documents his "doubts about the usefulness of secret services and secret agents, especially in the military field, and more especially when the results of their efforts are considered in the broad context of all Intelligence sources and operations."

Whaley, Barton. CODEWORD BARBAROSSA. Cambridge, Mass.: M.I.T. Press, 1973. x, 376 p. Bibliography, illustrations, index, notes, appendix, map.

> A major work and the most important on intelligence "signals" and strategic surprises since Roberta Wohlstetter's PEARL HARBOR: WARNING AND DECISION (see below). Excellent annotated bibliography, glossary of abbreviations, acronyms, code names, and definitions. Described by the author in his preface as "an intensive study of the eleven-month period preceding the German attack of 22 June 1941. The standard sources were culled, the intelligence warnings were collated, the networks of information flow were reconstructed, and the interpretations were analyzed. What emerged was not only an account of the intricacies of intelligence networks and communications systems in this critical period, and of the world leaders and intelligence experts who both ran these systems and were misled by them. What also emerged were the refutation of the generally accepted Wohlstetter communications model and the development of a new theory of strategic surprise."

Wise, David, and Ross, Thomas B. THE INVISIBLE GOVERNMENT. New York: Random House, 1964. 375 p. Notes, index.

> Two resourceful journalists teamed up to develop this account of the various organizational elements of the American intelligence community. Revealed are "special operations" of the CIA, with four chapters devoted to a description of the CIA in the Bay of Pigs landings in Cuba. Also described are activities in electronic espionage, black radio propaganda, and the use of spy satellites. Factually inaccurate in many cases, but a revealing account considering its date of publication.

Wohlstetter, Roberta. PEARL HARBOR: WARNING AND DECISION. Stanford, Calif.: Stanford University Press, 1962. 426 p.

A most complete study of the events leading to the surprise attack on Pearl Harbor. The author describes the availability of information in the months preceding the attack, especially communications intelligence, the handling of the information, and the effects it had at the national decision level. An exhaustive case study of strategic warning in which a concept is developed for identifying the critical indicators of warning among the volumes of information available before an event such as Pearl Harbor. Those critical indicators are "signals" amid the background information, termed "noise" by the author.

Barton Whaley, in CODEWORD BARBAROSSA (see above), an exhaustive study of the elements of deception in the German surprise attack on the USSR in World War II, argues: "The flaw in this [Wohlstetter] model is that it treats deliberate disinformation as part of the ambient background 'noise.' . . . By tying deception (disinformation) to noise, Wohlstetter not only misinterpreted BARBAROSSA as a case of ambiguity analogous to her classic Pearl Harbor surprise attack case but was even led to disregard very significant elements of Japanese deception planning in the Pearl Harbor case itself. Wohlstetter's is the most influential and widely applied model developed until now for understanding surprise. It is a useful tool for this purpose, but only where deception is not practiced."

Zacharias, Ellis M., in collaboration with Ladislas Farago. BEHIND CLOSED DOORS; THE SECRET HISTORY OF THE COLD WAR. New York: G.P. Putnam's Sons, 1950. 367 p. Index, notes on sources.

The authors, both experienced in the field of intelligence, develop the threat posed by the Soviet Union to the world, describe intelligence activities in the postwar period, and prescribe solutions to U.S. foreign policy problems.

B. ARTICLES, PAMPHLETS, CHAPTERS FROM BOOKS

Africa Research Group. INTELLIGENCE AND FOREIGN POLICY. Cambridge, Mass.: ca. 1972. 38 p.

The Africa Research Group describes itself as a "radical research/ action collective concerned with exposing and fighting American imperialist penetration of Africa." The pamphlet reproduces with introductory comment and notes a transcript of a Council on Foreign Relations Discussion Group meeting which took place on 8 January 1968, on the subject of intelligence and foreign policy. (A transcript of this discussion group meeting is also printed in the appendix to THE CIA AND THE CULT OF INTELLIGENCE, cited in chapter 16.) Also included in this pamphlet is a five-page report entitled "CIA Intervention in Africa."

Baldwin, Hanson W. An important series of five articles in the NEW YORK TIMES.

"Intelligence--One of the Weakest Links in Our Security. Survey Shows Omissions, Duplications." 20 July 1948, p. 6.

"Older Agencies Resent a Successor and Try to Restrict Scope of Action." 22 July 1948, p. 2.

"Intelligence III: Errors in Collecting Data Held Exceeded by Evaluation Weakness." 23 July 1948, p. 5.

"Competent Personnel Held Key to Success--Reforms Suggested." 24 July 1948, p. 5.

"Broader Control Set-Up is Held Need with a 'Watch-Dog' Committee for Congress." 25 July 1948, p. 15.

_____. "The Growing Risks of Bureaucratic Intelligence." REPORTER 29 (August 1963): 48-50, 53.

Barnds, William J. "Intelligence and Foreign Policy: Dilemmas of a Democracy." FOREIGN AFAIRS 47 (January 1969): 281-95.

A general discussion of the CIA and foreign policy by a former CIA analyst.

Barnet, Richard J. "The CIA's New Cover." NEW YORK REVIEW OF BOOKS, 30 December 1971, pp. 6-8.

Under the guise of a book review (of Victor Marchetti's THE ROPE DANCER, New York: Grosset and Dunlap, 1971) the author, a former State Department official, writes a highly critical essay on the CIA and its clandestine activities, including covert operations. He argues that contrary to news leaks indicating that the CIA's clandestine services are being downgraded, they are merely seeking to "professionalize" by taking deeper cover.

Belair, Felix, Jr. "C.I.A. Identifies 21 Asian Opium Refineries." NEW YORK TIMES, 6 June 1971, p. 2.

The author quotes extensively from an official CIA analysis of opium refining in the Burma-Laos-Thailand border area known as the "Golden Triangle." The article also quotes Congressman Robert H. Steele (R-Conn.), a former CIA agent and author of a report on the drug traffic in Southeast Asia.

Blachman, Morris J. "The Stupidity of Intelligence." In READINGS IN AMERICAN FOREIGN POLICY: A BUREAUCRATIC PERSPECTIVE, edited by Morton H. Halperin and Arnold Kanter, pp. 328-34. Boston: Little, Brown and Co., 1973. (Reprinted from Peters, Charles, ed. INSIDE THE SYSTEM: A WASHINGTON MONTHLY READER. New York: Praeger, 1970).

Blachman, a political scientist and former air force officer attached to tactical reconnaissance in Vietnam, describes "the way the military, and especially the Air Force, gathered and reported the results of its bombing of the North. Those reports greatly exaggerated the effects of the bombing, misleading the American public and, to the extent that they took the reports at face value, misleading both military and civilian policymakers." He concludes that "wrong decisions are continuing hazards as long as the Pentagon's civilian leadership, the Congress, and the public rely on the military's self-serving intelligence system."

Blackstock, Paul W. "CIA: A Non-inside Report." WORLDVIEW 9 (May 1966): 10-13.

A brief review of the role of the CIA, its status, image, and the problems of surveillance.

_____. CIA AND THE INTELLIGENCE COMMUNITY: THEIR ROLES, ORGANIZATION AND FUNCTIONS. St. Louis, Mo.: Forum Press, 1974. 14 p.

A primer or "learning module" for the layman and students. Among the topics discussed are intelligence and covert operations, the U.S. intelligence community under the Nixon reorganization, the CIA and Watergate, and the problems of congressional surveillance and control of both intelligence and covert operations.

_____. "The CIA Looks Good in the Pentagon Papers." PERSPECTIVE (the Sunday magazine section of the BALTIMORE SUN), 18 July 1971, p. K1.

An article on the improved image of the CIA as a result of its National Intelligence Estimates prepared during the war in Vietnam, as revealed in the Pentagon Papers.

_____. "Intelligence and Covert Operations: Changing Doctrine and Practice." University of South Carolina, Department of Government and International Studies, December 1973. 125 p. Mimeographed.

For main entry see chapter 4, section A.

_____. "A Look at the Intelligence Establishment." WORLDVIEW 14 (September 1971): 17-19.

A review of Harry Howe Ransom's THE INTELLIGENCE ESTABLISHMENT (cited in chapter 4, section A).

_____. [Book Reviews.] WORLDVIEW 17 (April 1974): 54-56.

A review of Lyman B. Kirkpatrick's THE U.S. INTELLIGENCE COMMUNITY (cited in this chapter, section A) and Patrick J.

McGarvey's CIA: THE MYTH AND THE MADNESS (cited in this chapter, section A). Blackstock takes the view that "for an analysis in depth of the many disturbing questions which Kirkpatrick leaves unanswered one must turn to less popular but more rewarding studies such as Harry Howe Ransom's classic, THE INTELLIGENCE ESTABLISHMENT (cited in chapter 4, section A).

Branch, Taylor. "The Censors of Bumbledom." HARPER'S MAGAZINE, January 1974, pp. 56-63.

A highly critical article by a contributing editor of HARPER'S on CIA efforts to censor and, if possible, to enjoin publication by Victor Marchetti and John D. Marks of THE CIA AND THE CULT OF INTELLIGENCE (cited in chapter 16). The author argues that "if the government wins its case, Marchetti and Marks will have unwittingly helped create the legal tools to make a vassal of every government employee who enters the sacred chambers of national security." (Marchetti is a former CIA aide who served for some time at the directorate level.)

Bruce, David K.E. "The National Intelligence Authority." VIRGINIA QUARTERLY REVIEW 22 (Summer 1946): 355-69.

A thoughtful review of the deficiencies of American intelligence in the pre-World War II period and a plea for the establishment of an independent national intelligence authority. The author was the commander of OSS in the European theater during the war and has since served as U.S. Ambassador to England, France, and Germany and headed the U.S. mission to the People's Republic of China.

Campbell, John Franklin. "The Intelligence and Propaganda Complexes." In his THE FOREIGN AFFAIRS FUDGE FACTORY, pp. 147-77. New York: Basic Books, 1971.

Campbell writes that "major concern has been expressed outside the system over the years that the intelligence system has not been under adequate policy controls." He argues that in both espionage and covert operations the CIA and related agencies have operated as laws unto themselves.

"Camp Peary Exposed as CIA Training Base." VIRGINIA GAZETTE, 22 December 1972, pp. 1, 13.

A detailed report, including several revealing photographs of the 10,000-acre training camp called "the farm." The report is based on the result of four weeks of investigation by staffer Ed Offley and news editor W.C. O'Donovan.

"Camp Peary Linked to 'Assassination Teams'." VIRGINIA GAZETTE, 9 February 1973, p. 1.

> An article based on interviews on the subject with Victor Marchetti and Patrick McGarvey.

Cline, Ray S. "Policy without Intelligence." FOREIGN POLICY 17 (Winter 1974-75): 121-35.

> The author, a former deputy director (intelligence) of the CIA and head of INR, the U.S. State Department's Bureau of Intelligence and Research, has written a trenchant critique of the personalized, idiosyncratic Nixon-Kissinger style of foreign policy decision making. Their foreign policy style emphasized secrecy to such an extent that the National Security Council (NSC) and related supportive intelligence bureaus were in effect bypassed or ignored. This important, authoritative article, which includes as contrasting case studies the 1962 Cuban missile crisis and the U.S. military alert of October 24, 1973, not only criticizes the neglect of intelligence by the Nixon administration, but also recommends changes in procedure designed to restore the NSC and the intelligence estimative function to the effectively supportive roles for which they were designed. The author expresses the hope that "the President and Secretary of State can build confidence and common understanding within and with the foreign policy and intelligence bureaucracy which they control, mainly by using it and engaging its skills in decision-making." An important article by an extremely knowledgeable source dealing with basic principles as well as operations.

Cooper, Chester L. "The CIA and Decision-Making." FOREIGN AFFAIRS 50 (January 1972): 223-36.

> An excellent account of the activities of the Office of National Estimates (comprised of the Board of National Estimates and the National Estimates Staff) which works for the director of Central Intelligence. In the article, experienced intelligence analyst Cooper describes the content of some of the National Estimates produced, especially those produced during the Vietnam War. The author calls for changes, and after the article appeared, the Office of National Estimates was disestablished and a group of National Intelligence Officers was formed to replace the old office and board.

Costa, John, and Evans, Gary Lee. LEGISLATION INTRODUCED RELATIVE TO THE ACTIVITIES OF THE INTELLIGENCE AGENCIES, 1947-1972. Washington, D.C.: Congressional Research Service, Library of Congress, UB 250 U.S.A. 73-22 F, 1973. 63 p. Appendices.

> This pamphlet provides a comprehensive list of bills proposed in the Congress between the years 1947 and 1972 relating to U.S.

intelligence agencies. A brief legislative history of each bill is provided along with its text. Since the passage of the National Security Act of 1947, which established the CIA and the National Security Council, and the passage of the 1949 Security Act modification relating to the organization and functions of the CIA, nearly 200 bills have been introduced in Congress which are relative to intelligence organizations. The pamphlet further reveals that the majority of these bills represented attempts to establish a Congressional committee to oversee the activities of the CIA of which only two reached the floor of Congress. Both surviving bills were defeated by more than two-thirds majority.

Daugherty, William E., and Janowitz, Morris, comps. A PSYCHOLOGICAL WARFARE CASEBOOK. Baltimore, Md.: Johns Hopkins Press, 1958. xxiii, 880 p.

> Chapter 7 contains selected writings by scholars on the "Role of Intelligence, Research, and Analysis in Psychological Warfare" (pp. 425-549). The basic premise is that psychological warfare depends on intelligence for all aspects of its operation.

Donovan, William J. "Intelligence: Key to Defense." LIFE, 30 September 1946, pp. 108-20.

> A sympathetic critique of prewar intelligence and of wartime OSS by its founder and director. Includes suggestions for postwar organization.

Dulles, Allen W. "Intelligence Estimating and National Security." DEPARTMENT OF STATE BULLETIN 42 (March 1960): 411-16.

Evans, Allan. "Intelligence and Policy Formation." WORLD POLITICS, October 1959, pp. 84-91.

> A former official in the State Department's Bureau of Intelligence and Research (INR) discusses the intelligence problem as seen from the directorate level in INR.

Evans, Allan, and Gatewood, R.D. "Intelligence and Research: Sentinel and Scholar in Foreign Relations." DEPARTMENT OF STATE BULLETIN 42 (June 1960): 1023-27.

Finney, John W. "War Signals Misjudged, U.S. Official Concedes." NEW YORK TIMES, 31 October 1973, pp. 1, 16.

> An analysis of the failure of both U.S. and Israeli intelligence to predict the outbreak of the fourth Middle East war on October 6, 1973. The author writes: "In remarks that seemed critical of the intelligence community's performance, Secretary of State Kissinger

said in a news conference October 12 that three times in the week immediately preceding the outbreak of war United States and Israeli intelligence agencies had been asked for assessments. They had come back with the conclusion, he said, that 'hostilities were unlikely to the point of there being no chance of it.' To Mr. Kissinger, this illustrated 'the gravest danger of intelligence assessments'--trying--'to fit the facts into existing preconceptions and to make them consistent with what is anticipated.' This is a judgment now widely shared in the intelligence community."

Graham, Daniel O. "Estimating the Threat: A Soldier's Job." ARMY 23 (April 1973): 14-18.

Lieutenant General Graham, formerly deputy director of estimates in the Defense Intelligence Agency, later deputy director of the CIA for the intelligence community (D/DCI [IC]) and then head of DIA, argues in this candid, revealing article that the function of estimating military threats to U.S. security properly belongs to DIA. "The lack of confidence in the threat estimates emanating from military intelligence agencies . . . stemmed from a series of bad overestimates, later dubbed 'bomber gap,' 'missile gap,' and 'megaton gap.'" However, he argues, with the reorganization of DIA in November 1970, a new directorate of estimates has corrected past errors. As a result: "The time is ripe for the military profession to reassert its traditional role in the function of describing military threats to national security. Both the military user and the military producer have come a long way since the 'missile gap' days. DIA has hit its stride in the production of respectable military estimates. . . . There is no longer a need, in my judgment, to duplicate DIA's efforts in other agencies."

Groth, Alexander. "On the Intelligence Aspects of Personal Diplomacy." ORBIS 7 (Winter 1964): 838-48.

Hamilton, Andrew. "The CIA's Dirty Tricks under Fire at Last." PROGRESSIVE, September 1973, pp. 14-22.

In 1973 the author served in the office of program analysis of the National Security Council. Although the main focus of the article is on the CIA's clandestine services, it is an excellent general review of the agency's recent history and reorganization under the Nixon administration. The author argues that "the Administration's approach . . . will be to cope with the CIA's current crisis merely by making its covert operations even more truly clandestine, and by restricting them in size to reduce the risk of exposure."

Harkness, Richard, and Harkness, Gladys. "The Mysterious Doings of CIA." SATURDAY EVENING POST, 30 October 1954, pp. 19-21, 162, 165; 6 November 1954, pp. 34-35, 64, 66, 68; and 13 November 1954, pp. 30, 132-34.

These three articles are the locus classicus of unofficial CIA boasts that the agency was involved in the overthrow of King Farouk in July 1952; of the Iranian Premier, Dr. Mossadegh, in August 1953; and of the Communist-controlled Arbenz regime in Guatemala in May 1954. The cold war tone of the articles is indicated by the conclusion to the account of the overthrow of Dr. Mossadegh: "It is the guiding premise of CIA's third force that we must develop and nurture indigenous freedom legions among captive or threatened people who stand ready to take personal risks for their own liberty."

Helms, Richard M. "Spying and a Free Society," excerpts from an address, 14 April 1971, as reprinted in U.S. NEWS & WORLD REPORT, 26 April 1971, pp. 84-86.

Hersh, Seymour M. "CIA Head Names Espionage Chief: Colby Becomes Director of Clandestine Operations." NEW YORK TIMES, 1 March 1973, p. 19.

An informative article which provides details of several important changes at the directorate level in the CIA.

Hilsman, Roger. "Intelligence and Policy-Making in Foreign Policy." In READINGS IN THE MAKING OF FOREIGN POLICY, edited by Andrew M. Scott and Raymond H. Dawson, pp. 447-56. New York: Macmillan, 1965.

_____. "The Intelligence Process." In READINGS IN THE MAKING OF FOREIGN POLICY, edited by Andrew M. Scott and Raymond H. Dawson, pp. 456-66. New York: Macmillan, 1965.

_____. "Intelligence through the Eyes of the Policy Maker." In SURVEILLANCE AND ESPIONAGE IN A FREE SOCIETY, edited by Richard H. Blum. Praeger Special Studies in International Politics and Government series. New York: Praeger, 1972. xxxii, 319 p.

A report by the planning group on intelligence and security to the Policy Council of the Democratic National Committee in which the one-time head of State Department intelligence provides his interesting views.

Hobbing, Enno. "CIA: Hottest Role in the Cold War." ESQUIRE, September 1957, pp. 31-34.

A journalistic account of CIA covert operations with some interesting details on recruitment and use of defectors from behind the iron curtain.

Jervis, Robert. "Hypotheses on Misperception." WORLD POLITICS 20 (April 1968): 454-79.

Karnow, Stanley. "Access by Hill to CIA Data Recommended." WASHING-
TON POST, 29 March 1972, p. 4.

An article based on testimony given at a hearing of the Senate
Foreign Relations Committee during which two former senior employees of the CIA urged that selected congressional committees
be provided regularly with intelligence studies on U.S. foreign
relations and "matters of national security." Chester L. Cooper,
formerly with the Office of National Estimates, "suggested that
Congress be authorized to receive the National Security Study
Memoranda" produced by the NSC. Herbert Scoville, Jr., formerly CIA's director of science and technology, "asserted that the
administration has deliberately misused intelligence in its presenta-
tions to Congress to promote its own legislation," citing the 1969
Safeguard antiballistic missile program of the Nixon administration.

Kendall, Willmoore. "The Function of Intelligence." WORLD POLITICS, July
1949, pp. 542-52.

A critical analysis of Sherman Kent's book, STRATEGIC INTELLI-
GENCE (see this chapter, section A). The late Professor Kendall
challenges prevailing doctrine on the function, organization, and
role of intelligence.

Kent, Sherman. "Estimates and Influence: Some Reflections on What Should
Make Intelligence Persuasive in Policy Deliberations." FOREIGN SERVICE
JOURNAL, April 1969, pp. 16-18, 45.

Taking the point of view of the intelligence producer, Kent writes
that "in many cases, no matter what we tell the policy-maker,
and no matter how right we are, and how convincing, he will
upon occasion disregard the thrust of our findings for reasons beyond our ken. If influence cannot be our goal, what should it
be? Two things. It should be to be relevant within the area
of our competence, and above all it should be to be credible
. . . . To wish simply for influence can, and upon occasion
does, get intelligence to the place where it can have no influence
whatever. By striving too hard in this direction intelligence may
come to seem just another policy voice, and an unwanted one at
that. On the other hand, . . . unself-conscious intelligence
work, even in the speculative and highly competitive are a of estimates, may prove (in fact, has proved many times) a key deter-
minant in policy decision."

Kissinger, Henry J., and the National Security Council Staff. NATIONAL
SECURITY STUDY MEMORANDUM-1 (NSSM-1) in the CONGRESSIONAL
RECORD. Vol. 118, part 3. 92d Cong., 2d sess., May 10, 1972,
pp. 16748-836; May 11, 1972, pp. 17186-89.

Prepared in early July 1969, this was the first such NSC "Study
Memorandum" produced by the agency, based on studies prepared

in the Departments of State, Defense, and the CIA. NSSM-1 reviews widely differing intelligence estimates of the political and military situation in Vietnam, and concludes, in part: "It is noteworthy that the gap in views that does exist is largely one between policy makers, the analysts, and the intelligence community on one hand, and the civilian and military operators on the other."

Knorr, Klaus. "Failure in National Estimates: The Case of the Cuban Missiles." WORLD POLITICS, April 1964, pp. 455-67.

The author defends the intelligence system's failure to give earlier warning of the emplacement of Soviet nuclear missiles in Cuba in 1962.

Langer, William L. "Scholarship and the Intelligence Problem." PROCEEDINGS OF THE AMERICAN PHILOSOPHICAL SOCIETY 92 (March 1948): 43-45.

A brief summary of the role of the Research and Analysis branch of OSS during World War II, and a plea for the necessity of its continuing function in the postwar period. Langer is an eminent American historian who served in that organization.

Lasswell, Harold D. "Policy and the Intelligence Function: Ideological Intelligence." In his THE ANALYSIS OF POLITICAL BEHAVIOR, pp. 55-68. London: Routledge & Kegan Paul, 1951.

Leacacos, John P. "Intelligence: The Raw Material of Diplomatists." In FIRES IN THE IN-BASKET: THE ABC'S OF THE STATE DEPARTMENT, pp. 468-537. Cleveland: World Publishing Co., 1968.

Excellent functional analysis which is neither a hatchet job nor a snow job. A comprehensive review of the operations of the Bureau of Intelligence with many details on recent crises is found on pages 481-500.

McGarvey, Patrick J. "DIA: Intelligence to Please." In READINGS IN AMERICAN FOREIGN POLICY: A BUREAUCRATIC PERSPECTIVE, edited by Morton H. Halperin and Arnold Kanter, pp. 318-28. Boston: Little, Brown and Co., 1973.

The author demonstrates that "the output from DIA is more inclined to serve the interests of the military services than the needs of good decision-making by their civilian superiors. . . . At the least, recognizing that the information supplied is unreliable, the Secretary [of Defense] may rely on alternate sources (where available) or proceed on the basis of deficient data. At the worst, the Secretary will fail to recognize the particular distortions in the intelligence reports he receives. To this extent, he will make decisions based on information designed less to reflect reality than to enhance careers and protect organizations." (From the abstract by Halperin).

Marchetti, Victor. "CIA: The President's Loyal Tool." NATION, 3 April 1972, pp. 430-33.

> The author, who was on the CIA director's staff until his resignation in 1970, writes: "The CIA is no accidental, romantic aberration; it is exactly what those who govern the country intend it to be--the clandestine mechanism whereby the executive branch influences the internal affairs of other nations. In conducting such operations, particularly those that are inherently risky, the CIA acts at the direction and with the approval of the President or his Special Assistant for National Security Affairs. . . . Only when one understands that, despite claims to the contrary, the CIA is basically concerned with interfering in the affairs of foreign countries, and that the agency carries out this mission with the approval and at the request of the country's political leaders, can one begin to deal with the issue. It is not a matter of reforming the CIA. The need is to reform those who govern us, to convince them that they must act more openly and honestly, both with the people whom they represent and with the other nations of the world."

Neumann, Robert G. "Political Intelligence and Its Relation to Military Government." In AMERICAN EXPERIENCES IN MILITARY GOVERNMENT IN WORLD WAR II, edited by Carl J. Friedrich and Associates, pp. 70-85. New York: Rinehart, 1948.

> An excellent article by a political scientist (formerly in political intelligence work attached to G-2, First and Third U.S. Armies) discussing the need for political intelligence as an integral part of military intelligence, and its role in military government.

NEWSWEEK, editors of. "The CIA--An Attack and a Reply: A Former Staff Officer Criticizes CIA Activities; A Former CIA Executive Defends Its Operations." NEWSWEEK, 11 October 1971, pp. 78-84.

> An important and revealing controversy between Victor Marchetti, the former staff officer, and Lyman B. Kirkpatrick, Jr., the former CIA executive. A classic exposition of two sharply contrasting views of the agency, and especially the role of its clandestine services.

_____. "The New Espionage American Style." NEWSWEEK, 22 November 1971, pp. 28-40.

> A quasi-official survey of the U.S. intelligence community and its reorganization under the Nixon administration. With respect to the CIA's clandestine services, this report concludes: "The gaudy era of the adventurer has passed in the American spy business; the bureaucratic age of Richard C. Helms and his gray specialists has settled in."

Oberdorfer, Don. "Helms to Oversee U.S. Spy Network." WASHINGTON POST, 6 November 1971, pp. 1, 15.

A detailed article on changes in the U.S. intelligence community following the announcement on November 5, 1971, by President Nixon, of "a long-awaited reorganization . . . creating a government-wide coordinating role for CIA Director Richard Helms and bringing military agencies under closer civilian control. . . . " The aim of the reorganization, according to the White House announcement, was to improve "efficiency and effectiveness." Although the statement did not say so, high-ranking officials were known to feel that the military intelligence apparatus had grown too large and costly in comparison to the amount of useful information it produced.

"The Pike Papers: House Select Committee on Intelligence CIA Report." SPECIAL SUPPLEMENT TO VILLAGE VOICE, October 1976, pp. 18-24.

The New York weekly tabloid VILLAGE VOICE reprinted portions of the secret House of Representative's Select Committee on Intelligence report of its investigations of the U.S. intelligence community. The portion referenced here records the committee's findings on the performance of the intelligence community during several world crises. The Vietnam Tet Offensive by North Vietnam and Vietcong forces, the invasion of Czechoslovakia by the Soviets, the Mid-East wars, the crisis in Portugal, and the Cyprus crisis are among the incidents in which the performance of the community is assessed. See chapter 19 for full annotation of this reference.

Ransom, Harry Howe. "How Effective Is Central Intelligence?" CHRISTIAN SCIENCE MONITOR, 1 December 1958, p. 13.

A general discussion of the intelligence function, and description of its evolution in the United States after World War II.

_____. "How Intelligent is Intelligence?" NEW YORK TIMES MAGAZINE, 22 May 1960, pp. 26, 80-83.

A discussion of the problem of managing espionage activities in a democratic society, written shortly after the downing of an American U-2 reconnaissance plane over the Soviet Union in early May 1960.

_____. "Secret Mission in an Open Society." NEW YORK TIMES MAGAZINE, 21 May 1961, pp. 20, 77-79.

An analysis of the problem of responsible political control of secret operations, written in the wake of the Bay of Pigs fiasco.

_____. STRATEGIC INTELLIGENCE. Morristown, N.J.: General Learning Press, 1973. 20 p. Selected bibliography.

Designed as a "learning module" for students and laymen, this is easily the best brief general discussion of strategic intelligence available. Among the topics discussed are the nature of intelligence, its importance in decision making, process and organization, and strategic intelligence as a research frontier. The latter section is based on an extensive survey made in 1971-72 with the aid of a grant from the Russell Sage Foundation.

Robinson, Donald. "They Fight the Cold War under Cover." SATURDAY EVENING POST, 20 November 1948, p. 30.

Written in 1948, within the first year of the CIA's existence and apparently with the agency's help, this article reveals the extensive overseas political operations of CIA agents.

Rosenthal, Jack. "A.E.C. Chief to Replace Helms as C.I.A. Director: Schlesinger, 43, Chosen--Intelligence Official to be Envoy to Iran." NEW YORK TIMES, 22 December 1972, pp. 1, 8.

Based on President Nixon's announcement of 21 December 1972. In the opinion of knowledgeable officials, it means the end of an era of professional intelligence operatives and the beginning of an era of systems management.

Sapin, Burton M. "Intelligence, Planning, and Policy Analysis." In AMERICAN DEFENSE POLICY, edited by Mark E. Smith and Claude J. Johns, Jr., pp. 416-32. Baltimore, Md.: Johns Hopkins Press, 1965.

Steinhauser, Thomas C. "A Winning Team: How the NMCC Works." ARMED FORCES JOURNAL, May 1972, pp. 48-49.

A brief article on the National Military Command Center (NMCC) in the U.S. Department of Defense, and its close working relationship with the DIA (Defense Intelligence Agency).

Stern, Laurence. "$1.5 Billion Secret in Sky: U.S. Spy Unit Surfaces by Accident." WASHINGTON POST, 9 December 1973, p. A1.

An article on the National Reconnaissance Office (NRO) operated out of the office of the secretary of the air force, which supervises the U.S. overhead surveillance program employing the U-2 and SR-71 planes and a variety of reconnaissance satellites.

Szulc, Tad. "The View from Langley." OUTLOOK (the Sunday magazine of the WASHINGTON POST), 21 October 1973, pp. C1, C5.

An article on CIA intervention in Chilean affairs under Allende, based on the secret testimony of CIA Director William E. Colby before the House Subcommittee on Inter-American Affairs. The transcript of this testimony "was made available . . . by sources in the intelligence community."

"U.S. Foreign Intelligence Community Reorganized by President Nixon." DE-PARTMENT OF STATE BULLETIN 65 (November 1971): 658-59.

Unna, Warren. "CIA: Who Watches the Watchman?" HARPER'S MAGAZINE, April 1958, pp. 46-53.

An informative journalistic account of the CIA's role in the Washington decision-making process in the 1950s, with emphasis on the question of congressional surveillance.

Welles, Benjamin. "First Congressional Restraints Are Imposed on C.I.A." NEW YORK TIMES, 13 February 1972, p. 3.

An important article on congressional surveillance of the CIA. The reporter notes: "The foreign aid authorization bill, signed by President Nixon on Monday, includes for the first time in a quarter-century new controls on the operations, cost and person-nel of the Central Intelligence Agency. . . . The controls were inserted at various points in this year's aid bill largely through the efforts of Senators Clifford P. Case, Republican of New Jer-sey; Frank Church, Democrat of Idaho, and Stuart Symington, Democrat of Missouri. They are members of the Foreign Relations Committee [who] have protested increasingly in recent months that Congress has too little knowledge of, let alone control over, the agency's activities, particularly in Southeast Asia."

_____. "H-L-S [Helms] of the C.I.A." NEW YORK TIMES MAGAZINE, 18 April 1971, pp. 34-35, 37, 39, 41-42, 43, 46, 48, 52, 54.

An informative article on the director of the CIA, analyzing his role and influence in national security affairs. Contains a discus-sion of covert operations, including the agency's acquisition of Soviet Premier Nikita Khrushchev's "Secret Speech" denouncing Stalin's errors.

_____. "Secrecy Redefined: 'New' CIA--with Colby's Brand on It." CHRIS-TIAN SCIENCE MONITOR, 5 March 1974, p. 2.

A review of the CIA under the direction of William Colby, with emphasis on the abolishing of the Board of National Estimates and its replacement by a staff of national intelligence officers. Ac-cording to Welles, Colby has indicated that CIA involvement in analysis of world events or in science, research, and technology need no longer be kept secret.

. "U.S. Intelligence Arm--Weakened? Mideast War Reveals Flaws."
CHRISTIAN SCIENCE MONITOR, 29 October 1973, pp. 1, 5.

A well-informed article, based on interviews with intelligence experts, reviewing the "intelligence gap" in the Mideast Arab-Israeli
war. The line taken is that "Nixon-administration budget cuts in
the United States intelligence community over the past three years
have seriously weakened the nation's intelligence arm. . . . Spy
satellite and electronic intelligence both have been heavily cut
back. Moreover, Mr. Nixon's rapid-fire personnel shifts with
three directors of Central Intelligence--Richard M. Helms, James
R. Schlesinger, and William Colby--in six months have impaired
the nation's intelligence arm. The CIA's tangential involvement
in the Watergate scandal, moreover, has improved neither its
morale nor its image."

Wicker, Tom, et al. An important five-part series authored by Tom Wicker
and other members of the Washington, D.C. staff of the NEW YORK TIMES
reveals and discusses specific operations of the CIA as well as its policy, organization, and controls.

."CIA: Maker of Policy, or Tool?" NEW YORK TIMES, 25 April
1966, pp. 1, 20. "How CIA Put 'Instant Air Force' into Congo."
NEW YORK TIMES, 26 April 1966, pp. 1, 3.

"CIA Spies from 100 Miles Up; Satellite Probes Secrets of Soviet."
NEW YORK TIMES, 27 April 1966, pp. 1, 28.

"CIA Operations: A Plot Scuttled." NEW YORK TIMES, 28
April 1966, pp. 1, 28.

"The CIA: Qualities of Director." NEW YORK TIMES, 29 April
1966, pp. 1, 18.

Wilensky, Harold L. "Intelligence, Crises, and Foreign Policy: Reflections
on the Limits of Rationality." In SURVEILLANCE AND ESPIONAGE IN A
FREE SOCIETY, edited by Richard H. Blum, pp. 236-66. New York: Praeger,
1972.

A report by the Planning Group on Intelligence and Security of
the Policy Council of the Democratic National Committee.

Wise, David. "Colby of C.I.A.--C.I.A. of Colby." NEW YORK TIMES
MAGAZINE, 1 July 1973, p. 15.

A detailed study of the clandestine operations career of the designated successor to William Colby as director of Central Intelligence, by one of the coauthors of THE INVISIBLE GOVERNMENT
(see Wise and Ross, this chapter, section A). In addition to cataloging some twelve separate covert operations of the CIA, the author
discusses personality and organizational changes in the clandestine
services of the agency.

Wohlstetter, Roberta. "Cuba and Pearl Harbor." FOREIGN AFFAIRS 43 (July 1965): 691-707.

A comparison of the strategic surprises in the Pearl Harbor attack and in the Soviet emplacement of missiles in Cuba two decades later.

_____. "Intelligence and Decision-Making." In READINGS IN THE MAKING OF AMERICAN FOREIGN POLICY, edited by Andrew M. Scott and Raymond H. Dawson, pp. 431-47. New York: Macmillan, 1965.

C. GOVERNMENT DOCUMENTS

Commission on Organization of the Executive Branch of the Government. [Hoover Commission, 1949] "Task Force Report on Foreign Affairs." Appendix H, p. 95. Washington, D.C.: Government Printing Office, January 1949; "Foreign Affairs, A Report to the Congress," pp. 15, 16, 56, 57. Washington, D.C.: Government Printing Office, February 1949; "Task Force Report, National Security Organization." Appendix G, pp. 4, 32, 76-78. Washington, D.C.: Government Printing Office, January 1949.

_____. [Hoover Commission, 1955] "Intelligence Activities: A Report to the Congress." Washington, D.C.: Government Printing Office, June 1955. ix, 76 p. Also published as House Doc. no. 201, 84th Cong., 1st sess., 1955.

An unclassified report of the intelligence task force of the second Hoover Commission. The task force was chaired by General Mark W. Clark. It investigated the functions of the intelligence community, including the CIA. The task force discovered an undue emphasis on covert action over intelligence collection and analysis in the CIA, and criticized the quantity and quality of its intelligence coverage of the USSR. A congressional oversight committee was recommended, only to be turned down by the overall commission. Improved management of intelligence in the CIA was also recommended. Another committee, under the chairmanship of General James Doolittle, was organized to investigate CIA's clandestine services. The report was classified.

Dulles, Allen W. "Memorandum Respecting . . . Central Intelligence Agency . . . ." Submitted to Senate Committee on Armed Services, 25 April 1947. In NATIONAL DEFENSE ESTABLISHMENT: HEARINGS ON S. 758, pp. 525-28. 80th Cong., 1st sess., 1947.

A concise statement of Dulles's views as of 1947 on a central intelligence organization. The Dulles memorandum is also printed in appendix A of Harry Howe Ransom's CENTRAL INTELLIGENCE AND NATIONAL SECURITY, pp. 217-24. (See chapter 4, section A).

U.S. Bureau of the Budget. "Intelligence and Security Activities of the Government." A Report to the President. Washington, D.C.: 20 September 1945. Mimeographed.

U.S. Congress. Act to Provide for the Administration of the CIA . . . And for Other Purposes. Public Law 110, 81st Cong., 1st sess., 20 June 1949, 63 Stat. 208.

> This act was designed to strengthen the administration of the CIA. It gave additional powers to the director, both in protecting the secrecy of CIA operations and in the unvouchered expenditure of money.

U.S. Congress. National Security Act of 1947. Public Law 253, 80th Cong., 26 July 1947, 61 Stat. 495, 50 USC Supp. 403.

> Section 102 contains provisions establishing the CIA. This is the CIA's basic charter.

U.S. Congress. PEARL HARBOR ATACK: HEARINGS BEFORE THE JOINT COMMITTEE ON THE INVESTIGATION OF THE PEARL HARBOR ATTACK. 39 vols. 79th Cong., 1st sess., 1946.

> The official record of the testimony, evidence, and findings of the 1945–46 Pearl Harbor inquiry. Contains much material on intercepts and intelligence organizations.

U.S. Congress. House. Committee on Armed Services. AMENDING THE CENTRAL INTELLIGENCE ACT OF 1949: REPORT TO ACCOMPANY H.R. 16306. 89th Cong., 2d sess., 11 August 1966.

_____. INQUIRY INTO THE U.S.S. PUEBLO AND EC-121 PLANE INCIDENTS. 91st Cong., 1st sess., 28 July 1969. Rept. no. 91-12.

U.S. Congress. House. Select Committee on Intelligence. U.S. INTELLIGENCE AGENCIES AND ACTIVITIES: THE PERFORMANCE OF THE INTELLIGENCE COMMUNITY: HEARINGS. Part 2. 94th Cong., 1st sess., 11, 12, 18, 25, 30 September and 7, 30, 31 October 1974. 937 p.

> Part of the hearings of the House of Representatives special committee investigating the intelligence community, chaired by Congressman Otis G. Pike. Recorded in this report is the expert testimony of witnesses regarding the intelligence available, and its use in the decision process of the nation regarding the Arab-Israeli War of 1973, the Tet offensive of the Vietnam War, the Turkish invasion of Cyprus, and the coup d'etat in Portugal in April 1974.

U.S. Congress. Senate. Committee on Armed Services. NATIONAL DE-
FENSE ESTABLISHMENT: HEARINGS ON S. 758. 80th Cong., 1st sess.,
1947. 3 parts.

Part 3 contains testimony on central intelligence.

U.S. Congress. Senate. Committee on Government Operations. Subcommittee on National Policy Machinery. INTELLIGENCE AND NATIONAL SECU-
RITY: REPORT. 86th Cong., 2d sess., 1960.

U.S. Congress. Senate. Committee on Naval Affairs. "Report to the Secretary of the Navy. Unification of the War and Navy Departments and Postwar
Organization for National Security." [Eberstadt Report] 79th Cong., 1st sess.,
22 October 1945.

In June 1945 Secretary of Navy James V. Forrestal commissioned
his friend and investment banker, Ferdinand Eberstadt, to study a
merger of the navy and war departments, a structure for centralized decision making, a separate air force, and a National Security
Council. Eberstadt also believed that a central intelligence role
for analysis and for coordination of departmental intelligence was
also needed. A section of the Eberstadt report was drafted by
Rear Admiral Sidney Souers, deputy chief of naval intelligence,
who, in January 1946 became the first director of Central Intelligence. Souers's recommendations included a coordination role for
central intelligence, not the creation of an independent central
intelligence agency. See especially pages 12-13 and 159-63 of
the report. Eberstadt also chaired a task force of the first Hoover
Commission of 1949 (see above).

U.S. Congress. Senate. Committee on Rules and Administration. REPORT,
JOINT COMMITTEE ON CENTRAL INTELLIGENCE AGENCY. 84th Cong.,
2d sess., 23 February 1956. S. Rept. no. 1570.

The committee supported, by an eight-to-one vote, the proposal
to establish a joint congressional committee on the CIA. Contains
the outlines of the argument in favor of such a move as well as
the dissenting argument.

U.S. Congress. Senate. Committee on the Judiciary. Subcommittee to Investigate the Administration of the Internal Security Act and other Internal
Security Laws. COMMUNIST FORGERIES. HEARINGS. 87th Cong., 1st
sess., 2 June 1961.

Testimony of Richard Helms, assistant director, CIA, concerning the
preparation by Soviet and other Communist intelligence agencies
of fabricated and forged news articles, documents, and intelligence
reports (see chapter 21, section C).

_____. "Interlocking Subversion in Government Departments." Hearings. 83d Cong., 1st sess., 25 June 1953.

Contains testimony relative to the organization within the Department of State for the conduct of intelligence during the period 1945-47. Also included are reprints of important documents and correspondence of the period. See especially pages 854-82 of the report.

_____. "The Wennerstroem Spy Case, How it Touched the U.S. and NATO." 88th Cong., 2d sess., 1964.

Reveals details of the disclosures to the Soviets of information on U.S. weapons and plans and the possible effects on U.S. Western defense posture, by Swedish Air Force Colonel, and Soviet spy, Stig Wennerstroem.

U.S. Congress. Joint Economic Committee. Subcommittee on Priorities and Economy in Government. ALLOCATION OF RESOURCES IN THE SOVIET UNION AND CHINA--1975: HEARINGS. Part 1. 94th Cong., 1st sess. Executive Sessions, 18 June and 21 July 1975. Appendix, charts, graphs, tables.

A remarkable report in that it contains the testimony of the director of the CIA regarding the status of the Soviet and Chinese economies and the capabilities of the two countries in military weapons production, plus the testimony of the director of the Defense Intelligence Agency (DIA) regarding the expenditures of both countries for military weapons production. The report is essentially a first in the publication in unclassified form of estimates of Soviet and Chinese economic potential and the percentages of gross national product devoted to military production. The methodologies used by both intelligence agencies is discussed frankly. The appendix is a reprint of a study prepared by the director of Net Assessments of the Office of the Secretary of Defense in which the methodologies for economic and military assessments used by the intelligence agencies is discussed. Net assessments, a relatively new technique, is a means by which U.S. and Soviet (or Chinese) economic and military potentials are compared for planning purposes.

U.S. Department of State. Bureau of Intelligence and Research. INR: INTELLIGENCE AND RESEARCH IN THE DEPARTMENT OF STATE. Doc. no. 0-496-792. Washington, D.C.: Government Printing Office, 1973. 19 p.

Includes organization chart of the bureau. A concise, well-written pamphlet on the role, functions, and organization of INR. The following excerpts summarize its origin, role, and functions:

"The need for specialized research capabilities was the reason for the creation, in 1946, of a centralized unit

within the Department of State which could devote itself exclusively to the processing, analysis, and evaluation of data collected from all parts of the world by
all the agencies of the U.S. Government, particularly the CIA, the FBI, and the Defense Department
intelligence agencies. This center is the Bureau of Intelligence and Research (INR). . . .

"INR culls the elaborate information-gathering apparatus of the Government for missing data and collates
and disseminates material which can be of use, indicating its relevance to foreign affairs. Staffed by a
close-knit group of experienced officers, the Bureau
can focus quickly the full range of information relevant
to topical questions of foreign policy. It operates in-
dependently of the Department's geographic and functional policy bureaus, which concentrate on the formulation of policy in their respective areas rather than
on a systematic view of what is happening all over
the world. . . . "

D. THE PENTAGON PAPERS

Gravel, Michael, ed. THE SENATOR MIKE GRAVEL EDITION--THE PENTA-
GON PAPERS. 5 vols. Boston: Beacon Press, 1971. Vols. 1-4, documents;
vol. 5, index and critical essays by Noam Chomsky and Howard Zinn. 4,100 p.

Contains a comprehensive interdepartmental task force study of 8
May 1961, entitled "A Program of Action for South Vietnam,"
and many other directives and reports on covert operations and
intelligence activities. See especially:

"Lansdale Team's Report on Covert Saigon Mission in
1954 and 1955" (vol. 1, doc. 95, p. 95)

"The Overthrow of Ngo Dinh Diem, May-November
1963" (vol. 2, pp. 201-76)

"OCO to CORDS" (vol. 2, pp. 609-23)

"Efforts to Improve Intelligence on Progress of the War"
(vol. 3, pp. 32-34)

"Initiation of Covert Operations" (vol. 3, pp. 149-54)

"Plan 34-A--September Schedule" (vol. 3, doc. 185,
p. 553)

See also the entry for this work in chapter 19.

Sheehan, Neil, and Kenworth, E.W., eds. THE PENTAGON PAPERS. New
York: Quadrangle, 1972. xxx, 677 p.

The original "revelations" by the editors of the NEW YORK TIMES, who broke the story, contains a number of assessments of intelligence estimates as well as an interpretive account of military and related covert operations.

UNITED STATES-VIETNAM RELATIONS, 1945-1967. 12 vols. Washington, D.C.: Government Printing Office, 1971.

The official government release of the Pentagon Papers, many of which were withheld from publication for security reasons. They are an invaluable source of documentary materials concerning the use and misuse of intelligence. Reproduced for the first time are the text of a Special National Intelligence Estimate, SNIE 53-2-61, dated 5 October 1961, "Bloc Support of the Communist Effort Against the Government of Vietnam" (Bloc 11, pp. 292-94), and a digest of National Intelligence Estimate no. 53-63, dated 17 April 1963, "Prospects in South Vietnam" (Bloc 12, pp. 522-24).

Chapter 6

MILITARY INTELLIGENCE

Military intelligence can be strategic or tactical in scope. Often it is a mixture of both. The higher the military headquarters involved, the more strategic in nature is the intelligence it uses or produces; the lower the echelon, the more purely tactical is the intelligence, with more concentration on the enemy in front and less on the broad economic, political, scientific, and sociological aspects of whole nations. Thus, entries will be found throughout this information guide on various aspects of military intelligence of a strategic nature.

The objective in this section is to focus on a selection of references which provide insights into the more tactical and less strategic aspects of intelligence on the national level. Andregg's MANAGEMENT OF DEFENSE INTELLIGENCE deals with military intelligence at the Headquarters, Department of Defense, and Joint Chiefs of Staff levels, the highest component of strategic intelligence. At the intermediate level there are works on intelligence for joint commands (the U.S. Armed Forces Staff College's INTELLIGENCE FOR JOINT FORCES), combined commands (Strong's INTELLIGENCE AT THE TOP), and lower echelon (Ind's ALLIED INTELLIGENCE BUREAU). There are many books and articles on combat or tactical intelligence doctrine, and on ground force, naval, and air force service tactical intelligence of either the United States or of certain foreign countries.

However, much of the literature on combat or tactical intelligence is fast becoming dated. Combat or tactical intelligence is changing rapidly and there are few comprehensive studies in the literature, although a few articles are included in this chapter and in chapter 10.

Three interrelated trends are mentioned here:

First, technological innovations in surveillance and reconnaissance sensors, computers, and communications are making possible an entirely new look in combat or tactical intelligence. Among the most important advances are improved and more time-responsive information acquisition means with greater range, information processing and display advances, and data links for the quick dissemination of information or intelligence. Combat intelligence is fast becoming more machine-intensive whereas it has always been thought of as a job which only humans could perform. In this regard see Dickson and Roth-shild's article, "The Electronic Battlefield," cited in this chapter, and the two Senate Subcommittee reports on electronic battlefield investigations noted in chapter 10.

Second, conflicts such as the one in Vietnam, and counterinsurgency or liberation conflicts, add economic, political, and sociological factors to the conduct of military operation and therefore to the intelligence support needed for them. Only one study has been written specifically on this area, although there are numerous news articles on U.S. Special Forces operations in Vietnam and on the CIA-sponsored operation Phoenix--a combination combat-intelligence and combat-counterintelligence action.

Third, for the past several years modern communications have made it possible for the president, the secretary of defense, or the chairman of the Joint Chiefs of Staff to be present, in effect, on the bridge of a destroyer on blockade duty off Cuba, in the cockpit of a fighter bomber over North Vietnam, or in the command operations center of an infantry division deployed in Germany. Consequently, consideration of the details of low-level combat intelligence has been forced to the highest strategic and national levels of decision making. The North Vietnamese and Vietcong forces fighting in South Vietnam could never pose a direct threat to the security of the United States, yet major discussions occured in Washington before and after the Tet offensive of 1968 on the order-of-battle estimates of these forces right down to the size of battalion units. Press releases at that time reported the decision makers in Washington simply did not believe the enemy strength figures reported by General Westmoreland in Vietnam. They believed the figures on the Vietcong and North Vietnam Army to be inflated in order to justify sending more U.S. troops to the battle area. Congressional hearings were held on the effects of bombing (Bomb Damage Assessment in air tactical intelligence terms) against North Vietnam and newspapers showed copies of aerial photographs taken over North Vietnamese targets. The distinctions between strategic (national) and tactical (combat) intelligence are becoming less clear as higher level intelligence staffs and agencies involve themselves in ever lower levels of combat intelligence. It appears that combat intelligence is becoming less a function of direct and personal support to the commander in the field and more and more a matter of strategic or national policy and decision making. Evidence of this trend is provided by recent news articles reporting efforts to control all intelligence fiscally and managerially at a central level under the director of the Central Intelligence and dominated by the CIA.

Among the many volumes of official histories of World War II and the Korean War (and those being written on the Vietnam War), no single volume on intelligence has been identified, and the coverage of intelligence in each of the volumes varies greatly. Many specific unit or staff histories, after-action reports, and studies have been written on intelligence, but have not become available publicly, secrecy classification being only part of the problem. For example, MacArthur's G-2, Major General Willoughby, stated in the preface of his book, MACARTHUR: 1941-1951, that his staff prepared a "General Intelligence Series running to some 6,000-odd pages." Most of this material written in the field probably ended up in the offices of the chiefs of military history of the three military services and may be available to researchers.

Annual yearbooks and strategic surveys which provide reliable information on the world's nuclear and strategic forces are described in the introduction to part II, Strategic Intelligence.

A. BOOKS, TRAINING MANUALS, TEXTS, MEMOIRS

Andregg, Charles H. MANAGEMENT OF DEFENSE INTELLIGENCE. Washington, D.C.: Industrial College of the Armed Forces, 1968. 52 p. Bibliography, tables of organization.

> This instructional monograph, written by an official of the Defense Intelligence Agency after attendance at the Industrial College, reviews the organizational and procedural changes to military intelligence brought about by the post-World War II revolution in unification and defense-wide management and by the creation of the Defense Intelligence Agency in 1961. Andregg describes the evolution of defense intelligence, the organization of the Defense Intelligence Agency, and the Defense Intelligence Management System.

Collier, Richard. TEN THOUSAND EYES. New York: Dutton, 1958. 320 p. Illustrations, appendix (Cast of Principal Characters). Foreign eds. TEN THOUSAND EYES. London: Collins, 1958; LA GUERRE SECRETE DU MUR DE L'ATLANTIQUE. Paris: Presses de la Cite, 1958; ZEHNTAUSEND AUGEN. Stuttgart, Germany: Diana Verlag, 1960.

> This is the best account of the use of civilians to gather military intelligence behind enemy lines. This book relates how thousands of men and women in occupied France became amateur spies for two years prior to D-Day to provide bits and pieces of information on the German defenses of their Atlantic Wall between Cherbourg and Le Havre. The operation was run and coordinated by the Free French Intelligence Service in London with the help of British intelligence and was so successful that General Omar Bradley, who led the First U.S. Army ashore on D-Day, called it an "incredible and brilliant feat, so valuable that the landing operation succeeded with a minimum of loss of men and material." Richard Collier, free-lance writer and editor, used published and unpublished material, and interviewed many participants including the head of Free French Intelligence, Colonel Andre Dewavrin ("Colonel Passy"), to produce this authentic record of the successful use of many low-level spies, in a remarkably coordinated way, for the collection of specific and valuable tactical military information.

Davidson, Phillip B., and Glass, Robert R. INTELLIGENCE IS FOR COM-
MANDERS. 2d ed. Harrisburg, Pa.: Military Services Publishing Co., 1952.
184 p.

> A concise manual for commanders and intelligence staff officers
> alike. Its primary purpose is to help the commander know the
> value of intelligence, but it also assists intelligence officers in
> understanding the functioning of various intelligence agencies.
> The authors, who were instructors at the army's Command and
> General Staff College at the time they wrote the book, went on
> to become successful high-level intelligence officers--General
> Glass as chief of staff of the Defense Intelligence Agency and
> Lt. General Davidson as deputy assistant secretary of defense for
> intelligence.

Fleming, Peter. OPERATION SEA LION: THE PROJECTED INVASION OF
ENGLAND IN 1940, AN ACCOUNT OF THE GERMAN PREPARATIONS AND
THE BRITISH COUNTERMEASURES. New York: Simon & Schuster, 1957.
323 p. Index, bibliography, photographs, map, illustrations.

> A thorough and objective study, based on German as well as Brit-
> ish sources, of the German plans to invade England and the Brit-
> ish plans to repel the projected invasion. Of particular interest
> are chapters 11 and 12, which describe the battle between the
> intelligence staffs on both sides of the channel.

Garthoff, Raymond L. SOVIET MILITARY DOCTRINE. Glencoe, Ill.: Free
Press, 1953. 587 p. Index, bibliography, notes, glossary, charts.

> A soundly documented pioneer study with insights into Soviet com-
> bat intelligence doctrine. Some information on the organization
> for intelligence in the wartime High Command and Stavka.

Grant, Robert M. U-BOAT INTELLIGENCE 1914-1918. Hamden, Conn.:
Archon, 1969. 192 p. Illustrated.

> An account of how the development of naval intelligence in inter-
> ception of radio signals, cryptography, radio direction finding,
> prisoner interrogation, and analysis of captured documents led to
> actual U-boat sinkings in World War II.

HANDBOOK OF GERMAN MILITARY FORCES (TM-E30-451) and HANDBOOK
OF JAPANESE MILITARY FORCES (TM-E30-480). Gaithersburg, Md.: Military Press, 1970. 550 p. each. Illustrations, index, maps.

> These two U.S. Army technical manuals were reprinted for sale by
> the Military Press. The German forces manual is dated 15 March
> 1945, and the Japanese forces manual, October 1944. Each was
> classified restricted and represented the knowledge of the enemy,
> obtained through intelligence, on tactics, organization, order of
> battle, and weapons and equipment. These handbooks represent

important military intelligence products of the War Department during World War II.

Hay, John H., Jr. TACTICAL AND MATERIEL INNOVATIONS. Vietnam Studies, Department of the Army. Washington, D.C.: Government Printing Office, 1974. 197 p. Index, illustrations, maps, glossary.

A monograph which discusses some of the more important tactical and materiel innovations in Vietnam from the viewpoint of the infantry division commander. Some discussion is devoted to the realization that traditional methods of collecting, analyzing, and disseminating intelligence information were inadequate to the needs of the Vietnam War. Describes the development of acoustic, magnetic, and seismic sensors, platforms for airborne reconnaissance, and surveillance and observation devices--forerunners of the automated battlefield.

Heymont, Irving. COMBAT INTELLIGENCE IN MODERN WARFARE. Harrisburg, Pa.: Stackpole, 1960. 244 p.

In this most recent of the professional texts on combat intelligence, Colonel Heymont has put together an analysis that is a must for reading, study, or reference. The book was translated and published in Moscow in 1963.

Ind, Allison W. ALLIED INTELLIGENCE BUREAU: OUR SECRET WEAPON IN THE WAR AGAINST JAPAN. New York: David McKay, 1958. 305 p. Illustrations, maps, index.

The Allied Intelligence Bureau (AIB) was the espionage and clandestine services arm of MacArthur's intelligence staff, made up of American, Australian, British, and Dutch personnel. Colonel Ind, American deputy to the Australian head of AIB, emphasizes the activities of the Australian coast watchers, concealed on Japanese-held islands, in collecting information on naval and shipping movements and aircraft overflights. He also describes the intelligence gathering and paramilitary operations of the guerrilla bands in the Philippines, providing operational and methodological insights. The sabotage operations of the Services Reconnaissance Department of AIB against the enemy-held Celebes Islands and Borneo and against shipping in Singapore harbor are also described. For more on intelligence operations in the Philippines see Wise's SECRET MISSION TO THE PHILIPPINES (this chapter).

Koch, Oscar W., and Hays, Robert G. G-2: INTELLIGENCE FOR PATTON. New York: Whitemore Publishing Co., 1972. 167 p.

The late General Koch was Patton's assistant chief of staff, intelligence (G-2) and in this all-too-short book he describes his own tested methods of collecting battlefield information and producing tactical intelligence. He also tells how Patton utilized Koch's intelligence in making command decisions in the battles after the North Africa campaign, before the invasion of Germany.

Leverkuehn, Paul. GERMAN MILITARY INTELLIGENCE. New York: Praeger; Longon: Weidenfeld and Nicolson, 1954. vii, 209 p. Illustrations, organization charts.

During World War II the author was chief of German military intelligence (Abwehr) in Turkey and the Near East, and describes some of his experiences. However, he has also attempted to write a history of the Abwehr that spells out its organization and functions. The Abwehr was a joint army, navy, and air force intelligence organization of the general staff, headed by an admiral, Canaris. Its establishment preceded by about thirty years the setting up of a joint military intelligence organization in the United States, the Defense Intelligence Agency. For an account of the takeover of military intelligence in 1944 by the Nazi party intelligence agency see Walter Schellenberg's THE LABYRINTH (chapter 14, section F).

McChristian, Joseph A. THE ROLE OF MILITARY INTELLIGENCE 1965-1967. Vietnam Studies, U.S. Department of the Army. Washington, D.C.: Government Printing Office, 1974. 182 p. Index, glossary, organization charts, photographs.

The author was General Westmoreland's chief of intelligence during the period 1965-67. This is a comprehensive account of the role and development of military intelligence during that period. Described in detail are the concepts and organizations developed for the conduct of combined intelligence activities with the Vietnamese armed forces. Until an official history of the Vietnam War is published by the army this is a valuable and useful account of the buildup period of U.S. combat intelligence in that area.

McLachlan, Donald. ROOM 39: A STUDY IN NAVAL INTELLIGENCE. Foreword by Admiral Louis Mountbatten. New York: Atheneum, 1968. xvii, 438 p. Index, notes, organization chart, appendix.

A dramatic account of the activities of British naval intelligence in Room 39 of the Admiralty. Room 39 was the nerve center of naval intelligence where raw information was analyzed resulting in orders for the British fleet in its battle against U-boats, the German navy, and merchant shipping. Chapter 2 contains a description and analysis of seventeen sources of intelligence information used as an input to Room 39 operations. The author, a professional editor and writer, served on the personal staff of the director of naval intelligence from 1940 to 1945, yet this book is much more than a memoir. It is a thorough discussion of the principles and philosphy of naval intelligence as conducted in World War II.

Mashbir, Sidney F. I WAS AN AMERICAN SPY. New York: Vantage Press, 1953. x, 374 p. Index, illustrations.

> The story of a remarkable military intelligence career, spanning thirty-five years as a National Guardsman, Regular, Reserve, and Army of the United States (AUS) officer, beginning as an intelligence specialist in the Mexican trouble in 1916 through the surrender of Japan in 1945. He was a language and area student in Japan for several years, engaged in intelligence during the period between the wars, and during World War II developed and headed the Allied Translator and Interpreter Section (ATIS) of MacArthur's intelligence staff, one of the best and most successful intelligence activities of the war. Along with Zacharias's SECRET MISSIONS: THE STORY OF AN INTELLIGENCE OFFICER (see below), this is one of the best books available on intelligence against Japan. Like Zacharias, Mashbir engaged in psychological warfare planning against the homeland of Japan, as well as against troops in the field.

Miles, Milton E., as prepared by Hawthorne, Daniel, from the original manuscript. A DIFFERENT KIND OF WAR: THE LITTLE-KNOWN STORY OF THE COMBINED GUERRILLA FORCES CREATED IN CHINA BY THE U.S. NAVY AND THE CHINESE DURING WORLD WAR II. Foreword by Arleigh Burke. Garden City, N.Y.: Doubleday, 1967. xv, 629 p. Index, appendices, illustrations.

> Shortly after the Pearl Harbor attack, Miles, who was then a commander, was ordered to establish weather stations in China and a coast watcher system to support the Pacific Fleet, and to collect information for possible landings on the China coast. From this original intelligence mission, the activity grew to the creation of the Sino-American Cooperative Association (SACO), an organization for the training, equipping, and operation of an extensive guerrilla force against Japanese occupation troops that eventually had more than 2,500 Americans and between 50,000 and 100,000 Chinese fishermen, pirates, police, and regular guerrilla forces. Miles also relates how jealousy and distrust of the Chinese head of SACO, General Tai Li, led the U.S. Army, State Department, and the Office of Strategic Services to duplicate intelligence and guerrilla operations in China.

Nelson, Otto L., Jr. NATIONAL SECURITY AND THE GENERAL STAFF: A STUDY OF ORGANIZATION AND ADMINISTRATION. Washington D.C.: Infantry Journal Press, 1946. vi, 608 p. Index, footnotes, charts, tables of organization.

> In this unique book General Nelson, a student and specialist on administration and organization, develops the history of the general staff of the U.S. Army from its emergence after the Spanish-American War, through various changes and reorganizations after World War I, and through World War II and the broadening of the

general staff concept to the Joint Chiefs of Staff. Throughout the nine chapters on the various stages of the development of the general staff, General Nelson includes sections on the evolution of the military intelligence staff elements and analyzes their relationship to the rest of the general staff.

O'Ballance, Edgar. THE ELECTRONIC WAR IN THE MIDDLE EAST: 1968-1970. Hamden, Conn.: Archon Books; London: Faber and Faber, 1974. 148 p. Index, maps.

The author of seven books on Middle-Eastern warfare, O'Ballance describes what he terms the first full-scale electronic conflict. He sees the war as a proxy conflict in which both the United States and the USSR battle-tested their sophisticated weapon systems, electronic sensors, electronic jammers, and countermeasure devices against each other, using the Israeli and Egyptian military forces and intelligence organizations as go-betweens. The author provides a useful account of the war that ended in a cease-fire in August 1970. He acquired his technical details on sensors and sensor countermeasures from briefings, interviews, and visits to the battlefield.

Phillips, C.E. Lucas. THE GREATEST RAID OF ALL. Boston: Little, Brown and Co., 1960. 270 p.

The "greatest raid" was on the port of St. Nazaire in March 1942, by a joint force of British commandos and naval units. The special force put out of action the only dry dock on the Atlantic coast that could service the German battleship Tirpitz, forcing the return of the Tirpitz to the north. The raid was based on sound geographic and combat intelligence, a near textbook example of the use of intelligence for a one-time armed raid against hostile port installations.

Pogue, Forrest C. THE EUROPEAN THEATER OF OPERATIONS: THE SUPREME COMMAND. U.S. Army in World War II Series; Office, Chief of Military History. Washington, D.C.: Government Printing Office, 1954. 610 p. Index, illustrations, charts, maps, bibliography, footnotes.

This history of Supreme Headquarters, Allied Expeditionary Forces (SHAEF) contains accounts of the various intelligence estimates made to support decisions before and after D-Day. It also includes information on German intelligence estimates of Allied capabilities, and information on the activities and operations of the SHAEF intelligence staff division (G-2 Division, SHAEF).

Roskill, S.W. THE SECRET CAPTURE. London: Collins, 1959. 156 p.

An account of naval intelligence during the critical Battle of the Atlantic. Stresses the intelligence value of the documents and equipment acquired from the capture of German U-boat 110 by the escort vessels of a westbound North Atlantic convoy from England in May 1941.

Schemmer, Benjamin F. THE RAID. New York: Harper and Row, 1976. 326 p. Index, bibliography, appendices, photographs, maps, aerial photographs.

The chronicle of the November 1970 raid on a camp at Sontay, North Vietnam, by American commandos in an attempt to liberate U.S. prisoners of war. The author, editor of the ARMED FORCES JOURNAL, wrote this authoritative book from an after-action report obtained through the Freedom of Information Act and from material obtained from planners and participants of the operation. The role of intelligence in the planning and conduct of the operation is described in detail. For example, from aerial photographs and from an agent inside Hanoi it was known that the prisoners had been moved due to flooding possibly caused by the CIA's secret rainmaking operations, yet the operations were not cancelled. The book contains some important insights into interworkings of Washington-based intelligence agencies and the Pentagon and national political decision makers during the Vietnam War.

Stagg, J.M. FORECAST FOR OVERLORD. New York: W.W. Norton & Co., 1972. 128 p. Illustrations, maps.

Eisenhower's chief meteorologist's account of the weather forecasts associated with the Normandy landings. Stresses the importance of presenting this type intelligence to the decision makers, the problems of dealing with the special requirements of air, naval, and land forces of two nationalities, and the reconciling of conflicting estimates made by weathermen of lower echelons all of whom thought their estimates the most reliable.

Stead, Philip John. SECOND BUREAU. London: Evans Brothers, 1959. 212 p. French ed. LE DEUXIEME BUREAU. Paris: Frayard, 1966. 240 p.

This was the first wartime history of the regular French military intelligence service, the Deuxieme Bureau of the General Staff, to be written in English by a British author who has specialized in this field. The author exposes the difficulties of conducting military intelligence and especially counterintelligence in occupied and unoccupied France after the armistice, and relates the problems in transferring personnel and files to North Africa after the landings there. Also cited in chapter 4, section E.

Strong, Sir Kenneth. INTELLIGENCE AT THE TOP: THE RECOLLECTIONS OF AN INTELLIGENCE OFFICER. Garden City, N.Y.: Doubleday, 1969. xiv, 366 p. Index, bibliography, illustrations. British ed. London: Cassell, 1968. xv, 366 p. Bibliography, index.

The first part of these memoirs deals with the early intelligence assignments of General Strong, especially as military attache in the British embassy in Berlin. The bulk of the book concerns World War II when General Strong was chief of intelligence for Allied Force Headquarters in Africa and then chief of intelligence for Supreme Headquarters, Allied Expeditionary Forces (SHAEF), where he remained throughout the war. The memoirs also cover postwar assignments of General Strong, first as founder and director of the Joint Intelligence Bureau in London, and then as director-general of intelligence in the Ministry of Defense. These assignments were at the national level and provide an excellent insight into postwar British intelligence reorganizations. The book is a gold mine of information and personal impressions of intelligence at the SHAEF level, the role it played in important battles and in the Italian armistice and Germany's surrender, and on the nature and methods of wartime military intelligence in a combined high-level headquarters.

_____. MEN OF INTELLIGENCE. New York: St. Martin's Press, 1972. 183 p. Index, illustrations.

The author examines the roles and decisions of a dozen chiefs of intelligence of four major powers from 1914 to the present. Almost half of the book is devoted to tracing the evolution of major intelligence decisions of Britain, France, and Germany through World War II.

Strutton, Bill, and Pearson, Michael. THE SECRET INVADERS. London: Hodder & Stoughton, 1958. 287 p.

An account of the British Combined Operations Pilotage Parties which, during World War II, collected defense, geographic, coast, and landing beach intelligence for the planning of amphibious operations, including the Normandy landings, by sending swimmers to make observations and measurements.

Thorpe, Elliott R. EAST WIND, RAIN; THE INTIMATE ACCOUNT OF AN INTELLIGENCE OFFICER IN THE PACIFIC, 1939-1949. Boston: Gambit, 1969. ix, 307 p. Index.

The autobiography of an experienced military intelligence officer. His career began in Hawaii before Pearl Harbor and continued through the Dutch East Indies, Malaya, Australia, the Philippines, Japan, and postwar Thailand. General Thorpe was MacArthur's chief of counterintelligence during World War II, his chief of civil intelligence in occupied Japan, and military attache to Thailand from 1948 to 1949. This book gives impressive insights into interrogation, escape and evasion, and censorship·techniques, but also provides candid commentary on the utilization of intelligence and on the controversial policy issues in the Pacific theater of operations. The title comes from the "winds message" which was broadcast on Japanese weather stations to signal the launching of surprise attacks.

Townsend, Elias C. RISKS: THE KEY TO COMBAT INTELLIGENCE. Harrisburg, Pa.: Military Service Publishing Co., 1955. xii, 82 p. Paperbound. Index, bibliography.

This short commonsensical text is a critical analysis of army combat intelligence doctrine of the mid-1950s and its relationship to the combat commander. Colonel Townsend, an instructor and intelligence specialist, makes a strong case for revision of the combat intelligence system to eliminate estimates or opinions of enemy intentions. Instead, Townsend would emphasize the speedy determination and factual presentation of the two major elements of combat intelligence--enemy location and strength.

U.S. Armed Forces Staff College. INTELLIGENCE FOR JOINT FORCES. AFSC Publication 5. Norfolk, Va.: 1965. 128 p. Rev. ed., 1967. 96 p.

This is the manual used in the Armed Forces Staff College for instruction in the doctrine and organization of military intelligence in support of joint army, navy, air force, and marine corps headquarters, and task forces. Since the creation of unified commands within the U.S. Armed Forces, the development of joint intelligence doctrine has been a necessity. This manual represents the basic guide for the conduct of intelligence for joint forces and for the organization and operations of the office of the assistant chief of staff, intelligence (J-2) within joint or unified command headquarters.

U.S. Congress. Senate. Committee on Foreign Relations. EARLY WARNING SYSTEM IN SINAI. 94th Cong., 1st sess., 1975. 264 p. Map, appendix.

Record of the testimony of witnesses regarding the installation of sensor systems in the Sinai, interposed between Israeli and Egyptian forces. The sensor "fence" would be an early warning system manned by U.S. nonmilitary personnel.

U.S. Department of the Army. Headquarters. COMBAT INTELLIGENCE. Field Manual 30-5. Washington, D.C.: Office of the Adjutant General, February 1971. ii, 205 p. Index, illustrations, charts, references, appendices.

This intelligence training manual is the most comprehensive published by the army. It includes references to doctrinal lessons learned in the Vietnam War and discusses the use of modern sensors for collecting information, target acquisition, night observation, and electronic warfare. Appendix A is a listing of all other manuals and regulations on the subject of intelligence and is therefore a bibliography of available army intelligence training literature. The manual contains chapters on the collection, processing, and dissemination of intelligence, and on counterintelligence, with special emphasis on order of battle intelligence, the mainstay of army combat intelligence.

U.S. Marine Corps. Headquarters. INTELLIGENCE. Washington, D.C.: 1967. 425 p.

Vagts, Alfred. THE MILITARY ATTACHE. Princeton, N.J.: Princeton University Press, 1967. 408 p. Bibliography.

An analysis of the history and evolution of the role of the diplomatically accredited military attache as an accepted espionage agent.

Whitehouse, Arch. ESPIONAGE AND COUNTERESPIONAGE: ADVENTURES IN MILITARY INTELLIGENCE. Garden City, N.Y.: Doubleday, 1964. xi, 298 p. Index, bibliography.

This prolific author of books on military subjects has pulled together a number of stories of military intelligence ranging from the American Civil War to the present, with emphasis on World Wars I and II.

Willoughby, Charles A., and Chamberlain, John. MacARTHUR: 1941-1951. New York: McGraw-Hill, 1954. xiii, 441 p. Index, illustrations, maps.

Although this is a book about MacArthur from the defense of the Philippines and battle of Bataan in 1941 to his dismissal during the Korean War in 1951, it was written by his assistant chief of staff, intelligence (G-2). Thus, it is against an intelligence background that the campaigns of MacArthur are presented. Although chapters 7, "MacArthur's Cloak and Dagger Men," and 8, "The Guerrilla Movement in the Philippines," are devoted exclusively to intelligence activities, all chapters contain descriptions of important intelligence operations during World War II and the Korean War, and the entire book must be studied for a complete picture of intelligence in these two Asiatic wars.

Wise, William. SECRET MISSION TO THE PHILIPPINES. New York: E.P. Dutton, 1969. 160 p.

In this short, highly readable book, Wise describes the Spyron operation in the Philippines. Spyron was an Allied Intelligence Bureau (AIB) operation from MacArthur's headquarters in Australia. It was established to collect intelligence for an eventual landing, to provide a system of coast watchers for information on Japanese naval and shipping movements and long-range aircraft early warning, to provide weather information, and to coordinate guerrilla

activities. The hero of Wise's book is navy commander Charles
"Chick" Parsons, who was a prominent Manila businessman before
World War II. He helped establish and organize intelligence and
resistance in the Philippines, and continued to be the driving
force behind many sea infiltrations by submarine from G-2 headquarters in Australia.

Wood, Derek, and Dempster, Derek. THE NARROW MARGIN: THE BATTLE
OF BRITAIN AND THE RISE OF AIR POWER 1930-1940. Rev. ed. New
York: Paperback Library, 1969. 505 p. Paperbound. Index, bibliography,
19 appendices.

The prologue of this remarkable book, which describes both the
British and German sides of the Battle of Britain, contains a detailed account of the electronic reconnaissance flights of the Graf
Zeppelin in 1939 to try to determine if British radar was operational. The lack of success of these first electronic reconnaissance
flights had a profound effect on German air tactics and targeting,
and thus on the outcome of the Battle of Britain. Chapter 5 provides an insight into the intelligence available to each side about
its adversary, with a comparative analysis of RAF and Luftwaffe
striking power at the time the battle began. Chapter 6 describes
the development of radar in Britain and the subsequent bringing
of scientific and technical intelligence to aerial warfare.

Zacharias, Ellis M. SECRET MISSIONS: THE STORY OF AN INTELLIGENCE
OFFICER. New York: G.P. Putnam's Sons, 1946. 351 p. Paperback ed.,
New York: Paperback Library, 1961. 351 p. Complete and unabridged.

A personalized account of the espionage battle against Japan before and during World War II. Admiral Zacharias was one of the
few officers who were trained for intelligence against Japan before
World War II, through assignments as language and area students
to Japan. His knowledge of Japanese enabled him to plan and
conduct an effective psychological warfare campaign. Along with
Mashbir's I WAS AN AMERICAN SPY (see above), the account
of another pre-World War II Japanese language and area student,
this is one of the best and most revealing books available on intelligence against Japan.

B. ARTICLES

Dickerson, Paul, and Rothchild, John. "The Electronic Battlefield: Wiring
Down the War." WASHINGTON MONTHLY, May 1971, pp. 6-14.

An extensive and comprehensive article on the army and air force
programs for deploying newly developed surveillance sensors in
Vietnam and along the Ho Chi Minh Trail in Laos, a concept revolu-
tionizing combat intelligence.

Military Intelligence

Enthoven, Alain C., and Wayne-Smith, K. "What Forces for NATO? And from Whom?" FOREIGN AFFAIRS 48 (October 1969): 80–89.

In this article analyzing the need for U.S. forces in Europe, the authors discuss the controversy over the intelligence estimates on the size of the Warsaw Pact military forces which pose a threat to NATO. Their contention is that the strength of the Warsaw Pact forces has been exaggerated and that the estimates lack proper analysis of the real makeup of the pact land forces.

Heiman, Grover. "Army: Beep to Bang." ARMED FORCES MANAGEMENT, July 1970, pp. 36–39.

An accurate and concise account of the army program to develop new surveillance and target acquisition techniques and material for combat intelligence gathering on the battlefield and to automate its distribution and display for quick utilization. An excellent graphic depicts the entire concept. See also the reports on investigations into the electronic battlefield programs of the services, cited in chapter 10 under U.S. Congress. Senate. Committee on Armed Services. Preparedness Investigation Subcommittee.

Norman, Lloyd H. "Westmoreland's J-2." ARMY 17 (May 1967): 21–25.

Norman, at the time the Pentagon correspondent for NEWSWEEK, describes the activities of Maj. Gen. Joseph A. McChristian, who between 1965 and 1967 was Westmoreland's Assostant Chief of Staff, Intelligence, J-2. Norman reports on the intelligence production, POW interrogation, and captured documents and captured documents and captured materiel exploitation centers organized and built by McChristian as part of the rapid development of combat intelligence in Vietnam.

Williams, Robert W. "Commanders and Intelligence: The Growing Gap." ARMY 22 (December 1972): 21-24.

A thoughtful article by an experienced intelligence officer. Williams suggests that the most serious reason for a growing communications gap between commander and intelligence is the widening separation of military intelligence from the combat arms it is supposed to support, and its relegation to higher echelons and separate agencies.

Chapter 7
COUNTERINTELLIGENCE AND SECURITY: UNITED STATES

Counterintelligence is often referred to as negative intelligence, since its primary objective is to block the efforts by those of inimical interests to obtain secret information and to conduct sabotage and subversion.

Active counterespionage, countersabotage, and countersubversion include specific and resolute operational measures designed to detect and identify individuals, groups, and organizations conducting espionage, sabotage, and subversion in order to neutralize their effectiveness or to exploit them through deception, disinformation, and manipulation.

Passive counterintelligence measures, on the other hand, are designed to conceal or protect information, individuals, and installations against espionage, sabotage, and subversion.

The security of classified information against unauthorized disclosure, access, or transmission is the responsibility of those who handle such information. Counterintelligence agencies assist them by providing (1) checks and inspections to detect weaknesses in security measures, (2) personnel security investigations to determine suitability for employment and to uncover espionage, and (3) security training and indoctrination which expose the methods of operation of foreign espionage organizations. For instance, during the 1950s and 1960s the FBI and various congressional committees published a number of works exposing Communist techniques of subversion. Other important passive counterintelligence measures are censorship and communications security. In order to evade censorship, microdot methods of concealing secret information were developed and used by agents to mail reports to their home bases. The burst or spurt radio transmitter was developed to reduce air time in agent reporting and thus to frustrate counterespionage communications interception and direction finding (DFing) efforts. The spurt transmitter used by Gordon Lonsdale in reporting to Moscow was captured by British counterespionage and photographs of the transmitter were later released in press articles and books describing the Portland Naval Secrets case in 1961. The importance of direction finding as a means of locating agent transmitters and as a wedge opening penetration to espionage networks is illustrated in H.J. Giskes's LONDON CALLING NORTH POLE (see chapter 15, section D2).

Library shelves are quite bare of comprehensive studies of overall counterintelligence organization, functions, doctrine, and tradecraft. The information available on negative intelligence is much worse than that available on the subject of positive intelligence. There is no counterintelligence source equivalent to Sherman Kent's work on intelligence, STRATEGIC INTELLIGENCE FOR AMERICAN WORLD POLICY or to Harry Howe Ransom's THE INTELLIGENCE ESTABLISHMENT (both cited in chapter 4, section A). The growth of open societies, with attendant antisecrecy sentiment, freedom of information, deliberate leaks and disclosures of classified information (the Pentagon Papers, for example), and resentment against surveillance, has created unique counterintelligence problems and implications of national and international importance. In chapters 8 and 9 of SPY IN THE U.S., Pawel Monat and John Dille provide one of the few insights into the counterintelligence problems associated with free speech and freedom of the press. In contrast, a considerable volume of literature has been created on the overclassification of government documents, the right to know, and the invasion of privacy by electronic surveillance methods.

The countersubversion role of counterintelligence has grown and altered significantly since most of the World War II literature was written, although a corresponding unclassified literature of explanation has not developed. Combating Communist-inspired subversive insurgency in the United States has been a priority policy of the cold war. The countering of subversive insurgency abroad has come to be carried out through covert and clandestine operations by the CIA's deputy directorate of operations (see part IV, Covert Operations) while countering domestic subversive insurgency has, as always, been the domain of the FBI. However, certain responsibilities have been delegated to other agencies, including the army's counterintelligence corps. In 1971 countering leaks and disclosures of classified information and other security problems became a matter of concern at the highest level, resulting in the establishment of the Special Investigations Unit under control of the White House staff--the unit later to be called the "Plumbers." Literature available on these activities is generally restricted to exposures of operations by the press followed by reports of investigations by Congress. There is no comprehensive study which analyzes a necessary counterintelligence role versus involvement in the domestic affairs of foreign sovereign nations or the surveillance and repression of individual groups at home.

There is a fair amount of literature available describing the counterespionage, countersabotage, and countersubversion activities and operations of the FBI. These include counterespionage and countersabotage roles in World Wars I and II, plus positive intelligence activities in the Western Hemisphere, economic intelligence activities in Latin America, counterespionage and countersubversion activities against the Soviet Union immediately following World War II (the Atom Spies, for example), and counterespionage and countersubversion during the "Big Red Threat Era." Memoirs of FBI counterspies such as Herbert Philbrick's I LED THREE LIVES and John Huminik's DOUBLE AGENT are illustrative of FBI counterespionage techniques. References to these memoirs and other reports of counterespionage operations and networks will be found in chapter

15. Comprehensive and objective literature describing more recent FBI counterintelligence activities against various domestic groups and organizations is far from adequate, and insights must be gleaned or pieced together from articles and press reports often written in the muckraking or expose tradition.

A. BOOKS AND MONOGRAPHS

Brown, Robert M. THE ELECTRONIC INVASION. New York: John F. Rider Publisher, 1967. 184 p. Paperbound. Illustrations, index.

The author of this electronic equipment surveillance handbook is the editor of a leading mobile radio industry magazine and a licensed private investigator in New York and New Jersey, with experience in personal and corporate surveillance. The guide provides information on techniques, devices, and circuitry, as well as users and suppliers of electronic bugging and de-bugging equipment. A good reference, with an excellent index. Useful for checking on the accuracy of other writings describing electronic bugging and wiretapping incidents and events.

Collins, Frederick L. THE FBI IN PEACE AND WAR. New York: G.P. Putnam's Sons, 1943. Rev. and enl. by Lester Dember. New York: Ace Books, 1962. 320 p. Paperback ed.

An account of the FBI's fight against Nazi and Japanese espionage and sabotage during World War II. In addition there is a limited description of the operations of the FBI's Special Intelligence Service in combating Axis espionage in Central and South America and in preventing cross-border operations into the United States. Descriptions of post-World War II counterespionage operations are sparse, with little detail on the Soviet atom bomb spy rings and a too-brief description of the capture of Rudolf Abel.

Dulles, Allen Welsh. THE CRAFT OF INTELLIGENCE. New York: Harper & Row, 1963. 277 p. Index, bibliography, photographs.

Since the role of the CIA in counterintelligence is primarily one of counterespionage outside the continental limits of the United States, it is this forward line of defense against espionage that Dulles emphasizes in chapter 9 of this work. Of considerable interest are the descriptions of radio direction finding as a means of detecting clandestine agent transmitters during World War II. In chapter 16 Dulles laments the ease with which information is obtained in the United States and the problems this poses to security agencies.

Farago, Ladislas. WAR OF WITS; THE ANATOMY OF ESPIONAGE AND INTELLIGENCE. New York: Funk & Wagnalls, 1954. ix, 379 p. Notes, illustrations, index of names.

This prolific author on intelligence discusses the evolution and some of the theory of counterintelligence, and describes some of the activities of the various counterintelligence agencies, including censorship activities.

Felix, Christopher [pseud.]. "Counterespionage Versus Security, and Other Deviltry." In his A SHORT COURSE IN THE SECRET WAR, pp. 143-54. New York: E.P. Dutton, 1963.

A retired intelligence operations specialist discusses some of the fundamentals of counterespionage and security. Counterespionage, he believes is an operational activity, conceived with intimate, controlled, and purposeful contact with the "enemy," for the primary purpose of penetrating the opposition's own secret operations apparatus with the objective of eventual deception. Security, on the other hand, is protective and defensive, and seeks to sever all contact with the "enemy" as being too dangerous.

Godfrey, E. Drexel, Jr., and Harris, Don R. BASIC ELEMENTS OF INTELLI-GENCE; A MANUAL OF THEORY, STRUCTURE AND PROCEDURES FOR USE BY LAW ENFORCEMENT AGENCIES AGAINST ORGANIZED CRIME. Washington, D.C.: Government Printing Office, 1971. xiii, 150 p. Appendices, bibliography, illustrations.

An excellent manual produced by the Technical Assistance Division, Office of Criminal Justice Assistance, Law Enforcement Assistance Administration, U.S. Department of Justice.

Goulding, Phil G. CONFIRM OR DENY; INFORMING THE PEOPLE ON NATIONAL SECURITY. New York: Harper & Row, 1970. xiii, 369 p. Index.

An ex-assistant secretary of defense for public affairs under Robert McNamara and Clark Clifford describes the conflicts that arose between the demands of the press and the requirements of national security, while trying to inform the public regarding crises and explaining major defense issues in a nuclear world. The author has selected misadventures occurring between mid-1965 and early 1969 in order to provide an insight into the pressures affecting decisions to provide or withhold information. Four of the episodes chosen are intelligence-related: the interception of an American photo-reconnaissance plane by a French jet aircraft in a prohibited area above an atomic plant in 1965; the attack on the intelligence ship U.S.S. Liberty in the Middle East in 1967; the antiballistic missile (ABM) controversies of 1967; and the capture of the intelligence ship U.S.S. Pueblo in 1968.

Hoover, J[ohn]. Edgar. MASTERS OF DECEIT: THE STORY OF COMMUNISM IN AMERICA AND HOW TO FIGHT IT. New York: Henry Holt & Co., 1958. x, 374 p. Index, bibliography, glossary, appendices.

The foreword states: "Every citizen has a duty to learn more about the menace that threatens his future, his home, his children, the peace of the world--and that is why I have written this book." Experts on Hoover and the FBI have an opinion that Hoover did not write this book, and may have never read it. However, the theme of a vast Communist conspiracy was one that was basic to almost everything he did and certainly was basic to the way he directed the FBI. Part 4 of the book contains the description of the espionage, sabotage, and subversion activities of the Communist party underground--the illegal apparatus. Techniques are described along with some collection priorities imposed by Moscow on the illegal apparatus. The material in the book came from files on FBI counterintelligence cases and activities. Good index with appendices providing lists of international Communist organizations and publications along with a chronology of dates and events relating to the history of communism in the United States.

Hyde, H. Montgomery. THE QUIET CANADIAN: THE SECRET SERVICE STORY OF SIR WILLIAM STEPHENSON. Foreword by David Bruce. London: Hamish Hamilton, 1962. xii, 255 p. American ed. ROOM 3603: THE STORY OF THE BRITISH INTELLIGENCE CENTER IN NEW YORK DURING WORLD WAR II. Foreword by Ian Fleming. New York: Farrar, Straus & Co., 1963. 257 p. Index, bibliography, illustrations.

This is the story of the Canadian Sir William Stephenson who established and directed the British Security Coordination (BSC) in New York as an agency to operate British intelligence, counterintelligence, and special operations in the Western Hemisphere before and following U.S. entry into World War II. Hyde has written or coauthored more than twenty-five other works. However, in the case of this book, because he was on the staff of the BSC and a friend of the chief, he was able to draw on the personal archives of Stephenson for material. The book emphasizes counterintelligence activities and describes some of the successes of the British system of censorship and passport control for detection of espionage. BSC worked closely with the FBI in the United States as well as in South and Central America in counterintelligence activities and operations. Authoritative, with a brief bibliography and good index.

Monat, Pawel, and Dille, John. SPY IN THE U.S. New York: Harper & Row, 1962. 208 p.

Monat, Polish army intelligence colonel and military attache in the Polish embassy in Washington, D.C., from 1955 to 1958, defected to the United States and has told his story through LIFE magazine editor Dille. Chapters 8 and 9 describe the ease by which information can be gained in the United States, and thus provides some insight into the problems of counterespionage and security information.

Ottenberg, Miriam. THE FEDERAL INVESTIGATORS. Englewood Cliffs, N.J.: Prentice Hall, 1962. 348 p. Index.

The only book describing the activities of all of the investigative agencies of the government by a Pulitzer Prize-winning reporter of the WASHINGTON STAR. Describes counterespionage and countersubversion activities of the FBI, security activities of the army, navy, air force, and State Department, as well as other investigative agencies and elements of the government.

Perkus, Cathy, ed. COINTELPRO: THE FBI'S SECRET WAR ON POLITICAL FREEDOM. Introduction by Noam Chomsky. New York: Monad Press, 1975. 190 p. Illustrations, reprints of official FBI papers.

This book contains nine essays based on research and interviews plus information obtained from recently released documents of the FBI under the Freedom of Information Act. The essays are enlarged versions of articles that appeared in the socialist newsweekly MILITANT. COINTELPRO is the code name for the FBI's counterintelligence program to track down subversion in the United States. Of special interest is the fact that there are a great many FBI documents reprinted in the book from the COINTELPRO program.

Peyroles, Jacques [Perrault, Gilles]. THE SECRET OF D-DAY. Translated by Len Ortzen. Boston: Little, Brown and Co., 1965. 249 p. Index, bibliography.

Quite the best compilation of available accounts of counterespionage and security operations designed to protect the D-Day place and date, and to deceive German intelligence with false information, especially to convince the German command that the invasion would take place not in Normandy but in Pas de Calais. The author, who received the Prix de la Resistance for this work, describes the battles between German and Allied espionage systems, and highlights the penetration and deception roles of Allied counterintelligence. Also cited in chapter 17, section B.

Tully, Andrew. "The Hollow Nickel." In his CIA: THE INSIDE STORY, pp. 230-42. New York: William Morrow & Co., 1962.

A journalistic account of the counterintelligence cooperation between the CIA and FBI in the detection and exposure of Soviet espionage agent Rudolf Invanovich Abel.

Ungar, Sanford J. FBI: AN UNCENSORED LOOK BEHIND THE WALLS. Boston: Atlantic; Little, Brown and Co., 1976. 682 p. Index, bibliography, glossary, organization chart, illustrations, appendix.

The most definitive and balanced history of the FBI written by an outsider. This is not a book exclusively about intelligence and counterintelligence in the FBI, but it does contain throughout information on the intelligence and counterintelligence activities of

the bureau. Chapter 6 is devoted exclusively to counterintelligence. The author, Washington editor of ATLANTIC MONTHLY
and writer of an award-winning book on the Pentagon Papers, had
access to FBI files and records, and was given permission to supplement this material by interviews with past key figures of the
bureau. He has concentrated on the operational aspects of the
FBI machine, and has provided useful insights on how the bureau
acted to protect the United States from suspected international
Communist conspiracy. Important information is revealed on the
FBI's surveillance of the leftists, extremists, and terrorists during
the height of the cold war, as one means of combating hostile intelligence infiltration and the spread of subversion. Of particular
interest are the inside views one obtains regarding the tensions between the FBI and the other intelligence agencies. No footnotes
are available for expansion of source material or checking on the
author's interpretation of the data.

Whitehead, Don. THE FBI STORY. New York: Random House, 1956. 368 p.
Index, notes.

An excellent history of FBI counterintelligence and security activities through the mid-1950s by a successful journalist who had the
full cooperation of J. Edgar Hoover and FBI personnel. There
are sections on counterespionage and countersabotage activities
against German intelligence in World Wars I and II. The account
of the operations of the FBI's Special Intelligence Service in positive intelligence and economic warfare in Latin America during
1940-46 is of special interest since this expansion of function
caused bureaucratic squabbles with other intelligence agencies,
especially the OSS. There is also a chapter on counterespionage
and countersubversion activities against the Communist conspiracy
in the early days of the cold war.

Wise, David. THE POLITICS OF LYING: GOVERNMENT DECEPTION, SE-
CRECY AND POWER. New York: Random House, 1973. 415 p. Bibliography, notes, index.

An informing, stinging critique of government deception, secrecy,
and relations with the press including the technique of press leaks.
See also the annotations in chapter 8, section A, and chapter 19.

B. ARTICLES AND REPORTS

Blackstock, Paul W. "Political Surveillance and the Constitutional Order."
WORLDVIEW 14 (May 1971): 11-14.

An analysis of the broad political and constitutional implications
of surveillance of civilians by U.S. Army counterintelligence agencies investigated by Senator Sam Ervin's Subcommittee on Constitu-

tional Rights. The author argues that political surveillance erodes the foundations of the democratic state.

"Classifying and De-classifying of Papers." WASHINGTON POST, 22 June 1971, p. A11.

A copy of an affidavit presented in open session in the U.S. District Court during the Pentagon Papers affair by George MacClain, director of security classification management in the Office of the Deputy Assistant Secretary of Defense for Security Policy. The affidavit is a detailed and authoritative description of the classification and declassification process. The affidavit cites Executive Order 10501, "Safeguarding Official Information in the Interests of the Defense of the United States" (originally put into force by President Eisenhower on 5 November 1953, and amended over the years), as the basic authority for classification and declassification, and identifies Department of Defense Instruction 5210.47, "Security Classification of Official Information," 31 December 1964, and Department of Defense Directive 5200.10, "Downgrading and Declassification of Classified Defense Information," 26 July 1962, as implementing regulations of the Executive Order. Other implementing instructions include "Industrial Security Manual for Safeguarding Classified Information" (available through the Government Printing Office) and Army Regulations 380-5, "Military Security."

Goldberg, David M. "Cold War Thaw Revives U.S. Card-Carrying Communists." WASHINGTON POST, 26 August 1973, p. F1.

Columnist Goldberg describes the signs of the thaw that has convinced many Americans that the Communist threat has eased and there is no longer a danger of overthrow of the U.S. government.

"How Detente Opens Doors for Soviet Spies in the U.S." U.S. NEWS & WORLD REPORT, 23 February 1976, pp. 18-19.

A survey article on the rise of the numbers of Soviet-bloc spies in the United States as relations with the Soviet Union expand and at a time when Congress is investigating U.S. spying abroad and in the United States. The article provides figures on the increase in the number of Soviet spies over the past five years, and lists those enlarged missions to the United States, 70 to 80 percent of the members of which are assigned some intelligence task by Moscow.

"Memorandums Urged Nixon to Set Up Program of Spying." WASHINGTON POST, 8 June 1973, p. A15.

This article contains copies of top-secret memorandums written by ex-Nixon aide Tom Charles Huston in July 1970 recommending a comprehensive program for improving domestic intelligence. The decision memorandum proposes the organization of an Interagency Group on Domestic Intelligence and Internal Security (IAG) with members consisting of representatives of the FBI, CIA, Defense Intelligence Agency, National Security Agency, and the counterintelligence agencies of the army, navy, and air force. The memorandums were first printed in the 7 June 1973 issue of the NEW YORK TIMES.

"1970 Intelligence Plan." WASHINGTON POST, 23 May 1973, p. A10.

Text of the statement issued by President Nixon relative to his efforts in 1970 to improve domestic intelligence and to stop leakage of national security secrets. Noting that coordination among intelligence agencies had fallen short of national security needs and that the FBI had shut off liaison with the CIA and other agencies, the president sought advice, established an Intelligence Evaluation Committee, and approved the creation of a special investigations unit, later to become known as the "Plumbers," to stop disclosures and leaks and to look into other sensitive security matters.

Political Rights Defense Fund. A CHALLENGE TO THE WATERGATE CRIMES. New York: 1974. 8" X 11" brochure. 39 p.

Produced for the purpose of raising money, this brochure reproduces documents concerning the $27 million damage suit filed in July 1973 by Leonard Boudin, the defense lawyer in the Ellsberg case, on behalf of the Socialist Workers Party. Also included in the collection are copies of numerous press clippings about the suit, the government reply, and FBI documents regarding a counterintelligence program against the New Left movement and directives placing a mail cover (censorship) on the Socialist Workers Party.

Rositzke, Harry. "America's Secret Operations: A Perspective." FOREIGN AFFAIRS 53 (January 1975): 334-51.

In an important article concerned mainly with counterintelligence functions, the author, a twenty-seven-year veteran of the OSS and the CIA, argues convincingly that propaganda and paramilitary operations do not belong in a secret intelligence service even if they are worth doing at all. Further, the author does not believe that covert political operations designed to sway elections in foreign countries or to overturn governments belong in a secret intelligence organization. The author argues, however, that there will continue to be occasions when support of a few individuals for intelligence purposes cannot (and should not) be separated from a measure of support for their political ends. There should be a means whereby the president, or a local ambassador, would be able to support a foreign political or labor leader who cannot afford to accept American largesse publicly. See also the annotation for this article in chapter 16.

Shloss, Leon. "DOD Security: The New Look." GOVERNMENT EXECUTIVE 1 (October 1969): 44-46.

The article, by GOVERNMENT EXECUTIVE's senior editor, describes new efforts by Director for Security Policy Joseph J. Liebling to get the "gumshoe" stigma off security, and to replace it with a reasonable policy consistent with national security and national interests. The changes noted in the article occurred when Secretary of Defense Laird gave Assistant Secretary of Defense Robert F. Froehlke new responsibilities in both intelligence and security. Liebling worked under Froehlke.

Szulc, Tad. "Secret Reports Keep Air Force Informed on Radicals." NEW YORK TIMES, 29 January 1971, p. 10.

A detailed article on the activities of the Office of Social Investigations (OSI) of the air force, which has responsibility for both counterintelligence and criminal investigations. Specially noted is the Significant Counterintelligence Briefs (SCIB), a secret bimonthly publication of the OSI, intended to keep air force commanders apprised of internal threats.

Ungar, Sanford J. "Internal Security Dies Quietly at Justice." WASHINGTON POST, 27 March 1973, pp. A1, A9.

The article announces the abolition of the Internal Security Division of the Justice Department and the transfer of its functions to the Criminal Division. The background of the Internal Security Division is traced, and it is suggested that its abolition was a sign of diminishing fear of the threat of subversion and the requirement to fight it.

U.S. Congress. House. Committee on Un-American Activities. GUIDE TO SUBVERSIVE ORGANIZATIONS AND PUBLICATIONS (AND APPENDICES), REVISED AND PUBLISHED DECEMBER 1, 1961 (INCLUDING INDEX). 87th Cong., 2d sess., 1961. House Doc. no. 398. xxxvii, 248 p. Index.

This handbook consists of a compilation of 663 organizations or projects and 122 publications declared to be Communist-front or outright Communist enterprises in official statements by federal agencies, and 155 organizations and 25 publications cited to be Communist or Communist-front by state or territorial investigating committees. Outright Communist enterprises and Communist-front organizations are defined in the introduction to the guide. The need for this guide and the Subversive Activities Control Board (SACB) has been questioned since mid-1971, and received publicity with the appointment of Otto Otepka to SACB after his suspension from a State Department security post. The board was abolished in 1973.

U.S. Congress. Senate. Committee on the Judiciary. Subcommittee on Constitutional Rights. MILITARY SURVEILLANCE OF CIVILIAN POLITICS. 93d Cong., 1st sess., 1973. 150 p. Tables, charts.

The best single source of detailed information on the organization, functions, and activities of military counterintelligence agencies, especially U.S. Army agencies. The Senate report traces the origins, history, and purposes of domestic intelligence with generous references and reprints of directives and policies establishing counterintelligence needs and priorities. The appendix contains a copy of the Intelligence Annex to the army's Civil Disturbance Plan and a copy of the Intelligence Information Collection Plan which developed from the army's Civil Disturbance Plan, both unique insights to behind-the-scenes intelligence activities in available counterintelligence literature.

U.S. Department of Justice. REPORT OF THE ATTORNEY GENERAL TO THE CONGRESS OF THE UNITED STATES ON THE ADMINISTRATION OF THE FOREIGN AGENTS REGISTRATION ACT OF 1938, AS AMENDED FOR THE CALENDAR YEAR 1972. Washington, D.C.: Government Printing Office, 1973. 208 p. Paperbound.

This is a report to the Congress (and the nation) of the nature, source, and content of political propaganda disseminated by agents of foreign governments, foreign political parties, or other foreign principals registered under the Foreign Agent's Registration Act. The report consists of analysis of the important trends noted during 1972 in the propaganda material distributed, an alphabetical list of all foreign agent registrants for the year 1972, and a listing according to geographical area or nationality of registrants.

Chapter 8

SECRECY AND SECURITY VERSUS FREEDOM OF INFORMATION AND THE RIGHT TO PRIVACY

The publication of the Pentagon Papers and the Anderson Papers plus leaks of government secret documents has created considerable controversy regarding national security and national interests in light of the importance of freedom of information and the right to privacy. A list of titles selected from the growing literature on this subject is contained in this chapter.

A. BOOKS AND MONOGRAPHS

Barker, Carol M., and Fow, Matthew H. CLASSIFIED FILES: THE YELLOW-ING PAGES--A REPORT ON SCHOLAR'S ACCESS TO GOVERNMENT DOCU-MENTS. New York: Twentieth Century Fund, 1972. 115 p. Four appendices, including the text of the Freedom of Information Act.

> Written by research associates of the Twentieth Century Fund, the report is an excellent analysis of the problem of security versus freedom of information.

Chevigny, Paul. COPS AND REBELS: A STUDY OF PROVOCATION. New York: Pantheon, 1972. 332 p.

> A study of political surveillance by the intelligence arm of the New York City Police Department. The author, a New York Civil Liberties Union lawyer, served as one of the defense attorneys for three members of the Brooklyn Black Panther Party who were arrested for attempted robbery and possession of illegal weapons through the efforts of a police undercover agent. Chevigny argues that undercover agents tend to step across the boundary dividing the collector of intelligence from the agent provocateur. He cites numerous examples.

Dorsen, Norman, and Gillers, Stephen, eds. NONE OF YOUR BUSINESS: GOVERNMENT SECRECY IN AMERICA. Introduction by Anthony Lewis. New York: Viking Press, 1974. xvii, 362 p. Notes, bibliography.

> A conference was held in New York in May 1973 by the Committee

for Public Justice and the New York University Law School. The results are published as an assortment of essays by leading public figures, historians, lawyers, journalists, and political scientists whose overall thrust is an exploration of the political implications of governmental secrecy within a democratic society. Each contributor has a different perception about the degree of public scrutiny that should be afforded to classified government information; however, most of the participants favor the formation of a more open government that would function with the support of an informed, intelligent electorate. Professor M.L. Stein's discussion of the prevalence of secrecy in local government forges an interesting link between local secrecy and national attitudes towards secrecy as displayed in Watergate. Morton H. Halperin and Jeremy J. Stone highlight several of the CIA's "dirty tricks" abroad and recommend the dismantling of the CIA covert operations department.

Halperin, Morton H., et al. THE LAWLESS STATE. THE CRIMES OF THE U.S. INTELLIGENCE AGENCIES. New York: Penguin Books, 1976. 328 p. Paperbound.

The authors, all working for reform in government, provide a documented and footnoted compilation of the misdeeds of the U.S. intelligence agencies from the CIA abroad to the FBI in the United States. Morton Halperin, while a member of the National Security Council staff in the Nixon administration, had his telephone bugged. He has since led a fight for reform and has made requests for information about the activities of intelligence organizations under the Freedom of Information Act.

Ladd, Bruce. CRISIS IN CREDIBILITY. New York: New American Library, 1968. vii, 247 p. Index, selected bibliography, chapter notes.

Written by a former reporter and congressional staff assistant, this is an excellent, well-researched and well-written study which aims "to discuss the credibility problem in a manner which will enable the reader to comprehend its broad scope. . . . It deals exclusively with three practices of the executive branch--secrecy, lying, and news management."

Marchetti, Victor, and Marks, John D. THE CIA AND THE CULT OF INTELLIGENCE. New York: Knopf, 1974. 398 p. Index, appendix.

Marchetti and Marks, both experienced intelligence officers, combine in this book to disclose CIA political and espionage covert operations since the early 1950s. Prior to publication, the manuscript met with substantial opposition on the basis that it would "result in grave and irreparable injury to the interests of the United States." The book was printed before a final censorship decision was made; it appeared with 168 blanks while 171 restored passages were printed in bold face for easy identification. The American

Civil Liberties Union defended the manuscript against censorship. Since the publication of this unique book, CIA Director William E. Colby and President Gerald Ford have proposed that legislation be passed which would prevent the future publication of books by ex-intelligence officials, when such publication would be harmful to the protection of intelligence sources and methods.

An annotation describing the contents of this book, which made bestseller lists during the summer of 1974, can be found in chapter 16.

REPORT TO THE PRESIDENT BY THE COMMISSION ON CIA ACTIVITIES WITHIN THE UNITED STATES. Washington, D.C.: Government Printing Office, June 1975. 299 p. Paperbound.

This is the text of the final report of Vice-President Nelson Rockefeller and his seven-man panel which investigated allegations, made chiefly by NEW YORK TIMES correspondent Seymour Hersh (see section B, this chapter), that the CIA had conducted massive operations within the United States during the 1960s and early 1970s. The report, released to the public by the president during a nationally televised press conference on 10 June 1975, contains specifics on the CIA's domestic intelligence operations such as infiltration of anti-Vietnam War groups and the interception and examination of U.S. mails. Findings, conclusions, and thirty recommendations are included in the report. It contains seven appendices: appendix 3 is the CIA charter from the National Security Act of 1947, as amended. Appendix 6 contains proposed changes to these statutes. Altogether a unique look behind the scenes of CIA's activities and operations.

Szulc, Tad. COMPULSIVE SPY: THE STRANGE CAREER OF E. HOWARD HUNT. New York: Viking Press, 1974. ix, 180 p. No index.

This book by a former NEW YORK TIMES correspondent is much more than a biographical sketch of the principal figure in the Watergate break-in, E. Howard Hunt. The first section, "The Backdrop " (pp. 1-44) is an excellent analysis of the "national security" measures taken by the Nixon administration; these measures led directly to Watergate. In this regard the book is more a study of counterintelligence and security under the special conditions of the period than a biography. The author's thesis is that "both Watergate and those associated with it were . . . the result of a strange American historical process with roots in the early years of the cold war. This process culminated in a plan, first conceived in Richard M. Nixon's White House in 1970, to apply cold war techniques of foreign intelligence operations to political surveillance, espionage, and sabotage against Americans at home. Watergate, therefore, was actually launched in July 1970, when President Nixon approved a top-secret plan for domestic intelligence operations, although the psychological climate for it had existed for a long time among the men who thought it up."

Turner, William W. HOOVER'S F.B.I.: THE MEN AND THE MYTH. Los Angeles: Sherbourne Press, 1970. xv, 352 p. Appendix, no index.

The author was an FBI agent for ten years and writes from that perspective. A third of the book is autobiographical, and the other sections are critical studies of the late director, J. Edgar Hoover, and of the organization itself. An informed, balanced account and a valuable source. See also the annotation for this work in chapter 15, section A.

West, Rebecca [pseud.]. THE NEW MEANING OF TREASON. New York: Viking Press, 1964. viii, 374 p.

The author traces the treasonous activities of the various people who agreed to spy for the Soviet Union in England and the United States during the 1950s and '60s. The book is a revision of her important classic of 1947--THE MEANING OF TREASON. Among the spies whose treason the author assesses are the atomic bomb spies, McLean and Burgess, Harry Houghton, Winifred Gee, Peter and Helen Kroger, George Blake, and William Vassal. Most of the books and articles cited in this section of the bibliography are concerned with the harm to personal freedom caused by the investigations and surveillance of counterespionage and security agencies. This book reveals the other side of the coin--the harm to national security by too little attention to protection of classi- fied information and investigation of traitors. The author condemns the casual acceptance of spying for the Soviet Union.

Westin, Alen F. PRIVACY AND FREEDOM. New York: Atheneum, 1967. 487 p. Index, bibliography, notes.

Written by a lawyer and political scientist and sponsored by the Special Committee on Science and Law of the New York City Bar Association and the Carnegie Corporation, this is the definitive work on the subject of privacy and freedom. A comprehensive bibliography of several hundred items includes technical literature on surveillance tools and techniques. Chapters 4 through 7 pro- vide the best coverage available of the application of technologi- cal developments for surveillance purposes.

_____, ed. INFORMATION TECHNOLOGY IN A DEMOCRACY. Cambridge, Mass.: Harvard University Press, 1971. 499 p. Index, bibliography.

The editor describes this work as "an edited collection of original and secondary materials about government use of information tech- nology . . . [which] includes descriptions of information technol- ogy systems by the agency spokesman and consultants who have created them, providing readers with the operating assumptions, systems objectives, and stages of development as the managers of these systems see these happenings."

Wise, David. THE AMERICAN POLICE STATE: THE GOVERNMENT AGAINST THE PEOPLE. New York: Random House, 1976. 437 p. Index, author's notes.

The author, a political journalist experienced in writing about U.S. intelligence organizations (see THE INVISIBLE GOVERNMENT, chapter 5, and THE POLITICS OF LYING, above), provides a well-organized and thoroughly documented account of the misdeeds of the CIA, FBI, and National Security Agency (NSA). He traces the use of intelligence and police organizations for political purposes or spying on Americans through seven administrations from Roosevelt to Nixon and Ford. Although much of the material has been taken from the Watergate and Nixon impeachment inquiries, the Rockefeller Commission Report and the House (Pike Committee) and Senate (Church Committee) investigations of the intelligence community, this is no mere rehash of already exposed allegations. The book could provide a guide to illegal wiretapping, mail opening, cable reading, bugging, physical surveillance, and break ins perpetrated by intelligence (and police) agencies in the name of national security. Wise provides some suggestions for curtailing these activities.

_____. THE POLITICS OF LYING: GOVERNMENT DECEPTION, SECRECY AND POWER. New York: Random House, 1973. 415 p. Bibliography, notes, index.

An attack on government deception, secrecy, and the security classification system by an ex-newsman and author who, with Thomas B. Ross, has written extensively on intelligence. Because of this acquired knowledge of intelligence, much of the material on deception and secrecy revolves around intelligence-associated incidents. Contains some good insights into the decision-making process where public figures are forced by crises and disclosures of operations to try to deceive Americans for a variety of reasons, including valid security considerations. Also cited in chapter 7, section A, and chapter 19.

B. ARTICLES AND REPORTS

Barnds, William J. THE RIGHT TO KNOW, TO WITHHOLD AND TO LIE. The Council on Religion and International Affairs (CRIA), Special Study no. 207. New York: CRIA, 1969. 86 p.

An essay with dissenting commentaries. Barnds, a Senior Research Fellow at the Council on Foreign Relations, was formerly with the Office of National Estimates of the Central Intelligence Agency.

Crewdson, John M. "Ford Asks Intelligence Disclosure Curb." NEW YORK TIMES, 19 February 1976, pp. 1, 30.

The reporter describes the provisions of a message to the Congress from President Ford in which the president seeks legislation impos- ing criminal and civil sanctions on government employees who are authorized access to intelligence secrets and who willfully reveal this information. The request to Congress stemmed from the publi- cation of books by Victor Marchetti and John D. Marks (THE CIA AND THE CULT OF INTELLIGENCE--see section A of this chap- ter) and by Philip Agee (INSIDE THE COMPANY: CIA DIARY-- see chapter 18). Excluded from the provisions of the requested legislation would be members of Congress or staffs of congressional committees. The message, however, does ask for legislation on opening of the mails for intelligence purposes and undertaking of electronic surveillance. Page 30 of the same issue of the NEW YORK TIMES contains the text of the presidential message.

Florence, William G. "A Madness for Secrecy." WASHINGTON POST, 12 December 1971, pp. C1, C4.

The author, ex-security expert for air force headquarters and secu- rity consultant to defense attorneys in the Daniel Ellsberg case, describes the abuse of secrecy rules. Examples are cited, some humorous.

Halloran, Richard. "Army Spied on 18,000 Civilians in 2-Year Operation." NEW YORK TIMES, 18 January 1971, pp. 1, 22.

An article describing the genesis of the army's role in collecting names of over 18,000 persons in computer banks, dossiers, and files from the summer of 1967 through the autumn of 1969. The army was given the function of providing intelligence and counter- intelligence to support a civil disturbance plan following the riots in Newark and Detroit in 1967 and the anti-Vietnam march on the Pentagon in October 1967.

Hersh, Seymour M. "Huge CIA Operation Reported in U.S. against Antiwar Forces, Other Dissidents in Nixon Years." NEW YORK TIMES, 22 December 1974, pp. 1, 26.

In this extensive article Hersh reveals that an investigation by the NEW YORK TIMES has established that the CIA conducted domes- tic intelligence and surveillance operations against antiwar acti- vists within the United States during the Nixon administration. These alleged operations, according to the article, are considered to be in violation of the 1947 charter of the CIA. Hersh reports his sources as believing that the domestic surveillance started in the 1950s and 1960s as part of legitimate counterintelligence opera- tions to determine penetration and support of antiwar groups by foreign intelligence organizations. Hersh's sources believe that

in the 1960s and early 1970s these operations grew into illegal efforts, such as recruiting informants in the United States to infiltrate some of the more militant dissident groups. Hersh wrote
follow-up articles in the 29 December 1974 and 5 January 1975
editions of the NEW YORK TIMES. His articles triggered the
establishment by President Ford of a special investigative panel
to look into possible CIA charter violations (see also REPORT TO
THE PRESIDENT BY THE COMMISSION ON CIA ACTIVITIES WITHIN
THE UNITED STATES, section A, this chapter).

Horrock, Nicholas M. "President Limits U.S. Surveillance of Citizen's Lives."
NEW YORK TIMES, 19 February 1976, pp. 1, 30.

TIMES correspondent Horrock describes the provisions of an executive order of 18 February 1976 prepared by President Ford, sharply
restricting the activities of intelligence agencies in intruding upon
the lives of American citizens. The thirty-six-page order limits
surveillance and bars such practices as burglaries, drug tests on
unsuspecting humans, and the illegal use of tax return information.
The limitations were imposed on activities of the intelligence community discovered and made public by the Rockefeller Commission
investigation and the Senate Select Committee (Church Committee)
and House Select Committee (Pike Committee) investigations of
1975 and 1976. Page 30 of the same issue of the NEW YORK
TIMES contains excerpts from the executive order.

Marks, John D. "On Being Censored." FOREIGN POLICY 15 (Summer
1974): 93-107.

An article by the coauthor (with Victor Marchetti) of THE CIA
AND THE CULT OF INTELLIGENCE (see section A, this chapter) in which he recounts the efforts of the agency first to suppress the book and second to delete 339 passages, a number later
reduced to 168. Marks argues the case that censorship, if successful, would establish "a legal precedent . . . that the government has the right to rule on the acceptability of writing done by
virtually all former officials. The public, as a result, may well
be deprived of one of its principal sources of information about
American foreign policy."

Pyle, Christopher H. "CONUS Intelligence: The Army Watches Civilian Politics." WASHINGTON MONTHLY, January 1970, p. 5.

A former captain in army intelligence, Pyle alleges the army investigated and maintained files on the activities of civilians un-
affiliated with the armed forces in the Continental United States
(CONUS). These charges received widespread publicity resulting
in demands by more than thirty members of Congress to the army
to know if the charges were true. Pyle became a consultant to
the Constitutional Rights Subcommittee (Ervin Subcommittee) of the

Senate Judiciary Committee which investigated the activities of the counterintelligence and security organizations of the army.

_____. "CONUS Revisited: The Army Covers Up." WASHINGTON MONTHLY, July 1970, pp. 49-58.

The author charges the army with continuing to watch civilian politics despite congressional inquiries and a lawsuit by the American Civil Liberties Union. Senator Fulbright had the original article printed in the 12 March 1970 issue of the CONGRESSIONAL RECORD (Senate), pages S3644-50, along with copies of his inquiry to the army and the army's response. Pyle has written his doctoral thesis on political surveillance.

Shearer, Lloyd. "What Price Secrecy?" PARADE, 22 August 1971, pp. 4-7.

An expose of the use and abuse of the government secrecy classification system. According to one estimate disclosed in the article, there are twenty million classified papers currently held in government, 99.5 percent of which should not be classified at all.

Stern, Laurence. "Hoover War on New Left Bared." WASHINGTON POST, 7 December 1973, p. A2.

NCB newscaster Carl Stern successfully sued for release of a 1968 FBI memorandum which directed offices to "expose, disrupt and otherwise neutralize" the New Left movement. This article describes the memorandum as well as a memorandum by Hoover of April 1971 discontinuing these counterintelligence programs (called COINTELPRO in the memos).

Stout, Jared. "Military Agents Had Secret Role at 1968 Conventions." EVENING STAR (Washington, D.C.), 2 December 1970, p. A8.

The article alleges that during the 1968 political conventions an army security agency radio intercept unit, elements of the army's Counter Intelligence Analysis Detachment (CIAD), and agents of army, navy, and air force counterintelligence units were active in collecting information, conducting surveillance on civilians, assisting the Secret Service in protecting presidential candidates, and providing security.

Symington, Stuart. "Congress's Right to Know." NEW YORK TIMES, 9 August 1970, sec. VI, p. 7.

In a long and detailed article Senator Symington describes the abuse of executive secrecy in the formation and conduct of foreign policy and associated military affairs and operations. An authoritative article that attempts to put secrecy and national security in proper perspective.

Teller, Edward. "Secrecy: No Longer a Security Asset." WALL STREET
JOURNAL, 15 July 1970, p. 12.

> In this lengthy article noted nuclear scientist Teller, who has had
> much experience with secrecy due to his work with atomic weapons
> development, presents the thesis that by the early sixties secrecy
> had become a political tool to shield leaders from criticism as
> much as a security measure to block access to classified informa-
> tion by espionage. During 1970 Teller was a member of the Task
> Force on Secrecy established by the Pentagon's Defense Science
> Board. The article, copyrighted by Public Affairs International of
> Princeton, New Jersey, was printed in many newspapers including
> the BALTIMORE SUN, 12 July 1970, and the WASHINGTON
> STAR, 19 July 1970.

Turn, R. PRIVACY TRANSFORMATION FOR DATABANK SYSTEMS. RAND
Monograph, no. P-4955. Santa Monica, Calif.: RAND Corp., March 1973.
50 p.

> "Privacy transformations--are techniques for increasing data secu-
> rity and privacy in computerized databank systems." This paper
> discusses cryptographic transformations used in communications sys-
> tems for protection against unauthorized use of data and programs
> in the databanks.

U.S. Congress. House. Committee on Armed Services. Special Subcommittee
on Intelligence. INQUIRY INTO THE ALLEGED INVOLVEMENT OF THE
CENTRAL INTELLIGENCE AGENCY IN THE WATERGATE AND ELLSBERG
MATTERS. 93d Cong., 1st sess., 23 October 1973. Doc. no. 93-25. 23 p.

> A summary report of five months of hearings of some twenty-four
> principal witnesses, including members of the CIA and former
> White House staffers. The purpose was to determine whether
> there was any CIA activity in the Watergate and Ellsberg break-
> in incidents which was contrary to the letter and spirit of the
> CIA charter. The investigation was conducted by the House in-
> telligence oversight subcommittee under the chairmanship of Lucien
> N. Nedzi (D-Mich.).

U.S. Congress. House. Committee on Government Operations. Subcommittee
on Foreign Operations and Government Information. SECURITY CLASSIFICA-
TION REFORM, HEARINGS. 93d Cong., 2d sess., 11, 25 July, and 1 August
1974. v, 756 p. Appendices.

> For three years prior to this report the Subcommittee on Foreign
> Operations and Government Information had focused attention on
> the nation's security classification system. In this report there is
> contained the testimony of many witnesses on a proposed Freedom
> of Information Act developed by the subcommittee. Included as
> a witness was Director of Central Intelligence William E. Colby
> who testified on the necessity of protecting by secrecy the sources

and methods of intelligence gathering. Twelve useful appendices
are included; appendix 3 is a study on the evolution of government information security from 1775 to 1973. The Freedom of Information Act is reprinted in this report.

U.S. Congress. House. Committee on the Judiciary. IMPEACHMENT OF
RICHARD M. NIXON, PRESIDENT OF THE UNITED STATES. 93d Cong.,
2d sess., 20 August 1974. Rept. no. 93-1305. 528 p.

A report of the Judiciary Committee detailing the articles of impeachment against Richard M. Nixon. Article 1 describes the
committee findings regarding unlawful entry into the headquarters
of the Democratic National Committee, by agents of the Committee for Re-election of the President. Part of the material supporting Article 1 of the impeachment resolution details the preparation, adoption, and implementation of a political intelligence
plan (the Liddy Plan), which included the use of electronic surveillance, for the acquisition of domestic political intelligence
useful in the re-election of Nixon. Other material includes evidence on the attempts to misuse the Central Intelligence Agency.

U.S. Congress. House. Committee on Un-American Activities. FACTS ON
COMMUNISM, VOLUME II, THE SOVIET UNION, FROM LENIN TO KHRUSH-
CHEV, STAFF STUDY. 87th Cong., 1st sess., 1961. iv, 367, xix p.

For counterintelligence and security see pages 96-103, "The Cheka";
pages 135-41, "The Police System"; pages 175-86, "Police and
Terrorism"; and pages 187-99, "Trials and Purges."

U.S. Congress. Senate. Committee on Foreign Relations. DR. KISSINGER'S
ROLE IN WIRETAPPING. 93d Cong., 2d sess., 1974. 409 p.

A complete report of the inquiry undertaken by the Senate Committee on Foreign Relations, at the request of Secretary of State
Kissinger, regarding his role in the wiretapping of seventeen newsmen and government officials during the period from 1969 to 1971.
The wiretapping was performed as a means of identifying those who
leaked secret classified information from the National Security
Council and White House.

U.S. Congress. Senate. Committee on the Judiciary. WIRETAPPING, EAVES-
DROPPING, AND THE BILL OF RIGHTS: HEARINGS BEFORE THE SUBCOM-
MITTEE ON CONSTITUTIONAL RIGHTS. (Ervin Subcommittee temporary manu-
script). 86th Cong., 1st sess., 1959. 2,008 p.

_____. WIRETAPPING FOR NATIONAL SECURITY: HEARINGS BEFORE A
SUBCOMMITTEE OF THE SENATE JUDICIARY COMMITTEE. 83d Cong., 2d
sess., 1954. 91 p.

U.S. Congress. Senate. Committee on the Judiciary. Internal Security Subcommittee. SOVIET INTELLIGENCE AND SECURITY SERVICES, 1964-1970:
A SELECTED BIBLIOGRAPHY OF SOVIET PUBLICATIONS. WITH SOME ADDI-
TIONAL TITLES FROM OTHER SOURCES. 92d Cong., 1st sess., 1972.
289 p. Author index.

>For a description and analysis of the contents see the listing and
>annotation in chapter 4, section B.

U.S. Congress. Senate. Select Committee to Study Governmental Operations
with Respect to Intelligence Activities. INTELLIGENCE ACTIVITIES AND THE
RIGHTS OF AMERICANS, Book II. 94th Cong., 2d sess., 26 April 1976.
Rept. no. 94-755. 396 p. Appendices, footnotes with bibliographic references.

>Book II of the final report of the intelligence investigative com-
>mittee of the Senate (chaired by Senator Frank Church) contains
>a remarkably thorough history of the evolution of domestic intelli-
>gence in the United States from 1936 to the present. Included
>are details on the roles of the CIA, the FBI, and the National
>Security Agency. Illegal activities such as mail openings, elec-
>tronic surveillance, and surreptitious entries into homes and of-
>fices are described. See chapter 4, section A, for main annota-
>tion.

"United States Foreign Intelligence." Executive Order of the President, no. 11905,
18 February 1976. In the FEDERAL REGISTER, Part II. Vol. 41, no. 34
(19 February 1976): 7703-38.

>A reprint of the presidential directive that reorganized the U.S.
>intelligence community in response to a report of an investigation
>headed by the vice-president (see REPORT TO THE PRESIDENT
>BY THE COMMISSION ON CIA ACTIVITIES WITHIN THE UNITED
>STATES, section A, this chapter), and two investigations of spe-
>cial congressional committees--one in the Senate and one in the
>House of Representatives. The directive establishes new commit-
>tees and oversight groups and sets down specific responsibilities
>and restrictions of intelligence agencies as regards activities with-
>in the United States.

Chapter 9

COUNTERINTELLIGENCE AND SECURITY: THE USSR

In the Soviet Union protection of the government and Communist party and suppression of opposition at home and abroad are traditional defense mechanisms
equal in importance to the more conventional armed forces. Secrecy, surveillance, and censorship are essential methods for the conduct of this defense.
While counterintelligence and internal security measures may be causing considerable problems and controversy in the United States, there is no question
of their strict application in the USSR. The tradition, however, does not date
from the revolution but from the days of the tsars. The tsarist security organization, the Okhrana, was responsible for suppression of two generations of
Russian revolutionists, who in turn were developing the techniques and methods,
and grooming the personnel to staff the new Soviet counterintelligence, security, and intelligence organization after the takeover.

The necessity for strict protective measures against counterrevolution, infiltration, wrecking, sabotage, and subversion was made clear in the months following the revolution by the activities and efforts of Western and Japanese intelligence and counterrevolutionary operations. These early counterrevolutionary
battles, which resulted in establishing more firmly the doctrine of suspicion and
security followed in the USSR, are described in Deacon's HISTORY OF THE
RUSSIAN SECRET SERVICE.

Today the civilian Committee for State Security (KGB) is responsible for counterintelligence, security, and intelligence functions, but unlike intelligence,
which is performed by other organizations in the USSR, the KGB has counterintelligence and security entirely to itself. The KGB is preeminent as the
custodian of the iron curtain. For example, it performs the counterintelligence
and security functions for all of the armed forces, at home or deployed outside
the Soviet Union. While the KGB is directly responsible to the Council of
Ministers, it is equally responsive to the desires and requirements of the party
Central Committee--in fact all counterintelligence and intelligence has its
focus in the Central Committee. In April 1973 the head of the KGB was made
a serving member of the Central Committee, the first to have this position
since Beria, Stalin's security chief. The implications of this move may be that
the more extensive international exchanges of personnel of the USSR abroad,

detente with the West, increased economic relations with the West and Japan, and internal dissident controversies will not alter the essential counterintelligence and security doctrine although methods may be changed.

Considering the absolute dedication to secrecy in the USSR, there is more information available in the literature regarding the KGB than could reasonably be expected. Most of it, however, is history, but history which traces in detail the evolution of the state security agency from a commission, to a commissariat, to a ministry, to a committee; with mergers and separations from the internal affairs ministry. All of these changes had political significance, but did not fundamentally change the organization, functions, and doctrine. For example, the comprehensive bibliography SOVIET INTELLIGENCE AND SECURITY SERVICES, 1964-70 published by the Senate Judiciary's Internal Security Subcommittee (see chapter 4, section B1), lists 715 titles out of a total of 2,507 in the bibliography under the rubric "State Security."

In addition to the multitude of names applicable to the same organization, there is another confusing factor regarding the literature on the KGB. In this one agency there are a combination of counterintelligence and internal security functions (some quite unlike any in the West--such as border guards and transportation security), external counterintelligence and positive intelligence and espionage functions, and covert political actions functions. Like the literature on the CIA, it is difficult to find definitive works that sort out and analyze various functions separately. However, a few scholarly works dealing with the subject proper are listed here, along with articles that tend to provide up-to-date insights into functional additions or changes.

A. BOOKS

Barron, John. KGB: THE SECRET WORK OF SOVIET SECRET AGENTS. Pleasantville, N.Y.: Reader's Digest Press, distributed by E.P. Dutton Co., New York, 1974. xiv, 462 p. Index, photographs, notes, bibliography, appendices.

> About five years ago the READER'S DIGEST editors began to assess the feasibility of a definitive book on the organization thought to be as important as any other organization in the Soviet Union-- the KGB (Committee for State Security). Senior editor John Barron was selected to collate the mass of data and to write the book since he had served with U.S. Naval Intelligence before becoming an award-winning newspaper reporter in Washington, D.C. A list of approximately fifty names of men and women who had been connected in some way with Soviet intelligence was compiled, and interviews with all but two were arranged over a period of years. Assistance was sought and obtained from the intelligence services of Great Britain, West Germany, the Netherlands, and some two dozen additional countries. The FBI and the CIA provided information and assistance in setting up meetings with ex-

Soviet agents. The foreign office of READER'S DIGEST provided assistance in searching publications for information in thirteen languages. From this data base were selected stories and episodes that exposed distinct activities of the KGB. Consequently there are dozens of case histories of KGB operatives. A list of 1,500 KGB agents engaged in espionage and clandestine operations outside the USSR is provided in the book.

Conquest, Robert. THE SOVIET POLICE SYSTEM. New York: Praeger, 1968. 103 p. Notes, bibliography.

A carefully documented study of the institutional history and structure of the Soviet police systems which concentrates on operations of its extralegal organs. The administrative framework of the system is traced from its beginnings in 1917 through the downgrading of its power as a political entity during the post-Stalin era. Methods of repression by the police within Soviet society are discussed, as are Soviet-directed police operations abroad. An extensive bibliography of primary sources in both Russian and English adds to the value of this work.

Copp, Dewitt S. INCIDENT AT BORIS GLEB: THE TRAGEDY OF NEWCOMB MOTT. Garden City, N.Y.: Doubleday, 1968. 280 p. Index, illustrations.

An account of Newcomb Mott, a twenty-seven-year-old textbook salesman from Sheffield, Massachusetts, who crossed into the USSR at remote Boris Gleb, a Soviet salient on the Norwegian border, in September 1965, and was arrested by the KGB. The author, an award-winning book and film writer with an interest in foreign affairs, describes the trial and conviction in Murmansk and the subsequent Soviet announcement that Mott had slashed his throat aboard a train enroute to a prison work camp to serve an eighteen-month sentence for violating the Soviet border.

Deacon, Richard [pseud.]. HISTORY OF THE RUSSIAN SECRET SERVICE. London: Muller; New York: Taplinger, 1972. 568 p. Notes, bibliography, index.

A detailed history of security services in Russia from earliest times to the present by the British author of A HISTORY OF THE BRITISH SECRET SERVICE (cited in chapter 14, section E1).

Deriabin, Peter, and Gibney, Frank. THE SECRET WORLD. Garden City, N.Y.: Doubleday, 1959. 334 p. Index, appendices, organization charts.

During the first part of his career in the KGB, Peter Deriabin was an internal security specialist. Therefore, almost half of the book is devoted to recounting his experiences in that portion of the state security organization, while the remainder details his activities in positive intelligence.

Hingley, Ronald. THE RUSSIAN SECRET POLICE: MUSCOVITE, IMPERIAL RUSSIAN AND SOVIET POLITICAL SECURITY OPERATIONS. New York: Simon & Schuster, 1970. xiii, 313 p. Index, bibliography, notes.

The outstanding work on the subject by a distinguished British so-vietologist who served with the Intelligence Corps of the Royal Army in World War II. Includes helpful notes and a highly selective bibliography of more than 300 listings. The author clearly describes and analyzes the changing political function of the security police and their complex relationships with other elements of the Russian government from the Oprichnina of 1565 to the KGB in the post-Khrushchev period. A unique book in that it is not an account of specific espionage operations, but rather a discussion of the techniques of intrigue, provocation, control of political dissidents, infiltration, and policing renegade Russian or Soviet citizens abroad who had been associated with the counterintelligence and internal security elements of the KGB or its antecedent organizations.

Levytsky, Boris. THE USES OF TERROR: THE SOVIET SECRET POLICE, 1917-1970. Translated by H.A. Piehler. New York: Coward, McCann, & Geoghegan, 1972. 349 p. Index, bibliography, notes, organization chart, tables.

English translation of a serious history of the evolution of Soviet political police from the revolution to mid-1970. (Lewytzkyj, Borys. DIE ROTE INQUISITION: DIE GESCHICHTE DER SOWJETISCHEN SICHERHEITSDIENSTE. Frankfurt/Main: Societats-Verlag, 1967. 395 p.).

Littell, Robert, ed. THE CZECH BLACK BOOK: Prepared by the Institute of History of the Czechoslovak Academy of Sciences. New York: F.A. Praeger, 1969. No index. Paperback ed. New York: Avon Books, 1969. x, 318 p.

This book provides a partial insight into the role of the KGB in the occupation of Czechoslovakia in August 1968. The book, originally entitled SEVEN DAYS IN PRAGUE, was hurriedly prepared one month after the occupation as a refutation of the Soviet claim that their intervention was essentially counter-counterrevolutionary and in the interests of "internal security"--a primary KGB responsibility.

Smith, Edward E. THE OKHRANA: THE RUSSIAN DEPARTMENTS OF PO-LICE, A BIBLIOGRAPHY. Stanford, Calif.: Hoover Institution of War, Revolution and Peace, 1967. 271 p. Index, glossary, bibliography.

Written with the collaboration of Rudolf Lednicky, this definitive bibliography includes an excellent introductory essay and some 843 items on the Okhrana, the last tsarist secret police; counterintelligence; intelligence; and internal security organization between the years 1880 and 1917.

Wittlin, Thaddeus. COMMISSAR: THE LIFE AND DEATH OF LAVRENTY PAV-
LOVICH BERIA. New York: Macmillan, 1972. 566 p. Index, selected bibliography, appendices, illustrations.

An account of Beria's rapid rise from a twenty-two-year-old graduate architect and informer for the tsarist secret police to chief
of security for the Republic of Georgia, after the revolution to
Stalin's chief counterrevolutionist and commissar of state security
and head of the NKVD. Polish-born historian Wittlin describes
Beria's role as head of intelligence, counterintelligence and security, propaganda, and as first head of the Soviet Union's atomic
weapons development program. He also describes Beria's organization of Smersh, the counterespionage and security force that, among
other things, conducted surveillance in the Soviet armed forces
during World War II. To obtain an understanding of the enormous
counterrevolution, counterintelligence, internal security, and espionage forces at work in the Soviet Union during the Stalin and
Beria era, the reader must navigate a lot of descriptive shoal waters in this flawed "psychological biography."

Wolin, Simon, and Slusser, Robert M., eds. THE SOVIET SECRET POLICE.
New York: F.A. Praeger; London: Methuen & Co., 1957. 408 p. Index,
bibliography, notes.

The editors have put together in one volume nine separate essays
on the development of state security in the USSR. Essays cover
the period from Cheka--the first Soviet intelligence, counterintelligence, internal security, and secret police organization after the
revolution in 1917--to the KGB of the post-Stalin 1956 era. The
essays deal primarily with counterintelligence and internal security
roles of state security, with only generalized treatment of external
espionage roles. This is one of the few books to deal extensively
with the border guards and armed units of the state security organization, and with the methods and doctrine of state security. The
nine essays by ex-Soviet citizens, however, are sparsely footnoted
and of varying quality. Contains an excellent reading list of materials in Russian and western languages.

B. ARTICLES AND REPORTS

Astrachan, Anthony. "Soviets Hit Telecasts by Satellite." WASHINGTON
POST, 13 October 1972, p. A23.

The Soviet ambassador to the United Nations submitted proposals
that would limit any possibility that the United States or China
would broadcast television programs directly from a satellite into
the homes of Soviet citizens. The proposals included the right to
jam such telecasts, censor, and even to destroy the relay satellite.

Barron, John. "Russia's Voices of Dissent." READER'S DIGEST 104 (May 1974): 139-43.

Senior editor Barron describes incidents in recent years of KGB efforts to suppress and eliminate dissidents in the USSR and how, in 1969, the KGB added an organizational element, the Fifth Chief Directorate, to enforce ideological conformity. Barron is the author of a recent study: KGB: THE SECRET WORK OF SOVIET SECRET AGENTS (see this chapter, section A).

Berger, Marilyn. "Soviets Halt Jamming of VOA Broadcasts." WASHINGTON POST, 13 September 1973, p. A12.

The article reports that the Soviets had stopped jamming Voice of America, British Broadcasting Corporation, and West German radio transmissions for the first time since the invasion of Czechoslovakia in 1968. Includes some speculation as to the reason for the cessation of the jamming.

Byrnes, Robert F. "American Scholars in Russia Soon Learn about the KGB." NEW YORK TIMES MAGAZINE, 16 November 1969, pp. 84, 87, 102.

A comprehensive and objective analysis of KGB surveillance against graduate students and scholars visiting the Soviet Union from Western and African countries, with examples cited involving those from the United States. The usual charges brought against students and scholars are for espionage, conducting anti-Soviet propaganda, and being "ideological saboteurs," and there is usually an offer to drop charges if the American will turn informer. The author, a professor of history at Indiana University and once head of the Inter-University Committee, suggests kinds of U.S. activities which tend to strengthen KGB suspicions of "subversive" activity.

Crankshaw, Edward. "Soviet Secret Police Shift to Soft Sell for Undermining West." WASHINGTON POST, 25 December 1967, p. C4.

The British expert on Soviet affairs analyzes the KGB in the light of the present world environment and relaxed international tension. He suggests that the Soviet leadership is forced by the present environment to move away from absolute hostility to the West, but is sure that while the KGB is still dedicated to rigid control and repression in the USSR, some of the methods may have altered. Organizational aspects of the KGB are detailed.

Doder, Dusko. "Kremlin Hounds U.S. Newsmen." WASHINGTON POST, 7 February 1971, p. C4.

A well-developed and objective article on the problems of American correspondents in the Soviet Union--the continual surveillance by the KGB and KGB provocations--and the links newsmen have established with Soviet political dissidents. The Soviet viewpoint regarding the meaning of free press is provided.

Dornberg, John. "In the Soviet Isolation Ward." NEWSWEEK, 28 December 1970, pp. 25-26.

The article details the secrecy, surveillance, travel restrictions, tapped telephones, bugged apartments, and searches that an American correspondent must put up with from Soviet state security.

Kaiser, Robert G. "Case 24: The KGB's Drive against Dissidents." WASHINGTON POST, 17 April 1973, pp. A1, A10.

In this lengthy article Moscow correspondent Kaiser summarizes the activities of the KGB operations (Case 24) against Soviet dissidents. Specifically, one objective of Case 24 was to prevent the publication of the dissident activities journal, THE CHRONICLE OF HUMAN EVENTS, which was suppressed early in 1973, but which reappeared again in the spring of 1974.

_____. "A Professor vs. the KGB." WASHINGTON POST, 19 May 1974, pp. C1, C4.

The WASHINGTON POST's Moscow correspondent has put together an unusual collection of documents concerning the harrassment of Soviet professor of literature Yefim G. Etkind. This harrassment is probably because Etkind is a friend to exiled dissident Solzhenitsyn. The article includes an account of a meeting of the Academic Board of Hertzen Teacher's Training College in Leningrad, which expelled Professor Etkind from his institute and from the Soviet Union of Writers. A copy of the certificate from the KGB used by the board is included. This certificate illustrates the type of surveillance and dossier kept on Soviet citizens.

Seeger, Murray. "Radio Hooligans Bug Soviets." WASHINGTON POST, 31 December 1973, p. A2.

Amateur radio broadcasters transmitting illegally in the USSR are becoming a problem and the focus of extensive police action. In many cases the "radio hooligans" transmit information that contradicts official news broadcasts, or retransmit recordings of foreign shortwave newscasts--two forms of anti-Soviet agitation and propaganda.

Shabad, Theodore. "Soviet Says B.B.C. Helps Espionage." NEW YORK TIMES, 17 December 1968, p. 10.

An analysis of an Izvestia counterintelligence and security warning article stating that the British Broadcasting Corporation's East European Division, which transmits to the USSR and Warsaw Pact countries, collaborates with the British Secret Intelligence Service by broadcasting prearranged musical passages and textual phrases at designated times to enable a British agent to prove his bona fides to a perspective contact or agent recruit.

Solzhenitsyn, Alexander. "Solzhenitsyn vs. the KGB." TIME, 27 May 1974, p. 51. Illustrated.

In this first short article since his exile to the West, Solzhenitsyn details how the KGB forged his handwriting and signature in letters to an emigre organization in Brussels in an apparent attempt to demonstrate his connection with anti-Soviet organizations and to establish a case for treason or anti-Soviet propaganda. Examples of Solzhenitsyn's handwriting and the KGB forgeries are shown in the article.

"Soviet Is Lifting Cloaks from Some of Its Spies." NEW YORK TIMES, 19 January 1969, p. 14.

This article tells of a film showing in Moscow neighborhood moviehouses entitled OFF SEASON, glorifying the exploits of a Soviet intelligence agent working in the West--probably the spy Gordon A. Lonsdale (real name: Konon T. Molodiy). This film is one indication of radical decisions made in 1964 to depart from traditional security policy, to lift the cloak of secrecy from some Soviet espionage activity, and to recognize the work of specific agents publicly. The glorifying of Richard Sorge, a Soviet intelligence agent operating in Japan prior to World War II, started the trend. He was posthumously awarded a Hero of the Soviet Union; a tanker and a street in Moscow were named after him; and his face was pictured on a four-kopek commemorative postage stamp. Later, Gordon A. Lonsdale was allowed to publish his memoirs, SPY: TWENTY YEARS IN THE SOVIET SECRET SERVICE, as was Kim Philby MY SILENT WAR (both cited in chapter 14, section D3).

Chapter 10

SCIENTIFIC AND TECHNICAL INTELLIGENCE

The U.S. Defense Department's DICTIONARY OF MILITARY AND ASSOCIA-
TED TERMS defines scientific and technical intelligence as intelligence per-
taining to (1) foreign developments in basic and applied research as well as
engineering techniques, (2) the technical characteristics, capabilities, limitations, and vulnerabilities of all foreign weapons and weapons systems, and (3)
the production methods employed in their serial manufacture. Since the post-
World War II explosion of knowledge has made scientific and technological
capability an important element of national power and politics, scientific intelligence provides early warning against technological surprise or the advent
of new weaponry. Scientific intelligence assessments determine who is ahead
in science and technology--a major adjunct to strategic foreign policy development. The doctrine for scientific intelligence was first developed in England
beginning in 1939 as information became available on new German developments in radar, bomber navigation, missiles and rockets, jet aircraft, atomic
research, and chemical warfare (see "Scientific Intelligence," by R.V. Jones,
in section B below, and "The Wizard War" in THE FINEST HOUR, by Winston
Churchill, in section A below). The United States began to develop its own
doctrine somewhat later as information available indicated that Germany might
beat us to the atomic bomb. See ALSOS, by Samuel Goudsmit, and THE ALSOS
MISSION, by Colonel Boris T. Pash, both in section A below. See also
Schaf's EVOLUTION OF MODERN STRATEGIC INTELLIGENCE--annotated in
chapter 4, section A--for a detailed history of the development of scientific
and technical intelligence from 1939 through 1964.

As in the case of so many other components of intelligence, World War II
gave technical intelligence its impetus towards a separate specialty. Trained
teams from the army's technical services scoured the battlefields of the world
in search of new weapons and equipment that might give the enemy an edge,
and even set up special combat operations in order to penetrate enemy territory
and capture a new piece of material or a weapons specialist or designer. See
THE ORDNANCE DEPARTMENT: PLANNING MUNITIONS FOR WAR, by
Green, Thomson, and Roots. At home and abroad the navy and army air forces
also had specialized technical intelligence collection teams to do the analytical and evaluation work on the captured material sent from the field. By
1943 a method had been worked out whereby analyses of the nameplates, mark-

ings, and serial numbers on captured weapons and equipment could be used to estimate enemy war production for strategic economic intelligence purposes and for the identification and location of factories for strategic bombing targeting. See "An Empirical Approach to Economic Intelligence in World War II," by Ruggles and Brodie. And, as weapons research and development was mobilized in the United States under the National Defense Research Committee, civilian scientists of this program began to use the enemy material obtained by the technical intelligence teams as a basis for countermeasure and new weapons design.

The postwar emergence of intercontinental nuclear weaponry saw the merging of scientific and technical intelligence into a single element of strategic intelligence at the national level. However, this same period was one in which direct access to foreign strategic intercontinental weapon systems for detailed and technical examination of characteristics and vulnerabilities was denied, although the Korean and Vietnam Wars provided opportunities for the capture and examination of foreign tactical weapons and equipment, and wars in the Middle East provided unique opportunities to examine late-model Soviet tactical material. See "Israel Offering to Barter Soviet Arms for the West's," by David Binder. The Moscow parades and flybys (called by some the "Moscow Disclosure System") on May Day and Red October Day provided a few glimpses of new missiles and heavy bombers, although the potential here for strategic deception was extensive. In any case, such casual glimpses did not satisfy the need for technical, engineering, and performance details. Because of this, extensive research and development programs were undertaken in the mid-fifties to provide our intelligence people a capability to "see" new aircraft, missiles, and submarines, even while the submarines were still undergoing early test and evaluation. By means of high resolution-high altitude photography and by means of powerful radars, our intelligence people were able to "see" missiles on test stands or in test flight from great distances, and to "hear" the details of performance of missiles while in test flight by interception of the emitted telemetry signals. In the early days these scientific and technical intelligence collection means were shrouded in the highest secrecy--even from most officials in Washington. However, the downing of the U-2 plane provided one of the first glimpses of this enormous undertaking and gradually, over recent years, more and more details have become available for public viewing. Phillip J. Klass in his SECRET SENTRIES IN SPACE has provided a remarkable expose of the development of these collection programs plus an analysis of why it was thought necessary to launch them. However secretly these means of collection of scientific and technical intelligence information are employed--some have termed them a form of technological espionage--they are now an accepted activity, at least between the governments of the United States and the USSR. In arms limitation agreements signed in Moscow they were called "National Means of Verification"; and the agreements included clauses to the effect that they were not to be interfered with or deceived.

The accomplishments of the long-range strategic surveillance sensors (aerial and space cameras, over-the-horizon radars, telemetry and electronic intelligence interception systems, seismic sensors, etc.) in the cause of intelligence and national security have been spectacular and substantial. However, there are important characteristics of ballistic missile systems, bombers, and submarines that cannot be "seen" or "heard" by these means--leaving much room for interpretation. Consequently quite a lot of the strategic dialogue in this country (arms limitation and antiballistic missile discussions, nuclear test ban provisions, or Defense Department budget justifications to the Congress), is based on findings of these surveillance systems which are subject to widely varying interpretations; they may be perceived as threatening to the United States, or not, with seemingly equally convincing interpretations.

Actually there is no great lack of information available in the open literature on descriptions and characteristics of foreign weapons, weapon systems, and material. For example, in each of its weekly issues, AVIATION WEEK AND SPACE TECHNOLOGY provides a sort of current intelligence reporting on new aerospace weaponry as well as on U.S. and USSR reconnaissance and surveillance systems, and once each year publishes an inventory issue of all major foreign missile and aircraft characteristics. INTERAVIA magazine does much the same thing, and JANE'S FIGHTING SHIPS, JANE'S ALL THE WORLD'S AIRCRAFT, and JANE'S WEAPON SYSTEMS are excellent technical intelligence handbooks with descriptions and characteristics of foreign material.

A. BOOKS

Babington-Smith, Constance. AIR SPY: THE STORY OF PHOTO INTELLIGENCE IN WORLD WAR II. New York: Harper, 1957. 266 p. British ed. EVIDENCE IN CAMERA. London: Chatto and Windus, 1957. 256 p. Index, illustrations.

> The author, a Royal Air Force photo interpreter, describes the development of photo-identification keys for German V-1 and V-2 missiles. This photo intelligence provided much needed solid evidence on characteristics and capabilities, led to the location of Peenemunde as the missile research and development center and proving ground, led to the first targeting of a weapon test center with its irreplaceable personnel by the strategic Bomber Command, and made possible the detection of V-1 and V-2 operational launch sites in Western Europe.

Blackman, Raymond V.B., ed. JANE'S FIGHTING SHIPS. London: Jane's Yearbooks; New York and Ontario: McGraw-Hill Co., 1972. 729 p. Photographs, illustrations, tables.

> Remarkably complete technical intelligence handbook of the characteristics and weaponry of the world's naval ships. Companion volumes deal with aircraft, missile systems, data acquisition and countermeasure systems, armored fighting vehicles, ordnance, and electronic and optical equipment.

Bulloch, John, and Miller, Henry. SPY RING: A STORY OF THE NAVAL SECRETS CASE. London: Martin Secker & Warburg, 1961. 224 p.

An account of identification and apprehension of the Soviet technical intelligence network in England, including Gordon Lonsdale and the Krogers, which was targeted against British and NATO underwater detection techniques.

Churchill, Winston S. "Hitler's Secret Weapon." In his THE SECOND WORLD WAR. Vol. 5: CLOSING THE RING, pp. 226-40. Boston: Houghton Mifflin, 1949.

An account of Churchill's appraisal of the intelligence available on German V-1 and V-2 missiles and the differences in the opinions of those who advised Churchill. Also an account of the bombing of Peenemunde and the warning which Churchill sent to President Roosevelt regarding intelligence on German missiles.

_____. "The Wizard War." In his THE SECOND WORLD WAR. Vol. 2: THEIR FINEST HOUR, pp. 381-97. Boston: Houghton Mifflin, 1949.

The author describes the "battle of the Beams" which was the scientific intelligence attack on German high-frequency electronic beacons used to guide Luftwaffe bombers to targets over England. British countermeasures were used to divert the beams without German knowledge.

Dulles, Allen W. "Collection--When the Machine Takes Over." In his THE CRAFT OF INTELLIGENCE, pp. 65-79. New York: Harper & Row, 1963.

In this chapter the former director of Central Intelligence describes early programs for monitoring Soviet nuclear tests, compares aerial photography and human espionage agents as sources of technical information, discusses the use of audio surveillance as an aid to espionage, and provides some examples of communications intelligence.

Goddard, George W., and Copp, DeWitt S. OVERVIEW: A LIFELONG ADVENTURE IN AERIAL PHOTOGRAPHY. Garden City, N.Y.: Doubleday, 1970. 415 p. Illustrations.

A history of aerial photography from 1917 through the Cuban missile crisis. Descriptions of the cameras, the film, and other features that made a significant contribution to intelligence gathering. Goddard is the father of aerial photography in the army and later in the air force.

Goudsmit, Samuel A. ALSOS. New York: Henry Schuman, 1947. 259 p. Index, illustrations.

Goudsmit was scientific chief of the Alsos Mission, a mixed military-civilian scientific intelligence unit designed to accompany Allied forces into Europe to seek out information on German scientific military developments, especially positive evidence on progress in atomic weapon development. Goudsmit describes the doctrine developed in choosing places, institutions, and people as targets to be located and exploited. Should be read in conjunction with THE ALSOS MISSION by Pash (cited below).

Green, Constance M.; Thomson, Harry C.; and Roots, Peter C. THE ORDNANCE DEPARTMENT: PLANNING MUNITIONS FOR WAR. U.S. Army in World War II Series: The Technical Services, Office, Chief of Military History. Washington, D.C.: Government Printing Office, 1955. xvii, 542 p. Index, illustrations, bibliography, footnotes.

One of the few official histories of World War II to give significant attention to the role of technical intelligence. Provides insights into the importance of technical intelligence in weapons design and also in providing protection against enemy weapons fire. Also reveals something of the organization of the Ordnance Corps for technical intelligence, and describes some of the joint and combined technical intelligence committees that sprang into being. Chapters 7 and 9, dealing with technical intelligence, are of special interest.

Heiman, Grover. AERIAL PHOTOGRAPHY: THE STORY OF AERIAL MAPPING RECONNAISSANCE. New York: Macmillan, 1972. 180 p. Index, bibliography.

A broad survey of the work of the camera and aircraft in aerial mapping and reconnaissance throughout history. Emphasizes the use of aircraft and photography as instruments of intelligence affecting military and national power.

Huminik, John. DOUBLE AGENT. New York: New American Library, 1967. 181 p. Illustrations, index.

An account by a scientist and engineer of his recruitment by Soviet embassy personnel in Washington, D.C., in 1960 for scientific and technological espionage purposes. The author spent six years as an agent of both Soviet intelligence and the FBI.

Infield, Glenn B. UNARMED AND UNAFRAID. New York: Macmillan, 1970. 308 p. Bibliography, index, illustrations.

A former pilot and major in the U.S. Air Force, the author traces the evolution of aerial reconnaissance from its beginnings in the Civil War to its sophisticated application in Southeast Asia and in Vietnam. Described in detail are reconnaissance operations in both Europe and the Pacific during World War II, and in Korea. Of special interest are descriptions of the photographic and electronic reconnaissance and surveillance flights around the periphery of the Soviet Union.

Irving, David. THE GERMAN ATOMIC BOMB: THE HISTORY OF NUCLEAR RESEARCH IN NAZI GERMANY. New York: Simon & Schuster, 1967. 329 p. Index, notes and sources, photographs, maps.

A fully documented account of German nuclear research and atomic bomb programs, set against the background of what Allied intelligence knew at each point, what measures it took to slow the program, the effects of these measures, and the interpretations of these actions by the Germans. In one brilliantly researched book the entire picture unfolds of the Allied intelligence effort against the German atomic bomb programs.

THE MARE'S NEST. Boston: Little, Brown and Co., 1965. 320 p. Appendix, index, illustrations.

An authoritative, well-written, and well-researched book by a British journalist on the combined Anglo-American scientific and technical intelligence campaign against German secret missile and rocket weapons. Details sources of information and analyses made, bureaucratic in-fighting, as well as skepticism of the intelligence by users such as Lord Cherwell, Churchill's scientific advisor. The author utilized Nazi war documents, private papers of British scientists, and more than 100 first-hand interviews in the writing of this book.

Klass, Philip J. SECRET SENTRIES IN SPACE. New York: Random House, 1971. xvii, 236 p. Illustrations, index.

A comprehensive study of the genesis and development of intelligence reconnaissance and surveillance space satellites in the United States and Soviet Union. It is knowledgeably set against the background of growing ICBM-nuclear threats, increasing political tension, and absolute requirements for intelligence information that could provide firm proofs to supplement conventional intelligence estimates. This technical but easily read book by the senior avionics editor of AVIATION WEEK AND SPACE TECHNOLOGY (which consistently publishes information on U.S. and USSR advances in intelligence spacecraft and aircraft), is a must for an overall appreciation of the role and characteristics of "secret" photographic, communications, and electronic intelligence spacecraft.

Langer, Walter C. THE MIND OF ADOLF HITLER: THE SECRET WARTIME REPORT. New York: Basic Books, 1972. 269 p. Bibliography, notes, index.

Langer, an American psychiatrist, was commissioned in 1943 to establish the Psychoanalytic Field Unit within the Office of Strategic Services (OSS) and to prepare a psychological analysis of Hitler using as source materials intelligence reports, interviews with men who knew Hitler, and Hitler's writings. This book is the report made by Langer, with certain additions. It is probably the pioneer effort of what has become an important but little-known activity of present-day intelligence--remote medical diagnostics and psychoanalysis of foreign leaders and political personalities. The introduction to the book contains all of the intelligence-associated background leading up to the report itself, which makes up the remainder of the book.

Lasby, Clarence G. PROJECT PAPERCLIP: GERMAN SCIENTISTS AND THE COLD WAR. New York: Atheneum, 1971. 338 p. Notes, index.

A definitive study of U.S. intelligence teams competing with French, Soviet, and British counterparts in a search for German scientists, engineers, and technicians and in a race for exploitation of Germany's wartime technology. The author, a professor of history, conducted interviews with more than 200 Paperclip personnel and studied extensive documentation held in government files. Important insights are revealed regarding the role of Paperclip in the emergent cold war, and in the little-known struggle for scientific supremacy in the immediate postwar period.

Leasor, James. GREEN BEACH. New York: William Morrow & Co., 1975. 292 p. Illustrations, no index.

This book is the account of the special technical intelligence aspects of the 5,000-man raid on Dieppe in occupied France in 1942. The author, prolific novelist and historian living in England, describes how Jack Nissenthall, expert in British and American radar technology, accompanied the raiding party in order to examine and evaluate a German air defense radar installation on a cliff above Green Beach, code name for the landing area. The author developed his material from extensive interviews with members of the radar intelligence team, especially Nissenthall.

Lovell, Stanley P. OF SPIES AND STRATAGEMS. Englewood Cliffs, N.J.: Prentice-Hall, 1963. 191 p.

The author, former director of research and development for OSS, relates some of his experiences in developing special weapons, devices, equipment, counterfeit Japanese occupation money, and myriad other gadgets and objects required to support an intelligence, subversion, and sabotage organization with operating elements throughout the world. Unfortunately, the author wrote the book from memory and consequently it lacks detail. However the literature is practically devoid of works on this aspect of intelligence.

McGovern, James. CROSSBOW AND OVERCAST. New York: William Morrow & Co., 1964. 279 p. Appendix, notes and sources, index, illustrations.

The author, himself an intelligence officer in Germany for five post-World War II years, researched original source material to assist in describing the intelligence attack on German V-1 and V-2 missile activity. That intelligence made possible Anglo-American countermeasure operations against research, test, manufacture, and field launch sites and transport networks (Operation Crossbow). He also describes operation Overcast, which was a top secret "battle-for-the-brains" project for locating German missile specialists, and other scientists and engineers, and bringing them to the United States one jump ahead of the Red Army.

Martelli, George, and Hollard, Michel. THE MAN WHO SAVED LONDON: THE STORY OF MICHEL HOLLARD. Garden City, N.Y.: Doubleday & Co., 1961. 258 p.

The account of how Michel Hollard and the French intelligence network specializing in technical intelligence targets, Reseau Agir, collected information on the technical aspects of V-1 flying bomb launch sites.

Medlicott, W.N. THE ECONOMIC BLOCKADE. Vol. 2. London: Her Majesty's Stationery Office and Longmans, Green & Co., 1959. 727 p.

Volume 2 of this official history of the Ministry of Economic Warfare covers the period from the summer of 1941 to the end of the war in 1945 and deals with the application of plans to strangle the economies of Germany, Italy, and Japan. Appendix IV deals with the intelligence organization of the ministry to support these plans. It emphasizes the increasing demand for technical specialists in every branch of industry, commerce, and finance as intelligence analysts. There was also an increasing need for specialists who could transfer technological and economic assessments into bombing targets for the Royal Air Force--that is, the transfer of intelligence to economic warfare applications.

Millar, George. THE BRUNEVAL RAID: FLASHPOINT OF THE RADAR WAR. Foreword by Admiral Louis Mountbatten. Garden City, N.Y.: Doubleday, 1975. xvi, 221 p. Index, notes, illustrations.

An account of a cross-channel raid in 1942 to capture a German radar at Bruneval, on the coast of occupied France. British paratroopers, commandos, the RAF, and the French underground combined to carry out this raid at the request of British scientific intelligence specialists analyzing German radar. Millar describes the activities of French and British intelligence, and especially the battles behind closed doors in London to gain acceptance of scientific intelligence findings. Millar, a journalist who also served as a British agent in France, obtained his material from the annals of the British Ministry of Defense and interviews with survivors of the raid and with Professor R.V. Jones, the "father" of British scientific intelligence in World War II.

Moorehead, Alan. THE TRAITORS. New York: Harper & Row, 1963. 236 p. Paperback ed. New York: Dell Publishing Co., 1965. 215 p. Bibliography, index.

> An account of Soviet atomic espionage of the World War II period with particular emphasis on Klaus Fuchs but also covering Allan Nunn May and Bruno Pontecorvo.

Pash, Boris T. THE ALSOS MISSION. New York: Award House, 1969. 256 p. List of mission personnel, illustrations.

> As commanding officer of the Alsos Mission, a scientific intelligence unit sent to Europe in 1944 to uncover information of German scientific military developments, particularly information on progress in atomic weapon development, Colonel Pash relates how procedures were developed for field operations against scientific targets.

Powers, Francis Gary, with Gentry, Curt. OPERATION OVERFLIGHT: THE U-2 SPY PILOT TELLS HIS STORY FOR THE FIRST TIME. New York: Holt, Rinehart and Winston, 1970. 375 p. Illustrations.

> U-2 pilot Francis Gary Powers describes in considerable detail his recruitment by the CIA, the vast scope of the CIA U-2 operations, his ill-fated reconnaissance flight over the Soviet Union on May 1, 1960, his imprisonment in the USSR and his return to the United States. The work contains insights into the KGB derived from his treatment and interrogations by that intelligence organization, and insights into the CIA derived from his debriefings.

Sanderson, James Dean. "The A-Bomb That Never Was." In his BEHIND ENEMY LINES, pp. 138-57. New York: Van Nostrand, 1959.

> A description of operations Swallow and Gunnerside, which were British Special Operations Executive (SOE) actions taken to destroy the Norwegian electrochemical plant, Norsk Hydro, and to prevent the heavy water made there from reaching Germany. Based on scientific intelligence information and analyses, the 1943 operation was designed to slow down the German atomic bomb program which was thought at the time to be ahead of the U.S. program. See also Knut Haukelid's SKIES AGAINST THE ATOM (chapter 17, section B).

Slater, Leonard. THE PLEDGE. New York: Simon & Schuster, 1970. 350 p. Paperback ed. New York: Pocket Books, 1971. 357 p. Index, sources.

> A remarkable account of a crash program to arm and equip an army to defend Israel after the British pull-out in May 1948. Co-

ordinated by the Israeli Haganah, the arms procurement and smuggling involved many Americans. The author relied primarily on first-hand interviews and correspondence, which he documents.

Smith, John T., and Abraham, Anson, eds. MANUAL OF COLOR AERIAL PHOTOGRAPHY. Falls Church, Va.: American Society of Photogrammetry, 1968. xv, 550 p. Index, illustrations, charts, tables, color photographs.

Technical discussion of aerial and space color photography (including infrared).

Stevenson, William. ZANEK: A CHRONICLE OF THE ISRAELI AIR FORCE. New York: Viking Press, 1971. vi, 344 p. Paperback ed. Toronto and New York: Bantam Books, 1971. 338 p. Index.

The Canadian journalist Stevenson relates in chapter 5 the technical intelligence operation of the Israelis in December 1969, which resulted in the capture of a complete S-12 Russian-built search radar from Egyptian territory.

Stockholm International Peace Research Institute (SIPRI). THE ARMS TRADE WITH THE THIRD WORLD. Stockholm: Almquist & Wiksell; New York: Humanities Press, November 1971. 910 p.

A complete technical intelligence handbook of the trade of major weapons--ships, aircraft, tanks, missiles--between eleven supplying nations and the Third World during the post-World War II period.

_____. "Non-seismic Detection of Underground Nuclear Tests." In WORLD ARMAMENTS AND DISARMAMENT SIPRI YEARBOOK 1972, pp. 437-60. Stockholm: Almquist & Wiksell; New York: Humanities Press; London: Paul Elek, 1972. Tables, bibliography.

Summarizes and analyzes publicly available information on the role of space satellites in detection and identification of underground nuclear tests. Also summarizes information on ground-based and satellite-borne detection methods for atmospheric and space weapons tests. Excellent bibliography containing 102 entries on this subject matter.

Translation World Publishers. THE TRIAL OF THE U-2: THE EXCLUSIVE AUTHORIZED ACCOUNT. Introduction by Harold J. Berman. Chicago: 1960. xxx, 158 p. Photographs, paperbound.

The record of the court proceedings of the trial of Francis Gary Powers held in Moscow August 17-19, 1960. The trial record was released in English translation by the Soviet government within a matter of days after the trial. In the extensive introduction Harold J. Berman, professor of law at Harvard University, discusses legal and moral aspects of espionage from aircraft and interprets events surrounding U.S. denials and admissions of the flight.

U.S. Department of Defense. STATEMENT OF SECRETARY OF DEFENSE MEL-VIN LAIRD BEFORE THE HOUSE ARMED SERVICES COMMITTEE ON THE FY 1973 DEFENSE BUDGET AND FY 1973-1977 PROGRAM. Secretary of Defense Melvin R. Laird's Annual Defense Department Report FY 1973: A National Security Strategy of Realistic Deterrence. Washington, D.C.: Government Printing Office, 17 February 1972. 203 p. Charts, tables, graphs.

Each year in February or March the Secretary of Defense prepares his annual statement as a prelude to his appearances before the Congress to defend the department's budget. It has become customary to include in this annual report a section outlining the threat to the United States derived from information available to the intelligence community. Pages 35 through 58 of this edition carry detailed descriptions of Soviet strategic weapons taken from scientific and technical intelligence estimates—especially declassified for this annual report. Also in this edition is the justification for the establishment of an assistant secretary of defense for intelligence as well as other changes in the defense intelligence community (pp. 133-36). This so called "Posture Statement" is available from the Government Printing Office each year and represents one of the best insights into strategic weapons assessments of the Soviet Union and Warsaw Pact countries. It also indicates the credibility which defense decision makers place on our scientific and technical intelligence collection and estimative capabilities.

U.S. Department of the Army. Headquarters. TECHNICAL INTELLIGENCE. Field Manual 30-16. Washington, D.C.: Office of the Adjutant General, August 1966. 76 p. Index, bibliography (references to other technical intelligence manuals), charts, tables.

A training manual which sets forth the army doctrine for technical intelligence and describes the procedures for its collection, production, and dissemination. It establishes broad principles regarding the role and employment of tech-intelligence personnel and field units.

B. ARTICLES AND REPORTS

Binder, David. "Israel Offering to Barter Soviet Arms for the West's." NEW YORK TIMES, 25 July 1967, p. 1.

The article describes a novel development in technical intelligence: the offer by Israel of up-to-date Soviet weapons and equipment to the intelligence services of the West for characterization, analysis, and countermeasure development.

Coates, G.P. "Reconnaissance Satellites." SPACEFLIGHT 3 (May 1961): 100-104.

An account of observation satellite orbits; photographic systems, both film-return and electro-optical; radar systems; and ground stations.

Frisbee, John L. "Electronic Warfare: Essential Element of Deterrence." AIR FORCE MAGAZINE, July 1972, pp. 36-41.

A useful review of the evolution of electronic warfare, and the implications of test cases of use of electronic warfare by U.S. aircraft in penetrating Soviet-made antiaircraft defenses in North Vietnam. The author assesses expected increased future importance of electronic warfare.

Galloway, Alec. "A Decade of U.S. Reconnaissance Satellites." INTERAVIA, April 1972, pp. 376-80.

Traces, from available published literature, the development of photographic reconnaissance spacecraft in the United States.

Garwin, Richard L. "Antisubmarine Warfare and National Security." SCIEN-TIFIC AMERICAN 227 (July 1972): 14-25.

A useful portrayal of the technical aspects of detection and iden-tification of submerged submarines.

Germain, Jean Rene. "Les Satellites de Reconnaissance." FORCES AERIENNES FRANCAIS (Paris) 266 (February 1970): 171-89. Illustrations.

A review of U.S. and USSR reconnaissance and surveillance space-craft, with characteristics, launch, and retrieval systems described.

Greenwood, Ted. "Reconnaissance and Arms Control." SCIENTIFIC AMERI-CAN 228 (February 1973): 14-19. Illustrations.

Greenwood's article is based on his paper, RECONNAISSANCE, SURVEILLANCE AND ARMS CONTROL (see below). This later version includes excellent diagrams and photographs.

_____. RECONNAISSANCE, SURVEILLANCE AND ARMS CONTROL. Adel-phi Papers, no. 88. London: The International Institute for Strategic Studies, June 1972. 28 p. Bibliography.

The author discusses the advantages of reconnaissance and surveil-lance systems over other methods of intelligence gathering as a means of verifying and monitoring arms control agreements that affect national security. He provides technical descriptions and applications of photographic and electronic reconnaissance space systems as well as the use of radar, over-the-horizon radar, satel-

lite systems, and shipboard sensors as means of surveillance of
missile tests. A useful bibliography of seventy-five entries of
separate magazine and newspaper articles is included.

Hersh, Seymour. "CIA Salvage Ship Brought Up Part of Soviet Sub Lost in
1968, Failed to Raise Atom Missiles." NEW YORK TIMES, 19 March 1975,
pp. 1, 48.

The article exposes details of project Jennifer, a remarkable technical intelligence operation in which U.S. intelligence retrieved
parts of a 1958-model Soviet submarine in the Pacific Ocean
northwest of Hawaii in water three miles deep. Information is
provided on how intelligence contracted with Howard Hughes to
have constructed a specially designed deep sea recovery vessel--
the Glomar Explorer--plus a companion submersible recovery barge,
designated the HMB-1, in which to transport the recovered submarine parts on the surface but hidden from view. See also the
following detailed and well-illustrated articles: "The Great Submarine Snatch." TIME, 31 March 1975, pages 20-27, and "CIA's
Mission Impossible." NEWSWEEK, 31 March 1975, pages 24-32.

Jones, R.V. "Scientific Intelligence." JOURNAL OF THE ROYAL UNITED
SERVICE INSTITUTION (London) 92 (August 1947): 352-69.

A summary of the scientific and technical intelligence activities
of the air staff in England during World War II by the man who
pioneered this effort and developed its doctrine and philosphy.
The article is chiefly concerned with detecting German developments in radio-navigational aids, radar, flying bombs, long-range
rockets, and atomic weaponry.

"Scientific Intelligence." RESEARCH (London) 9 (September 1956):
347-52.

The importance of scientific and technical intelligence, both in
revealing intentions of a potential enemy and in anticipating the
enemy's application of science and technology to weaponry is
brought out by Jones, using his wartime experiences as illustrations regarding intelligence organization and procedures.

Katz, Amrom H. "Observation Satellites: Problems and Prospects." ASTRO-
NAUTICS 5 (April 1960): 26-29ff; (June 1960): 26-29, 52-54; (July 1960):
28-29, 80-85; (August 1960): 30-31, 59-64; (September 1960): 32-33, 40-46;
(October 1960): 36-37, 66-71. Also published as OBSERVATION SATELLITES:
PROBLEMS, POSSIBILITIES AND PROSPECTS. RAND Paper P-1707. Santa
Monica, Calif.: RAND Corp., 25 May 1959. 128 p. Bibliography, photo-
graphs.

An introduction to almost every aspect of observation satellites,
including what might be observed and recorded, the sensors, the

resolutions achievable, the advantages of both video return and film return systems, and use for international arms control inspection. The author, a pioneer in aerial reconnaissance with the air force and head of RAND's Intelligence and Reconnaissance Group, is now with the Arms Control and Disarmament Agency. Extensive and useful bibliography.

Klass, Philip J. "More Spies in the Sky: How U.S.-Russia Watch Each Other." U.S. NEWS & WORLD REPORT, 13 August 1973, pp. 27-28.

A comparison of U.S. and Soviet reconnaissance programs shows that since 1968 the USSR has had a seven-to-one edge on numbers of spy satellites launched. Interprets meaning of U.S.-Russian arms limitation agreements in terms of capabilities of national technical means of verification.

"Soviets Push Ocean Surveillance." AVIATION WEEK & SPACE TECHNOLOGY, 10 September 1973, pp. 12-13.

A comparison of Soviet and U.S. ocean surveillance capabilities in which the Soviets are considered to be ahead, routinely using photo-reconnaissance spacecraft to locate elements of the U.S. fleet and to photograph shore installations.

"Reconnaissance and Surveillance." DATA: MAGAZINE OF MILITARY RDT&E MANAGEMENT 12 (April 1967): 11-63. Photographs.

This entire issue of DATA is devoted to articles by air force, navy, and marine corps specialists on tactical reconnaissance and tactical and strategic surveillance. Of note is an introductory article by Senator Strom Thurmond, "The Growth of Reconnaissance and Surveillance in Political Decisions," pp. 11-12.

Ruggles, Richard, and Brodie, Henry. "An Empirical Approach to Economic Intelligence in World War II." JOURNAL OF THE AMERICAN STATISTICAL ASSOCIATION 42 (March 1947): 72-91. Diagrams, tables.

In early 1943 the Economic Warfare Division of the American embassy in London started a program of utilizing technical intelligence information for economic intelligence purposes. The technique of analyzing markings and serial numbers obtained from captured German weapons and equipment was developed as a means of obtaining accurate estimates of German war production and strength. The authors describe the development of this technique and compare the accuracy of wartime estimates of production of certain items of weapons and equipment with the official statistics which became available on German war production at the end of the conflict.

Simons, Howard. "Our Eye in the Sky." WASHINGTON POST, 8 December 1963, p. E2.

Traces the early development of the Samos observation satellite with some analysis of political implications and Soviet reaction.

"Spies in Space: They Make an Open Book of Russia." U.S. NEWS & WORLD REPORT, 9 September 1968, pp. 69-72.

A compilation of data on U.S. intelligence capabilities in space observation at the time of the Czechoslovakian crisis of 1968.

Trainor, James. "Cuba Missile Threat Detailed." MISSILES AND ROCKETS, 29 October 1962, pp. 12-14, 47. Aerial photographs.

Details the types and locations of Russian missiles deployed in Cuba. Uses annotated aerial reconnaissance photographs to develop the story.

U.S. Congress. House. Committee on Armed Services. THE CHANGING STRATEGIC MILITARY BALANCE: USA VS. USSR. 90th Cong., 1st sess., July 1967. Rept. no. 80-785. 94 p. Charts, tables.

This interesting comparison of strategic weaponry of the United States and the USSR was prepared by a special subcommittee of the National Strategy Committee of the American Security Council at the request of the House Committee on Armed Services. The scientific and technical weapons assessment and comparison was based on unclassified sources only and demonstrates the amount of detail on foreign (USSR) intercontinental ballistic missiles, intermediate and medium range ballistic missiles, antimissile missiles, submarine-launched missiles, strategic bombers, and space weapons that is available in the open literature.

U.S. Congress. Joint Committee on Atomic Energy. HEARINGS ON STATUS OF CURRENT TECHNOLOGY TO IDENTIFY SEISMIC EVENTS AS NATURAL OR MAN-MADE. 92d Cong., 1st sess., 1971. v, 343 p. Illustrations.

A review of the technology available and seismic means used to detect and identify nuclear underground explosions in order to assess the reliability of national means of verification in event of complete test ban agreements.

_____. SOVIET ATOMIC ESPIONAGE. 82d Cong., 1st sess., April 1951. Rept. no. 81095. 222 p. Maps.

Part 1 of this study seeks to develop factual, authentic information about the four known atomic spies--Fuchs, Pontecorvo, May, and Greenglass--and the courier Gold. Parts 2 and 3 deal with allegations of spying for the USSR during World War II and with information relating to serious security breaches.

U.S. Congress. Senate. Committee on Aeronautical & Space Programs. SO-
VIET SPACE PROGRAMS, 1966-70. 92d Cong., 1st sess., 9 December 1971.
Doc. no. 92-51. Staff report prepared by the Congressional Research Service
and Law Library of the Library of Congress. Washington, D.C.: Government
Printing Office, 1971. 670 p. Index, tables, illustrations, appendices.

> Dr. Charles S. Sheldon II, foremost authority on Soviet space activi-
> ties, directed the preparation of this complete and factual report.
> See especially chapter 9, which is devoted to photographic and
> electronic intelligence satellites.

U S. Congress. Senate. Committee on Armed Services. Preparedness Investigation Subcommittee. HEARINGS BEFORE THE ELECTRONIC BATTLEFIELD SUB-
COMMITTEE. 92d Cong., 2d sess., 1971. Rept. no. 53-830. 221 p. Illustrations, charts, photographs.

> Details on the characteristics of new surveillance sensors developed
> by the air force, army, navy, and marine corps and used in Viet-
> nam and Laos to detect and locate enemy forces and for targeting
> air strikes against infiltration and supply trails.

_____. INTERIM REPORT OF THE SUBCOMMITTEE ON THE CUBAN MILI-
TARY BUILDUP. 88th Cong., 1st sess., 1963. Rept. no. 98018. 18 p.

> A review of the military developments and intelligence activities
> and operations, primarily aerial photographic reconnaissance and
> surveillance, undertaken by all elements of the U.S. intelligence
> community in connection with the Cuban missile crisis of 1962.

_____. INVESTIGATION INTO ELECTRONIC BATTLEFIELD PROGRAM. 92d
Cong., 1st sess., 1971. Rept. no. 56-743. 20 p.

> This report sets forth the findings and conclusions of an investiga-
> tion into the development and use of new surveillance sensors used
> in South Vietnam and Laos to locate enemy forces.

Chapter 11

COMMUNICATIONS AND ELECTRONIC INTELLIGENCE

Cryptology, the making and breaking of codes and ciphers, is the component of communications intelligence (termed Comint in the intelligence community) that seems to hold the most public interest. It has its own engrossing history which dates from the dawn of Western civilization, and cryptanalysis, the breaking of codes, has from time to time played a key role in the outcome of battles and the affairs of nations (see Barbara Tuchman's THE ZIMMERMANN TELEGRAM, for example). However, to the intelligence community other forms of communications intelligence gathering are also important. The advent of radio communications gave rise to developments in transmitter direction finding (DFing) and locating, traffic volume analysis, Morse operator identification ("fingerprinting"), radio signal analysis, communications network analysis, and more recently, voice printing analysis. These are all forms of communications intelligence possible without necessarily breaking the code guarding the content of the messages sent.

David Kahn's THE CODEBREAKERS; THE STORY OF SECRET WRITING is certainly the best single source of information on the history of cryptology. Although the author concentrates on the development of the methods of making and breaking codes and ciphers, and the roles these methods have played in specific historic events, there is also much that describes the broader aspects of communications intelligence (such as direction finding and traffic analysis) and the roles these techniques have played since their development. John Carroll's SECRETS OF ELECTRONIC ESPIONAGE is also a helpful source in the broader considerations of communications intelligence describing doctrine and techniques during the formative years of World War I and the rapid expansion years of World War II. Frederick W. Winterbotham's THE ULTRA SECRET, which achieved best-seller status in both its hard cover and paperback editions, is an outstanding account of how breaking the code of the German High Command and reading the contents of Hitler's orders to his field commanders was an important factor of Allied victory in Europe in World War II.

The development of radar provided another important long-range detection and tracking tool for intelligence. Large radars have been important in the strategic warning role (for example, the BMEWS radars--Ballistic Missile Early Warning System) and in the technical intelligence role of "watching" the trajectories of Soviet strategic missiles fired on proving grounds for performance test purposes. This "watching" is done from bases on the periphery of the USSR. This use of active radar for intelligence purposes is termed Radint, for radar intelligence. Additional technical intelligence information can be obtained on missile performance by the passive interception of the telemetry signals they emit during test flight. Telemetry intelligence (Telint) is a form of electronic intelligence.

Electronic intelligence, or Elint, was developed to a high form of specialization in World War II. It is defined as the passive "listening" to the radars of others. By such "listening" it is possible to obtain intelligence information regarding location, identification of type, and use of the radars (Elint order-of-battle); the detection of new radars for yet unknown purposes (technical intelligence); or information on which to design radar jammers (electronic countermeasures--ECM). For a detailed discussion of Elint and ECM, see John Carroll's SECRETS OF ELECTRONIC ESPIONAGE, below. See also Philip Klass's SECRET SENTRIES IN SPACE, in chapter 10, for descriptions of satellite Elint collection systems. Elint also includes "listening" to other forms of noncommunications electromagnetic emissions such as bomber navigation aids (see again John Carroll, below, and R.V. Jones, "Scientific Intelligence," in chapter 10).

Just as intelligence has its protective side in counterintelligence and security, signal intelligence (Sigint which includes both Comint and Elint) has its signal security designed to protect our communications systems and electronic emitters and to prevent unauthorized persons from gaining intelligence from them (see David Kahn's THE CODE BREAKERS, and the army's SIGSEC INSTRUCTIONAL PACKET). Communications security (Comsec) includes the development and proper use of codes and ciphers (cryptographic security), and it also includes transmission security--the use of very short-burst, high-speed transmitter systems, the frequent change of call signs, padding traffic with dummy messages, and radio silence. (See again David Kahn for descriptions of late developments in the National Security Agency in the field of Comsec.) Gordon Lonsdale, the Soviet spy in the British naval secrets case, for example, used a high-speed transmitter for communicating with Moscow (see Bulloch and Miller's SPY RING: A STORY OF THE NAVAL SECRETS CASE, in chapter 10). Electronic Intelligence Security (Elint Sec or Elsec) includes changing radar frequencies or locations or radar silence when "ferret" or Elint collection planes or ships are nearby. See John Carroll for the history of U.S. and Soviet "ferreting" operations and techniques designed to get the other side to turn on their radars. A more recent protective category of Elsec is the shielding of spurious radiations made by electric generators, radars turned on but not transmitting, or even computers that would disclose information or location to sensitive radiation intelligence (Rint) detection systems.

Extreme secrecy has always been associated with cryptology; membership in the intelligence community has never been sufficient grounds for access to this type information. The guarding of one's own cryptographic systems as a matter of signal security is understandable, and the leaking of information on the cryptanalytic success of another's cipher systems would cause them to be changed, bringing to an end years of work and all intelligence gain until the replacement system was broken. Strangely, very nearly the same degree of secrecy still shrouds activities during World Wars I and II, making a history more comprehensive than Kahn's virtually impossible to write. Furthermore, the same rules of security classification which protect cryptologic activities are generally applicable to the broader aspects of communications intelligence (direction finding, etc.) and to most of the electronic intelligence fields, although the potential intelligence loss, if compromised, would not be comparable to the loss in cryptologic intelligence. Although the literature is providing more and more insights into Comint and Elint activities, the revelations are in bits and pieces and in many types of books, magazines, trade journals, and newspapers. Disclosure of the intercept taps on East German communications located in a tunnel in Berlin is one such "bit," as was the disclosure of the U.S. Radint and Elint station located in Peshawar, Pakistan, and targeted against Soviet Central Asia (see William Coughlin's article in the WASHINGTON POST). AVIATION WEEK AND SPACE TECHNOLOGY reveals much regarding Radint, Elint, and ECM equipment and activities, and from time to time an author puts all the pieces together, as Klass did in his SECRET SENTRIES IN SPACE, and as Dr. Charles S. Sheldon of the Library of Congress did on Soviet space and space surveillance activities (see U.S. Congress. Senate. SOVIET SPACE PROGRAMS: 1966-70, in chapter 10).

A glossary of signal intelligence terms can be found in Kahn's book and definitions of terms can be found in the Department of Defense DICTIONARY OF MILITARY AND ASSOCIATED TERMS (cited in chapter 3).

A. BOOKS

Armbrister, Trevor. A MATTER OF ACCOUNTABILITY: THE TRUE STORY OF THE PUEBLO AFFAIR. New York: Coward-McCann, 1970. 408 p.

> Journalist Armbrister interviewed and traveled widely to accumulate data on the Pueblo affair, and was assisted by Commander Bucher himself. The book does not emphasize the intelligence aspects of the Pueblo but provides insight into the approval and risk assessment procedures incidental to intelligence missions.

Bucher, Lloyd M., and Rasovich, Mark. BUCHER: MY STORY. New York: Doubleday, 1970. 447 p.

> The captain of the U.S.S. Pueblo provides his own account of the mission of his ship, its capture, and his imprisonment.

Carroll, John M. SECRETS OF ELECTRONIC ESPIONAGE. New York: E.P. Dutton & Co., 1966. 224 p. Index, photographs, illustrations.

> A useful, short, but densely packed handbook of communications, electronic and radar intelligence techniques, hardware, and countermeasures, developed during both World Wars, the Korean War,

and the cold war. This information has been meticulously assembled by an associate professor of industrial engineering and former managing editor of ELECTRONICS MAGAZINE.

Davis, Burke. GET YAMAMOTO. New York: Random House, 1969. 231 p.

An account of the spectacular cryptanalytic incident in the Pacific during World War II, in which a radio intercept by a U.S. radio intelligence unit indicated that Admiral Isoroku Yamamoto, architect of the Pearl Harbor attack and an undisputed strategic leader, would visit Bougainville. This intelligence led to the interception of his plane by army air force fighters and his death.

Farago, Ladislas. THE BROKEN SEAL: THE STORY OF "OPERATION MAGIC" AND THE PEARL HARBOR DISASTER. New York: Random House, 1967. 439 p. Index, bibliography, source notes.

In a book filled with incidents and characters, an accomplished chronicler of intelligence history portrays the operations of both American and Japanese code-breaking operations from 1921 to December 7, 1941. Of special interest is chapter 21, which describes how the Japanese disguised their fleet movements prior to sailing to Pearl Harbor by changing communications call signs, sending dummy messages to foil traffic analysis, and by having fleet radio operators whose "fingerprints" were known to U.S. intercepters send messages from the homeland as if they were with the fleet. A useful bibliography and notes on sources provide rich material on both cryptologic and the usual espionage activities associated with Pearl Harbor.

_____. THE TENTH FLEET. New York: Paperback Library, 1964. 319 p. Paperbound.

Story of a little-known phase of the Battle of the Atlantic by an author on intelligence who was close to the action. The Tenth Fleet was a centralized antisubmarine command established during World War II to bring together all elements of intelligence and operations to defeat the German U-boats. The book describes in detail the intelligence efforts using radar, underwater sound, and radio direction finding (High Frequency Direction Finding, HF/DF, or HuffDuffs) for detecting and locating U-boats, and signal analysis of their radio transmissions to Germany for specific U-boat identification.

James, Sir William. THE CODE BREAKERS OF ROOM 40: THE STORY OF ADMIRAL SIR WILLIAM HALL, GENIUS OF BRITISH COUNTER-INTELLIGENCE. New York: St. Martin's Press, 1956. 212 p. British ed. THE EYES OF THE NAVY. London: Methuen & Co., 1955. 212 p.

The story of the director of British naval intelligence during World

War I by a member of Room 40. Emphasizes cryptanalysis of German communications.

Kahn, David. THE CODEBREAKERS: THE STORY OF SECRET WRITING. New York: Macmillan, 1967. xvi, 1,164 p. Index, bibliography, photographs, illustrations, notes. Abridged ed., paperbound. New York: New American Library, Signet Books, 1973. 476 p.

A scholarly world history of cryptology, eminently readable and highly informative, by a journalist-author, amateur cryptologist, and past president of the American Cryptogram Association. Although there is much in the book regarding the development of the technical aspects of cryptography and cryptanalysis, there is also much of interest regarding the evolution of organizations engaged in cryptology and the influence of cryptology on the course of war, battles, and world events. The chapters on Allied, Axis, and neutral cryptologic activities and organizations during World War II, and the 60 pages on the history and structure of the National Security Agency (NSA) in the postwar period, are especially informative. The bibliography plus the 155 pages of notes to the text represent a unique insight into signal intelligence source material.

Ransom, Harry Howe. "The Intelligence Community: Other Principal Members." In his THE INTELLIGENCE ESTABLISHMENT, pp. 126-33. Cambridge, Mass.: Harvard University Press, 1970.

The roles and functions of the National Security Agency in signal intelligence by a leading author on the subject of intelligence organization and procedures. See main entry, chapter 4, section A.

Sinkov, Abraham. ELEMENTARY CRYPTANALYSIS: A MATHEMATICAL APPROACH. New York: Random House, 1968. 189 p.

In a private communication to the compilers of this bibliography, David Kahn evaluates this book as an "excellent study of the basic cipher systems, with a very systematic explanation of the underlying mathematics . . . clear and thorough in explanation."

Thompson, George Raynor, and Harris, Dixie R. THE SIGNAL CORPS: THE OUTCOME. United States Army in World War II series, the Technical Services subseries. Prepared by Department of the Army, Office of the Chief of Military History. Washington, D.C.: Government Printing Office, 1966.

Recommended as an authoritative insight into the organization, activities, and problems of signal intelligence and signal security during World War II. Of special interest are chapter 10, "Signal Security and Intelligence," and chapter 11, "Electronic Combat: Countermeasure."

Tuchman, Barbara W. THE ZIMMERMANN TELEGRAM. New York: Viking Press, 1958. 244 p. Bibliography, index, notes.

A well-documented account of a significant achievement of British cryptanalysis during World War I. In January 1917 the British interception and deciphering of a telegram from Berlin would bring the United States to the aid of the Allies. The book describes the decoding and use of the telegram by the British.

Tully, Andrew. THE SUPER SPIES. New York: William Morrow & Co., 1969. 256 p. Index.

A popularly aimed book by a Washington columnist who has specialized in books that reveal the inner workings of the intelligence and security community. Contains an overall insight into communications and electronic intelligence activities set against a background of descriptions of elements of the entire U.S. intelligence community, but with special emphasis on the National Security Agency.

U.S. Congress. House. Committee on Armed Services. INQUIRING INTO THE U.S.S. PUEBLO AND EC-121 PLANE INCIDENTS. 91st Cong., 1st sess., 1969. Doc. no. 91-10. 1,170 p. Index, appendix.

A record of hearings held for the purpose of assessing the national security implications implicit in the loss of the Pueblo, the genesis of the concept of single, unprotected, intelligence-gathering ships, and the procedures used in determining the risk involved in Pueblo missions.

U.S. Department of the Army. Headquarters. SIGSEC INSTRUCTIONAL PACKET. Department of Army Pamplet no. 350-19. Washington, D.C.: Office of the Adjutant General, October 1971. ii, 105 p.

An instructional pamphlet on signal security (Sigsec) which includes both communications security (Comsec) and electronic security (Elsec). Covers both the technical and practical sides of Sigsec by providing interesting examples of the results of violations of communications security in various battles in World War II and the Korean and Vietnam Wars. Excellent for definitions of all the terms used in both signal intelligence (Sigint) and signal security (Sigsec).

Winterbotham, Frederick W. THE ULTRA SECRET. Foreword by Royal Air Force Marshal Sir John Slessor. New York and London: Harper & Row, 1974. xiii, 199 p. Index.

This is the remarkable revelation of how the British were able to decipher the most secret radio communications of the German High Command to the major field commanders, and from the field commanders to minor commands. It was written by a retired group captain who for ten years prior to 1939 was the senior air staff representative in the Secret Intelligence Service (SIS). In the early days of the war the author was largely responsible for the inception of the Ultra operation and subsequently for its working throughout the war. The author credits the original solution of the German Enigma coding machines to information obtained from a Polish employee of the coding machine factory. But Winterbotham admits that while this was the story he was given at the time, the Polish cipher bureau first made copies of the Enigma machine and turned one over to the British. More interesting than the technical aspects of the Ultra code-breaking operation are the strategic effects of knowing the German military strengths, dispositions, and intentions before key battles, and disseminating this information quickly to British and U.S. field commanders. The author discusses which of these field commanders best utilized the Ultra information. The book provides new insights into some of the most famous battles of World War II and is essential reading for the history of that war. Additional information on the Ultra operation is provided in Anthony Cave Brown's BODYGUARD OF LIES (see chapter 21, section B). THE ULTRA SECRET was written and published while Brown was researching additional source material.

Wohlstetter, Roberta. PEARL HARBOR: WARNING AND DECISION. Stanford, Calif.: Stanford University Press, 1962. 426 p. Bibliography, illustrations.

A well-documented study of the events leading to Pearl Harbor, with some emphasis on communications intelligence, its organization and interfaces with the decision makers in government. Also valuable as an insight into indications intelligence and the relationships between communications intelligence and indicators of hostilities.

Yardley, Herbert Osborn. THE AMERICAN BLACK CHAMBER. Indianapolis, Ind.: Bobbs-Merrill, 1931. 375 p.

A history of the first modern organization for cryptanalysis in the United States by its originator and director during the period of World War I through the 1920s.

B. ARTICLES AND REPORTS

Anderson, Jack. "How the CIA Snooped inside Russia." WASHINGTON POST, 10 December 1973, p. B17.

An account of a CIA communications intelligence operation in which the radio telephone traffic between the automobiles of the Soviet leaders in Moscow was monitored.

Communications & Electronic Intelligence

Coughlin, William J. "U.S. is Dismantling Peshawar Spy Base." WASHING-
TON POST, 10 April 1969, p. A15.

A resume of the history of the U.S. base in Peshawar, Pakistan.
This communications, electronic, and radar intelligence base was
targeted against the Soviet strategic weapons proving and test areas
in Central Asia.

Dommen, Arthur. "Enemy Radio Base Intercepted 1400 Military Messages."
WASHINGTON POST, 13 January 1970, p. A12.

An insight into the communications intelligence activities of the
North Vietnamese army in South Vietnam. Provides a description
of the equipment found by U.S. forces in a captured radio monitoring station, with added information on North Vietnamese radio
deception activities.

"Electronic Countermeasures: Special Report." AVIATION WEEK AND SPACE
TECHNOLOGY 96 (February 21, 1972): 38-107.

A series of twenty-six articles on various aspects of electronic intelligence and electronic countermeasures including articles on
Soviet activities.

Kahn, David. "Modern Cryptology." SCIENTIFIC AMERICAN 215 (July
1966): 38-46. Illustrations.

An excellent summary of some widely used cipher systems along
with something of the history of their origin. Also emphasizes
developments in cryptanalytical methods. The author, compiler of
the definitive survey on cryptology, THE CODEBREAKERS (see section A of this chapter), describes in some detail the evolution of
the one-time pad system and of rotor machines. The article is
made more interesting by references to specific instances in history where cryptology made important contributions. The illustrations meet the high standards of SCIENTIFIC AMERICAN.

_____. "Secret Writings: Selected Works on Modern Cryptology." BULLE-
TIN OF THE NEW YORK PUBLIC LIBRARY 73 (May 1969): 315-27.

An outstanding, selective annotated bibliography by an authority
in the field. The author states that his listing of the better works
"aims at helping the person approaching cryptology for the first
time to find his way around the field." An appendix to the paper
contains helpful references to areas of communications intelligence
broader than cryptology, and even provides references to works of
fiction in cryptology. The author's annotations are especially helpful and incisive.

Miller, Barry. "Soviet Radar Expertise Expands." AVIATION WEEK AND
SPACE TECHNOLOGY 94 (February 15, 1971): 14-16, and "Soviet Radars
Disclose Clues to Doctrine." AVIATION WEEK AND SPACE TECHNOLOGY
94 (22 February 1971): 42-50.

A two-part series on the characteristics and use of all types of
Soviet radars, with interpretations regarding implications for electronic intelligence and electronic countermeasures.

Morrow, Michael. "GI's at a Secret Base--Plenty of Time to Worry." WASH-
INGTON POST, 14 September 1972, pp. E1, E5.

A description of some of the activities at the U.S. Army Security
Agency communications intelligence base at Ramasun, Thailand.

"Snoopers: Looking and Listening." NEWSWEEK, 5 February 1968, p. 18.

A review of the roles and mission of the U.S.S. Pueblo. Part of
a larger article covering nonintelligence aspects of the Pueblo capture entitled "They Mean Business," pages 16, 17, 19-21.

"The Spy Planes: What They Do and Why." TIME, 25 April 1969, p. 17.

A short account of the mission and capabilities of the EC-121 signal intelligence collection aircraft shot down by the North Koreans.
Part of a larger article "A New Lesson in the Limits of Power,"
pages 15-16, on the political implications of the EC-121 shootdown.

"United States Air Force Security Service: A Major Air Command." AIR
FORCE MAGAZINE, May 1973, pp. 98-99.

A description of the missions and functions of the U.S. Air Force
Security Service, the signal intelligence organization of the air
force.

U.S. Congress. House. Committee on Un-American Activities. REPORT ON
SECURITY PRACTICES IN THE NATIONAL SECURITY AGENCY. 87th Cong.,
1st sess., 1962. 23 p.

A report surrounding the defection of National Security Agency
employees Bernon F. Mitchell and William H. Martin to Russia.

Wilson, George C. "Pueblo Crew Fitted to Spy on Russia." WASHINGTON
POST, 2 March 1969, pp. A1, A6.

A useful article detailing some of the qualifications of the Pueblo
crew for communications intelligence missions, and a description
of some of the specialized equipment.

Chapter 12

ESCAPE AND EVASION

World War II in Europe saw the beginning of the large-scale development of escape and evasion (E&E) as an increasingly important intelligence function. The British were the leaders in this expansion, understandably, since a program for the return of downed air crews, who represented a considerable investment in training and experience, was a matter of national necessity. Special elements of organization were set up in intelligence to plan, develop, and operate escape lines from occupied Europe, and a special research and development program was established to provide equipment and devices that would aid in escape and evasion (see Clayton Hutton, OFFICIAL SECRET). When the Americans entered the war, they participated in the development of E&E aids in the OSS technical equipment program and through the programs of the civilian National Defense Research Committee and the Office of Scientific Research and Development (NDRC/OSRC). Escape and evasion had different requirements in the Pacific theaters where jungle survival became part of the evolving E&E doctrine.

The literature is abundantly supplied with E&E books, mostly of British origin. However, with the Korean and Vietnam experiences, E&E books by Americans have increased in number. The best stories of escape and evasion during the Vietnam War have not yet been written.

Blair, Clay, Jr. BEYOND COURAGE. New York: David McKay Co., 1955. 247 p. British ed. London: Jarrolds, 1956. 247 p.

Stories of successful evasion by U.S. Air Force airmen shot down behind Communist Chinese and North Korean lines during the Korean War.

Crawley, Aldan M. ESCAPE FROM GERMANY: A HISTORY OF R.A.F. ESCAPES DURING THE WAR. New York: Simon & Schuster, 1956. 291 p. British ed. ESCAPE FROM GERMANY. London: Collins, 1958. 291 p.

A version of the official history of evasion and escape during World War II, written for use by the Air Ministry and edited for security purposes. Fully describes how captured airmen organized

and planned for escape from Luftstalags in Germany in accordance
with their training and code of conduct. The author was himself
a prisoner and headed an escape committee.

Howarth, David A. ACROSS TO NORWAY. New York: William Sloane,
1952. 286 p. British ed. THE SHETLAND BUS. London: Thomas Nelson
& Sons, 1951. 220 p.

An account of one escape and evasion operation during World War
II. The British and Norwegians operated a base in the Shetland
Islands from which small boats journeyed across the Norwegian Sea
to aid the resistance, as well as to take away evaders, escapees,
and refugees.

Hutton, Clayton. OFFICIAL SECRET. New York: Crown Publishers, 1961.
212 p. Illustrations. British ed. London: Max Parrish, 1960. 195 p.

The account of the research and development program in England
to produce aids, devices, and equipment that could be hidden or
disguised for the purpose of assisting in escape and evasion. Aids
designed and made in quantity for general issue included compasses
of all sizes--some disguised as uniform buttons--silk maps, dart
guns, boots with hidden compartments, emergency rations, and
many, many other items.

Sunderman, James F. AIR ESCAPE AND EVASION. New York: Franklin
Watts, 1963. 289 p. Index, bibliography.

The author, an air force colonel, has selected from official U.S.
Air Force and Royal Air Force records and documents, and from
published books, thirty-one accounts of escapes and evasions that
occurred during World War I, World War II, and the Korean War.
Not a definitive study, but one which clearly demonstrates the
imagination and ingenuity required for successful escapes.

U.S. Department of the Army. SURVIVAL, ESCAPE AND EVASION. Army
Field Manual 21-76. Washington, D.C.: Government Printing Office, 1968.
431 p. Index.

This is the army's training manual on the techniques and concepts
of evasion and escape. An examination of servicemen isolated
during World War II and the Korean and Vietnam Wars has shown
that survival is an essential element of evasion and escape. Thus
this manual has included chapters on survival in cold and tropical
areas as well as survival at sea and in internment and prisoner-of-
war camps. Chapters on interrogation and indoctrination techniques
used by potential enemies are also included.

Chapter 13

INDUSTRIAL ESPIONAGE

About a decade ago an estimate made for an American Management Association conference held in Manhattan stated that corporate losses due to spying and theft of processes was running at about $2 billion per year. Furthermore, the estimate revealed that by the mid-1960s industrial espionage had risen 50 percent over earlier years. Considering that ten years ago industrial espionage was an activity of such significant magnitude, it is surprising that not a great deal of definitive literature has been written on the subject in the United States, except for articles in business and research-oriented magazines and the press, plus a few good books. Richard Greene's BUSINESS INTELLIGENCE AND ESPIONAGE is a serious textbook treatment of the subject; Edward Engberg's THE SPY IN THE CORPORATE STRUCTURE--AND THE RIGHT TO PRIVACY is a readable treatment which also brings in the broader issue of the individual's right to privacy. England has produced some literature (see Peter Hamilton's ESPIONAGE AND SUBVERSION IN AN INDUSTRIAL SOCIETY: AN EXAMINATION AND PHILOSPHY OF DEFENSE FOR MANAGEMENT), and a more extensive literature exists in German (see Max Gurzenhauser's bibliography in chapter 1).

Industry in the United States has banded together for security protection through the establishment of the American Society for Industrial Security which has fifty-three chapters spread throughout the country. (Headquarters of the Society is at 2000 K Street, NW, Washington, D.C. 20006.) The organization's bimonthly magazine, INDUSTRIAL SECURITY, is a continuing source of information on the entire security field, and the society publishes special studies and guides from time to time. Industrial espionage is not restricted to competitive businesses of one country acquiring secrets from each other. There is an increasingly international aspect to the activity, and this has received very little coverage in the literature. Moreover, as a matter of national policy some countries assign to their intelligence services the special function of collection of commercial or military research and production secrets or designs from the companies of another country in order to save funds, cut lead times, or make up for a lack of facilities, personnel, or capabilities. For example, since the early 1920s, Soviet Russia has resorted to this form of industrial espionage on a planned and coordinated basis. (See David Dallin's SOVIET ESPIONAGE in chapter 14, section D1, for details regarding Soviet efforts in this field in the

1920s and 1930s.) So far as techniques and tools for the conduct of industrial espionage are concerned, all the items listed in chapters 7, 8, and 10 concerning use of electronic sensors, information technology, and invasion of privacy are also applicable here.

Alden, Burton H., et al. COMPETITIVE INTELLIGENCE: INFORMATION, ESPIONAGE, AND DECISION-MAKING: A SPECIAL REPORT FOR BUSINESSMEN. Watertown, Mass.: C.I. Associates, 1959. 78 p.

A study prepared by students of the Harvard Graduate School of Business. Based on responses from two hundred top-level executives, it shows that 27 percent knew of instances of spying in their businesses and 20 percent thought that the practice was increasing.

Baker, Anthony G. "Competitive Espionage." INDUSTRIAL RESEARCH 4 (April 1962): 20-23. Chart.

The author, managing editor of INDUSTRIAL RESEARCH, writes that as research and development competition in industry sharpens, the research laboratory has become the most tempting target for industrial spies, after the board of directors room. Several industries with formal intelligence operations were surveyed to determine the methods of business spying and countermeasures. The article includes an interesting chart on the requirements usually placed on business espionage agents, a list of innocuous activities that tip off the competition, and a statement of mission of the technical spy.

Brenton, Myron. "Industrial Espionage." In his THE PRIVACY INVADERS, pp. 139-50. New York: Coward-McCann, 1964.

The author has filled this chapter with examples of industrial espionage which demonstrate technique. Industrial espionage is one of today's activities which reduce "workaday privacy." Brenton distinguishes between business intelligence, which is the legal activity of analyzing articles in trade magazines and published market data, interrogating salesmen or suppliers, and comparative shopping; and illegal industrial espionage, which is the stealing of research and process secrets, plans, and designs. See also the annotation for this book in chapter 8.

Calkins, Clinch. SPY OVERHEAD: THE STORY OF INDUSTRIAL ESPIONAGE. New York: Harcourt, Brace, 1937. 363 p.

This is an account of a special part of industrial espionage--labor spying. In SPY OVERHEAD the author describes how industrialists, by hiring secret operatives to spy among workmen, attempted to prevent American labor from organizing itself. Calkins based her study and analyses on material obtained from the records of Senator La Follette's civil liberties investigative committee.

Engberg, Edward. THE SPY IN THE CORPORATE STRUCTURE--AND THE RIGHT TO PRIVACY. New York and Cleveland: World Publishing Co., 1967. x, 247 p.

Engberg, a former staff writer for FORTUNE magazine and one-time managing editor of BUSINESS INTERNATIONAL, provides a sharp and highly readable discussion of the art of industrial espionage. He also discusses industrial espionage in the context of the broader issue of the individual's right to privacy. The author details all the basic weapons included in the arsenal of the corporate spy engaged in the modern science of purloining business secrets, and discusses the countermeasures available--a sort of counterindustrial espionage. A definitive work encompassing the entire story from crude beginnings to the present state as well as its broader implications.

Furash, Edward E. "Industrial Espionage." HARVARD BUSINESS REVIEW, December 1959, pp. 6-8, 10, 12, 148, 150, 152-54, 156, 161-62, 164, 168, 170, 172, 173-74.

A detailed questionnaire survey of 1,558 business executives indicated that "for the business community as a whole industrial espionage is an insignificant and frowned-on practice. Many of them also feel that it has received publicity out of all proportion to the frequency that such activity actually occurs in business, and hope that such publicity will help control rather than encourage it."

Greene, Richard M., Jr., ed. BUSINESS INTELLIGENCE AND ESPIONAGE Homewood, Ill.: Dow Jones-Irwin, 1966. 312 p. Illustrations, bibliography.

A substantial textbook on industrial espionage and counterespionage edited by the president of R.M. Greene & Associates, who is also an experienced management consultant from California. The authors of the thirteen chapters and two appendices provide detailed information on concepts, methods, values, and ethics, including useful material for courses of instruction in the field or for establishing a business intelligence unit in an industrial organization. The editor states that since roughly $113 million per year go into estimating the strengths of business competition in the United States, a company cannot afford to be without a formal business intelligence element. Excellent overall bibliography at the end of the book with specific bibliographic references after most chapters.

Hamilton, Peter. ESPIONAGE AND SUBVERSION IN AN INDUSTRIAL SOCIETY: AN EXAMINATION AND PHILOSPHY OF DEFENSE FOR MANAGEMENT. Foreword by Sir Richard Jackson, former Assistant Commissioner CID, New Scotland Yard, and President of Interpol. London: Hutchinson, 1967. xviii, 230 p. Index, bibliography.

A detailed text devoted to exposing the true significance and dangers of industrial espionage. The author postulates that the industrial arena is the battlefield of the future, and therefore industrial intelligence will become as vital as--and indistinguishable from--its political and military intelligence counterparts. The author provides expert descriptions of the methods and techniques of industrial espionage and emphasizes means by which it can be fought. He goes into some detail to show similarities in doctrine and technique between industrial espionage and what he calls the "parent art" of political and military intelligence and espionage.

Wade, Worth. INDUSTRIAL ESPIONAGE AND MIS-USE OF TRADE SECRETS. Ardmore, Pa.: Advance House, 1964. 134 p. Index, bibliography.

Wade, chemist, patent attorney, and author, has written a handbook on all the major aspects of industrial espionage including the techniques used and the theft of trade secrets. He emphasizes security measures--both physical and managerial. The handbook was written for business executives, security personnel, and patent counsels. Extensive bibliography.

Part III
ESPIONAGE AND COUNTERESPIONAGE

Espionage is the clandestine collection of information through illegal means and methods carried on against the organized opposition of counterespionage agencies. As a clandestine activity it is analogous to organized crime, such as international drug traffic. In the United States, for example, one organization, the Federal Bureau of Investigation, has both counterespionage and police (or countercriminal) functions. Ironically, although there is a vast analytical literature in the field of criminology, much of it dealing with police techniques, there is almost nothing comparable in the field of espionage/counterespionage. Here the literature is almost entirely episodic (or historical/episodic) of the "great, true spy stories" category. Occasionally in recounting the exploits of a "master spy," an author will incidentally discuss methods and techniques, adding to the "human interest" of his story, but only as a matter of peripheral interest. The reason for this state of affairs is that as a matter of national security most governments classify as secret any serious discussion of intelligence sources and methods. Former intelligence aides, especially those who have been engaged in clandestine operations, are enjoined by law from writing about such methods, even in the form of personal memoirs, until enough time has passed that there is no longer any "security violation" involved. Because of such legal restraint, the literature for the most part is necessarily historical. An exception to this rule occurs when someone in the position of Alexander Orlov, a highly placed Soviet intelligence expert, defects to another country and reconstructs from memory a training manual or handbook of espionage, or when such a clandestine activities training manual is stolen or bought. Another exception occurs when someone like Philip Agee, one-time officer of the CIA in Latin America, disregards the legal aspects and writes a diary of his activities in intelligence and covert political warfare (see Agee's INSIDE THE COMPANY: CIA DIARY).

The field is further confused by the fact that beginning with World War II both the United States and Great Britain set up agencies (OSS and SOE, respectively) which trained agents not only to collect information behind enemy lines (espionage) but also to conduct sabotage and diversionary activities and to organize resistance and partisan movements. The strategic services mission, which Churchill called "to set Europe ablaze," soon took precedence over the espionage function. Following World War II, as an integral part of its "cold war mission" the Central Intelligence Agency also mounted covert operations designed to extend U.S. political influence or control or to thwart Communist seizures of power in various parts of the world. Books dealing with such operations are listed in a special section on covert operations.

Chapter 14
ESPIONAGE

A. GENERAL SURVEYS

There are only a few serious or scholarly works which deal with espionage and counterespionage systematically and analytically, such as those by Bulloch, Burn, Deacon, Felix, and Masterman (see below). The literature consists for the most part of popular journalistic surveys of "espionage establishments" of several states, or books on the "secret services" of a single state such as the United States, the USSR, or Germany--the three countries on which there is an extensive but largely unreliable bibliography of books produced for political warfare purposes.

Burn, Michael. THE DEBATABLE LAND. A STUDY OF THE MOTIVES OF SPIES IN TWO AGES. London: Hamish Hamilton, 1970. viii, 285 p. Books consulted, notes, index.

> A scholarly, brilliantly written survey of espionage during the Eliza-
> bethan age in England, followed by an analysis and comparison
> of the motives of spies then and in the post-World War II period.
> The only other analysis of such motives is in Christopher Felix,
> A SHORT COURSE IN THE SECRET WAR (see below). Burn's
> work is an outstanding example of careful scholarship combined
> with a depth of analysis which is extremely rare in the literature
> on espionage.

Cobban, Alfred. AMBASSADORS AND SECRET AGENTS, THE DIPLOMACY OF THE FIRST EARL OF MALMESBURY AT THE HAGUE. London: Jonathan Cape, 1954. 255 p. Bibliography, references, index.

> In his introduction the author writes, "Little has been written, ex-
> cept in works of imagination, on the role of secret services activi-
> ties in British diplomacy." Cobban examines such activities in de-
> tail in writing about the diplomacy of Sir James Harris, British
> minister to the Hague on the eve of the French Revolution.

Copeland, Miles. WITHOUT CLOAK AND DAGGER: THE TRUTH ABOUT THE NEW ESPIONAGE. New York: Simon & Schuster, 1974. 351 p. Index, appendices.

Copeland, author of THE GAME OF NATIONS (cited in chapter 16), ex-CIA official, ex-State Department official, and adviser to the intelligence and counterintelligence organizations of several foreign countries, has drawn on his unique background to write a sort of manual or handbook covering the inside information of espionage techniques. In this book Copeland describes the modern espionage activities of the CIA, and attempts to correct popular misconceptions, bringing intelligence out of its classic cloak of secrecy, and building a basis for general understanding. Also discussed are some aspects of the work of Britain's SIS, the Soviet's KGB, and the French SDECE.

Felix, Christopher [pseud.]. A SHORT COURSE IN THE SECRET WAR. New York: E.P. Dutton & Co., 1963. 314 p. No index. British ed. THE SPY AND HIS MASTERS. London: Secker and Warburg, 1963. 287 p.

The author, who was for many years a case officer directing important U.S. intelligence operations, reveals the reasons and methods used by nations in obtaining intelligence information by undercover means. This is one of the few books in the field which treats its subject analytically. It is a valuable adjunct to clandestine training manuals in its treatment of the recruiting and handling of agents. The chapters on the art of using cover are especially valuable. See also Felix's "The Unknowable CIA," REPORTER, 6 April 1967, pages 20-24, defending the CIA against its many critics.

Hagen, Louis. THE SECRET WAR FOR EUROPE: A DOSSIER OF ESPIONAGE. London: MacDonald, 1968. 287 p. Index of proper names. American ed. New York: Stein and Day, 1969. 287 p. Index, illustrations.

An excellent, detailed examination of outstanding cases of espionage in West Germany since 1945, foreword by Sir Kenneth Strong and a postscript essay entitled "Espionage and the Balance of Power" which concludes that "the intelligence services have assumed a new, vital and creative role in world politics. Espionage, after the threat of nuclear war, is today the strongest contributor to the maintenance of peace in the world."

Ind, Allison. A HISTORY OF MODERN ESPIONAGE. London: Hodder and Stoughton, 1965. 288 p. Notes, index, bibliography.

An expanded version of A SHORT HISTORY OF ESPIONAGE (see below). This study includes new material dealing with a number of outstanding British and Western European cases.

_____. A SHORT HISTORY OF ESPIONAGE. New York: David McKay Co., 1963. x, 337 p. Index.

Colonel Allison Ind, Army of the United States (retired), has written this abbreviated version of espionage history beginning in antiquity and continuing through the American Civil War, the Spanish American War, World War I, World War II, and through the postwar period to the Bay of Pigs in Cuba. Ind concentrates on appraisals of the methods of modern espionage in England, France, Germany, and the Soviet Union. His assessments of both espionage and counterespionage are vigorously expressed to provide valid analyses and he draws on his experiences as an intelligence specialist with the U.S. Army in the Far East from 1940 to 1961.

Morgan, Ted [Gramont, Sanche de]. THE SECRET WAR; THE STORY OF INTERNATIONAL ESPIONAGE SINCE WORLD WAR II. New York: Putnam, 1962. 515 p. Index, appendix.

A popularized expose of many espionage activities and covert operations of the CIA and foreign secret agencies during the tense cold war years of the 1950s. Deals with a number of specific espionage and internal security cases, mainly Soviet. Chapter 1, "Total Espionage," is a brief survey of such activities as they relate to the cold war; chapter 15, "The Future of Espionage," argues that "the CIA is considered a kind of freak in a democratic society, but it is allowed to exist (under increasing control, one hopes), because it has proved its necessity. The Soviet intelligence system, on the other hand, is the core of the regime and its disappearance could lead to the end of the Communist dictatorship in the Soviet Union as we have known it for forty years."

The appendix lists American diplomats expelled from the USSR between 1947 and 1961, and Soviet diplomats expelled from the United States between 1948 and 1961.

Rowan, Richard Wilmer. THE STORY OF SECRET SERVICE. Garden City, N.Y.: Doubleday, Doran, 1937. xii, 732 p. Notes, illustrations, no index.

See next item.

Rowan, Richard Wilmer, with Deindorfer, Robert G. SECRET SERVICE: THIRTY-THREE CENTURIES OF ESPIONAGE. New York: Hawthorn Books, 1967. xi, 786 p. Index, source notes.

Richard Rowan's authoritative and exhaustive history of espionage published as THE STORY OF SECRET SERVICE (cited above) was, according to Allen Dulles's remarks in the foreword of the 1967 edition, "the best single account of intelligence services down to the time he wrote it in 1937, and remains so today." In a monumental, scholarly study of eighty-eight chapters, Rowan traced the early amateur and hireling informers of the Roman Empire through

the development of more modern espionage organizations up to
1937. Before his death in 1964, Rowan chose Robert G. Deindorfer, a successful author on intelligence (editor of THE SPIES: GREAT
TRUE STORIES OF ESPIONAGE, New York: Fawcett, 1969) to
collaborate on an enlarged and revised edition of the 1937 classic.
In the 1967 edition Deindorfer, with the help of Rowan's widow
Ruth, has brought the history of intelligence activities and organizations up through World War II and the postwar period, emphasizing the sophistication of present-day espionage systems, in an
accurate and objective account of ninety-four chapters.

Seth, Ronald. THE ANATOMY OF SPYING. London: Barker, 1961. 256 p.
Index.

A popular look at the anatomy of espionage based on "the consideration of the exploits of great spies of the past." Glamorizes
the role of the spy. The exploits of the author, a former British
SOE agent and saboteur, emerge as larger than life.

Singer, Kurt, ed. THREE THOUSAND YEARS OF ESPIONAGE: AN ANTHOL-
OGY OF THE WORLD'S GREATEST SPY STORIES. New York: Prentice-Hall,
1948. Reprint. Freeport, N.Y.: Books for Libraries Press, 1970. xvi, 384 p.
Index.

In this early post-World War II anthology, Singer has brought together thirty-eight accounts of espionage beginning in biblical
times and ending with World War II and the immediate postwar
period. Published too early to include much of a definitive nature
on World War II and the postwar era, the anthology has little to
offer here. Singer, an author on intelligence with experience in
underground work in Germany prior to 1940, wrote five of the accounts. Five others were written by the intelligence history authority, Richard Rowan.

Wise, David, and Ross, Thomas B. THE ESPIONAGE ESTABLISHMENT. New
York: Random House, 1967. 308 p. Index.

Informative sketches of the espionage systems of the United States,
Great Britain, Russia, and Communist China, by the authors of
THE INVISIBLE GOVERNMENT AND THE U-2 AFFAIR. In a
final chapter the authors argue: "The Soviet Union and Communist
China have an active espionage apparatus. Under the circumstances, the United States needs its intelligence machinery. But it
can stop treating it as something sacrosanct, separate and apart
from the normal constitutional processes of congressional and executive control. If the American vision is to be sustained, the
American people must guard against the easy rationalization that
anything can be excused in defense of the American Way of
Life."

B. ANTHOLOGIES OF SPY STORIES

There are literally scores of anthologies of the "great, true spy stories" category, and new collections appear whenever journalists who specialize in the genre can find a publisher. Those selected for listing here are among the best known, and are representative of the better collections. Actually, such general surveys of espionage as those of Richard Rowan, THE STORY OF SECRET SERVICE, or Kurt Singer, THREE THOUSAND YEARS OF ESPIONAGE, both listed above in section A, are essentially collections of spy stories.

Hinchley, Vernon. SPIES WHO NEVER WERE. London: Harrap, 1965. 221 p.

The author, a former British intelligence officer, examines the legends which have accumulated around thirteen people accused of espionage and condemned by the press and public opinion as spies. Among the more notable cases are those of Dreyfus, Treibitsch Lincoln, Bruno Pontecorvo, Rutland, Elsbeth Scragmuller, Guy Burgess, and Alger Hiss.

Seth, Ronald. THE WORLD OF ESPIONAGE. London: Souvenir Press, 1962. 254 p. No index.

Contains more than twenty accounts of post-World War II espionage cases or incidents with the traditional closing notes on "Soviet Espionage" and "Soviet Spy Technique." Draws the moralizing conclusion: "Spies do not cause wars; they themselves are the product of war and the fear of war. Our objective should be to rid the world, not of one particular weapon, but of the fear of war."

1. General Anthologies

Dulles, Allan Welsh, ed. GREAT TRUE SPY STORIES. New York: Harper & Row, 1968. xvii, 393 p. Acknowledgments.

A collection of spy adventures ranging in time from Greek antiquity to the cold war. The former director of CIA and head of OSS in Switzerland during World War II has selected thirty-nine stories and has divided them into groups illustrating elements of the intelligence process: networks, counterespionage, double agents, codes and ciphers, and the technology of espionage. Dulles provides a review of intelligence literature in the foreword and in prefaces for each section containing material from his own experiences.

Wighton, Charles. THE WORLD'S GREATEST SPIES. TRUE-LIFE DRAMAS OF OUTSTANDING SECRET AGENTS. New York: Taplinger, 1962. 319 p. Index.

A journalistic review of fifteen spy cases from Mata Hari to Colonel Abel, preceded by an introductory chapter, "Espionage Through the Ages."

2. Women in Espionage

History has had its famous women spies, some of whom have directly or indirectly altered events through their secret service activities. Others, like Mata Hari, have merely established a false but persistent image that has altered the way people look at the idea of women in espionage. However, it was during the late thirties and World War II that the turning point arrived for women in intelligence, for it was during this period that for the first time significant numbers of women were utilized as field operatives and as research and analysis specialists and administrators in intelligence organization headquarters. In the field, some seemed well suited to act as network couriers, cut-outs or contacts, and radio operators (see chapter 8 of Alexander Foote's HANDBOOK FOR SPIES, cited in section D of this chapter), while others were agents or informants. Regardless of their role, they took the high risks involved. Michael R.D. Foot in his SOE IN FRANCE (see chapter 17, section A) stated that twelve of the fifty-three women agents parachuted or infiltrated by boat into France by SOE were executed in German concentration camps. As an example of recognition of their work, the East German government issued a set of commemorative postage stamps in honor of the martyrs of the Red Orchestra (Rote Kapelle) network, and women members were pictured on several of the stamps. Few accounts of women's contribution to the research and analysis side of intelligence exist in the literature of World War II. However, Constance Babington-Smith's AIR SPY: THE STORY OF PHOTO INTELLIGENCE IN WORLD WAR II is one fine example (see chapter 10, section A).

In a postwar development that might be considered utilizing the best of both worlds, the Soviets seem to have encouraged husband and wife espionage teams. Examples are Ethel and Julius Rosenberg of the atomic weapons espionage case, Helen and Peter Kroger of the Portland England naval secrets case (see Bulloch and Miller, SPY RING: A STORY OF THE NAVAL SECRETS CASE, cited in chapter 10, section A), and Evodkia and Vladimir Petrov who operated in Australia.

The day of full equality for women in intelligence has not yet arrived. However, the male conservative intelligence planners, personnel managers, and recruiters who hold that women have no place as field agents because of a supposed tendency to risk security for emotional entanglements are now fewer in number, and those who remain have less and less evidence to support their views. For women in the research and analysis side of intelligence the day of equality is nearer--newer, approved personnel career programs acknowledge and accept them in these roles. William E. Colby, head of the overall U.S. intelligence community as director of Central Intelligence and also head of the Central Intelligence Agency, has expressed a desire to see the number of women as professional intelligence officers rise sharply.

Fourcade, Marie-Madeleine. NOAH'S ARK. Translated by Kenneth Morgan. Foreword by Commander Kenneth Cohen. New York: E.P. Dutton & Co., 1974. 377 p. Illustrations, lists of agents under real and cover names, no index.

The author was the leader of an espionage network in France during World War II that the Gestapo called "Noah's Ark" because its members used animal names for their aliases. The network included about three thousand members and covered all of France. Officially called the Alliance Intelligence Service, the network obtained military information on German ground force order-of-battle, U-boat pens, Luftwaffe air order-of-battle, channel fortifications, and V-1 and V-2 launch sites in France. The network worked first for British intelligence in London and then for de Gaulle's intelligence. The author was directly responsible for the arrangements for spiriting General Henri Giraud out of France to Algiers by submarine. This incident was one of the very few action projects of the strictly information-gathering network. The author describes the acts of sacrifice, arrests and escapes of members of the network, and the few acts of treachery. Her book is dedicated to the exposition of the members of the network. Unfortunately there is all too little detail provided on the type of information obtained by this remarkable network.

Hoehling, Adolph A. WOMEN WHO SPIED. New York: Dodd, Mead & Co., 1967. xvi, 204 p. Index, bibliography, illustrations.

True stories of espionage by women from the American Revolution to the 1950s. Includes the story of Lydia Darrach, an agent for the Continental Army; Sarah Thompson of the Civil War; and Louise de Bettignies and Maria de Victorica (the Kaiser's woman in New York) of World War I. Stories from the World War II period include that of Velvalee Dickinson (who spied for Japan in the United States) and a collection of stories of SOE women agents for England. Also includes an account of photo-interpreter Barbara Slade, who covered German U-1 and U-2 launch sites for Royal Air Force Intelligence, and the post-World War II story of the intelligence and counterintelligence activities of Czechoslovakia's Milada Horákova. A good bibliography of feminine espionage is included.

Hutton, Bernard J.[pseud.]. WOMEN IN ESPIONAGE. New York: Macmillan, 1971. 192 p. Index, illustrations.

Formerly an editor for Czech and Russian Communist newspapers, and now a journalist in the West, the author disposes of the Mata Hari myth in the prologue of WOMEN IN ESPIONAGE, and then goes on to prove his case that women make capable agents--as capable as men and more difficult for counterespionage to detect. He describes the recruitment techniques used in the USSR for women agents along with their schooling and training (see also Hutton's SCHOOL FOR SPIES, New York: Coward-McCann, 1962), and follows this by accounts of six successful Soviet women agents who operated in Western countries in the post-World War II period. Hutton compares Chinese Communist, British, and U.S. philosophies regarding women agents to the Soviet techniques, giving as an example of Chinese Communist technique an account of Min Chian-sen (Lily Petal), an agent who for years operated in New York. There follows a variety of the stories of seven women agents of various countries active in the postwar period.

Hyde, H. Montgomery. CYNTHIA. New York: Farrar, Straus & Giroux, 1965. 240 p. British ed. CYNTHIA: THE SPY WHO CHANGED THE COURSE OF THE WAR. London: Hamish Hamilton, 1966. 180 p.

A well-told biography of Minneapolis-born Amy Elizabeth Thorpe (1910-63) who was an American agent of Allied intelligence working for British Secret Intelligence Service. One feat credited to "Cynthia" was obtaining the naval code of the Vichy French. The author was a member of the British intelligence organization in New York--British Security Coordination (BSC).

Singer, Kurt D. THE WORLD'S GREATEST WOMEN SPIES. London: W.H. Allen & Co., 1951. 199 p. Illustrations.

In this book, Singer, a prolific editor and compiler of espionage anthologies, has put together a collection of accounts of female spies who operated in various parts of the world from the thirties through World War II. Included are descriptions of the activities of Velvalee Dickinson, Lydia Von Stahl, and Mathilde-Lily Carre (for Mathilde's own story see her I WAS THE CAT, cited in chapter 17, section B). Also included is an account of the activities of Baroness Anna Wolkoff, an agent of the intelligence arm of the Nazi party, who subverted Tyler Kent of the U.S. embassy's communications security section in 1939-40.

Spiro, Edward [Edward H. Cookridge]. SISTERS OF DELILAH. London: Oldbourne Press, 1959. 224 p.

The author has selected a number of examples of feminine espionage, treating twelve as major incidents. In the main they cover the World War II period, and while some accounts are true, some are not. He accepts, for example, the story of Banda Wilhelmina Van Deeren, allegedly the daughter of Mata Hari, who was supposed to have been shot as a spy in December 1950 by the Chinese Communists in North Korea. The author leans a bit too heavily on the premise that most women agents depend on entrapment of men for their success.

C. THE UNITED STATES

Because of its classified nature, there are few serious books in English dealing primarily with U.S. espionage. Material on the subject is scattered throughout the general literature on the intelligence agencies and espionage establishments of the great powers and in memoirs of former agents. For reference to nearly 600 Soviet works in Russian on the CIA see chapter 4, section B1.

Agee, Philip. INSIDE THE COMPANY: CIA DIARY. New York: Stonehill, 1975. 640 p. Appendices, acknowledgments, organization charts, no index. Paperback ed. London: Penguin Books, 1975.

Agee, a former CIA employee for twelve years, has prepared a comprehensive expose of the CIA's clandestine activities and operations during the period 1960-68 in the countries of Ecuador, Uruguay, and Mexico. The book, written as a diary of day-to-day actions, provides a unique insight into the details of the operations and techniques of espionage and covert political operations. The first part of the book provides detailed descriptions of the author's recruitment into the CIA and his early training in the CIA's school. Appendices contain lists of individuals and organizations in Latin America supported or used by the CIA, a list of abbreviations which is in itself an insight into the details of the CIA's activities, and a collection of organization charts of the CIA. The book was originally published in England to avoid legal action; legal action was attempted by the CIA to prohibit its sale and publication in the United States. The American edition has a small number of corrections and additions.

Ford, Corey. DONOVAN OF OSS. Boston: Little, Brown and Co., 1970. 336 p. Index, bibliography.

An excellent, carefully researched biography of William J. Donovan, the late head of the wartime Office of Strategic Services and influential architect of postwar U.S. intelligence. The work is based both on open sources and on Donovan's private papers made available for the first time to the author. See also the annotation for this book in chapter 18, section B.

Hunt, E. Howard. UNDERCOVER: MEMOIRS OF AN AMERICAN SECRET AGENT. New York: Berkley Publishing Corp.; distributed by Putnam's and Sons, 1974. 338 p. Index, illustrations.

Autobiography of the now well-known Watergate operative, ex-CIA operative, and prolific intelligence fiction writer. Hunt describes his early life, his service with an OSS detachment in China, and his participation in various covert operations while a member of the CIA. However, about half the book is taken up with descriptions of the "Plumbers" operations and the subsequent Watergate scandal and investigations. During October 1974, while testifying under cross-examination at the Watergate coverup trial, Hunt stated that this book contained false statements, especially concerning the timing of events subsequent to the Watergate break-in. That portion must therefore be read discriminately.

Mashbir, Sidney Forrester. I WAS AN AMERICAN SPY. New York: Vantage Press, 1953. x, 374 p. Index, illustrations, appendix.

Memoirs of an army colonel whose intelligence career began on the Mexican border in 1916 and culminated in the G-2 section of General MacArthur's headquarters in the Pacific.

Murphy, Robert. DIPLOMAT AMONG WARRIORS. Garden City, N.Y.: Doubleday, 1964. x, 470 p. Index, illustrations.

The autobiography of a career diplomat who was designated by President Roosevelt as his personal secret agent to obtain information regarding North Africa before its invasion. In 1940 Murphy was charge d'affaires in wartime Vichy when he was recalled to Washington to be made a private information source for the president and for General Eisenhower. Returning to North Africa he set up his own information system and communications system for relaying information to be used in the invasion planning. Later he became the first political advisor on the personal staff of General Eisenhower. In that capacity he was involved in the invasion of Italy and the conquest and occupation of Germany. This book provides a different insight into the intelligence picture of World War II.

Penkovskiy, Oleg. THE PENKOVSKIY PAPERS. Translated by Peter Deriabin. Introduction and commentary by Frank Gibney. Foreword by Edward Crankshaw. Personal comment by Greville Wynne. Garden City, N.Y.: Doubleday, 1965. xiv, 411 p. Appendices, illustrations. British ed. London: Collins Clear-Type Press, 1965. With different photographs and chapter arrangement, and without personal note by Greville Wynne.

Ostensibly the memoirs of a Soviet colonel of army military intelligence working as a departmental deputy chief in Moscow, who provided information to U.S. and British intelligence from April 1961 to August 1962. The information included details on secret Soviet troop deployments and technical details on weapons developments, as well as information on political and economic capabilities and intentions. Penkovskiy provided the information in microfilm form (some five thousand photoprints, according to Soviet counterintelligence) to his British intelligence contact and handler, Greville Wynne. During three trips to London and Paris, Penkovskiy furnished volumes of specific information on current events in extensive debriefing sessions arranged by American and British intelligence. Arrested by Soviet counterintelligence, Penkovskiy was tried in Moscow along with Wynne, who had been arrested in Budapest while trying to reach Moscow for yet another contact with Penkovskiy. Penkovskiy was sentenced to death and Wynne was given a jail sentence. Later Wynne was traded for Soviet intelligence operative Gordon Lonsdale (see Greville Wynne's CONTACT ON GORKY STREET in chapter 14, section E).

While there is no doubt that Penkovskiy was a valuable source of secret information on the USSR at a critical time, there has been much skepticism that the memoirs were actually written by Penkovskiy as claimed; many believed they were compiled by CIA and British intelligence personnel as a cold war weapon against Soviet intelligence and the Soviet system. The controversy was ended in 1976, by the publication of the final report of the Senate Select Committee to Study Governmental Operations with Respect to Intelligence Activities (Church Committee). The Senate report stated that the book was prepared by CIA personnel who drew on actual case materials. Publication rights to the manuscript were sold to the publisher (who was unaware of CIA interests) through a trust fund which was established for the purpose. See chapter 4, section A, U.S. Congress, Senate, for reference to the Church Committee report.

Zacharias, Ellis M. SECRET MISSIONS: THE STORY OF AN INTELLIGENCE OFFICER. New York: Putnam, 1946. viii, 433 p.

The memoir of a naval officer who began his intelligence career as a Japanese language and area trainee in Tokyo before World War II. Rear Admiral Zacharias emphasizes the role he played in the psychological warfare campaign against the Japanese home islands, preceding their final surrender.

D. THE SOVIET UNION

1. General Surveys

Soviet intelligence agencies have traditionally concentrated on clandestine collection (espionage) as a major source of information. For this reason, with the exception of Alexander Orlov's HANDBOOK OF INTELLIGENCE AND GUERRILLA WARFARE (see chapter 4, section B2), most books dealing with Soviet intelligence are in fact studies of Soviet espionage, and are for the most part highly unreliable, sensationalized journalistic exposes published for political warfare purposes during the cold war or post-cold war periods. There are some authors who have exploited this lucrative field of journalism by writing several books each, going over much of the same material each time, rewritten or updated to include recent "revelations."

Dallin, David J. SOVIET ESPIONAGE. New Haven, Conn.: Yale University Press, 1955. xiv, 558 p. Notes, index.

A leading authority on Soviet Russia discusses in detail the Soviet espionage system, with special emphasis on operations in Europe and North America. A comprehensive and authoritative study free of the cold war propaganda which characterizes most books on the subject, although Dallin occasionally fails to distinguish between NKVD and GRU networks.

Espionage

Deacon, Richard [pseud.]. A HISTORY OF THE RUSSIAN SECRET SERVICE.
London: Muller, 1972. vii, 568 p. Notes, bibliography, index. American
ed. New York: Taplinger, 1972. viii, 568 p. Index, bibliography, illustrations.

In his introduction the author states, "This book is not intended
to be in any way ideological or propagandist, but an objective
assessment of the Russian Secret Service throughout history, giving
credit for brilliant work where it is due but pointing out weaknesses and failures." He covers several centuries in thirty-five
chapters. The work is full of operational details, summarizes most
of the special studies available in English, and is liberally laced
with evaluations. It is undoubtedly the best story of Russian espionage, but it leaves much to be desired as a scholarly history.
There are only a few notes to many of the most interesting and
controversial sources used, of which only a fraction are listed in
the bibliography. Disproportionate emphasis is often placed on
certain operations due to the overuse of a given source. In spite
of such shortcomings, however, the author has written a useful
survey if the sources from which it is drawn are carefully evaluated.

Deriabin, Peter, and Gibney, Frank. THE SECRET WORLD. Garden City,
N.Y.: Doubleday, 1959. 334 p. Index, appendix, organization charts.

The memoirs of a former staff officer of the Russian KGB. Both
authors of this book have been under contract to the CIA. For
this reason it is difficult to separate elements of disinformation
and cold war propaganda from the substratum of factual material
on which it is based, although the book is cited in almost all
bibliographies on the subject of Soviet espionage.

Huss, Pierre J., and Carpozi, George, Jr. RED SPIES IN THE U.N. New
York: Coward-McCann, 1965. 287 p. Index, illustrations.

Newspapermen Huss and Carpozi provide accounts of instances of
Soviet, and Soviet-influenced attempts to obtain official American
secret documents and information while being safe from prosecu-
tion if discovered because of United Nations diplomatic immunity
status.

Noel-Baker, Francis. THE SPY WEB. Introduction by Herbert A. Philbrick.
New York: Vanguard Press, 1955. 208 p.

One of the better cold war exposes of Soviet espionage. It was
written by a former junior SOE officer with the Free Greek Forces
in the Middle East.

Seth, Ronald. UNMASKED! THE STORY OF SOVIET ESPIONAGE. New
York: Hawthorn, 1965. 306 p. Index. British ed. FORTY YEARS OF SO-

VIET SPYING. London: Cassell, 1965. viii, 294 p.

In spite of the sensational title of the American edition, this is a competent survey of Soviet espionage by a former British intelligence officer who has since authored some thirty books on war and espionage. Remarkably free of cold war cant.

Spiro, Edward [Edward H. Cookridge]. THE NET THAT COVERS THE WORLD. New York: Henry Holt, 1955. 315 p. Index, glossary of terms, illustrations, appendix. British ed. SOVIET SPY NET. London: Muller, 1955. 264 p.

Written by a former British intelligence aide and professional journalist, this is a popular account of the Soviet espionage system, its history, organization, and functions. In an introductory chapter the author states his purposes as follows: "This book is not a 'denunciation' of the Soviet secret service, and only an 'exposure' in the sense that, for the first time, the organization and working of this formidable superhead of militant Communism is fully explained." Like all such popular surveys this work is "undocumented and often unverifiable."

2. Survey Articles

Heiman, Leo. "Cloak-and-Dagger Literature behind the Iron Curtain." EAST EUROPE 14 (January 1965): 54-56.

See next item.

Slusser, Robert M. "Recent Soviet Books on the History of the Secret Service." SLAVIC REVIEW 24 (March 1965): 90-98.

Both articles describe Soviet publicizing of the activities of secret intelligence services in the public press and literature. During this campaign, which began in 1964, Sorge, the East German Rote Kappelle members, Abel, and others surfaced and were honored.

U.S. Congress. Senate. Committee on the Judiciary. Subcommittee to Investigate the Administration of the Internal Security Act and Other Internal Security Laws. COMMUNIST BLOC INTELLIGENCE ACTIVITIES IN THE UNITED STATES: HEARING. 94th Cong., 1st sess., 18 November 1975. ix, 64 p. Index, organization chart, portraits.

This report contains the testimony of Josef Frolik, who for seventeen years before his defection to the CIA in 1969 was a senior member of the Czechoslovakian intelligence service. The witness describes in detail the organization of the various Czechoslovakian intelligence services and confirms the domination of these services by the Soviet KGB. Frolik provides details on many of the "dirty tricks" operations conducted against the United States by the Czechoslovakian service. Also detailed are the U.S. government organizations which are targets of Communist bloc intelligence and "dirty tricks."

3. Memoirs and Biographies

Bernikow, Louise. ABEL. Introduction by Burt Silverman. New York: Trident Press, 1970. 347 p. Bibliography, illustrations.

The author and Burt Silverman, a friend of Soviet espionage agent Rudolph Abel, spent two and a half years researching records and interviewing people who knew Abel or the other Soviet agent who betrayed him--Reino Hayhanen. Their research is the basis for this description of the spy and his nine years in various hotels and rooming houses in New York. The book provides an unusual look at an accomplished field agent as he lived his cover.

Deakin, F.W., and Storry, G.R. THE CASE OF RICHARD SORGE. New York: Harper & Row, 1966. 373 p. Index, bibliography, notes, illustrations.

Operating as a Nazi journalist, and so completely trusted by the German embassy staff in Tokyo that he edited the embassy newsletter, Sorge for years headed a Red Army espionage network in the Far East. Sorge was credited with providing Moscow with the first information that Japan would attack to the south instead of toward Russia. Deakin, a historian, and Storry, an authority on Japan, searched new German and Japanese sources for material for this interpretation of the Sorge story. Excellent bibliography on the many writings about this espionage agent.

Ginsburg, Samuel [Walter G. Krivitsky]. IN STALIN'S SECRET SERVICE. New York: Harper, 1939. xvi, 273 p.

An important memoir by one of the highest-ranking Soviet defectors. The author was the chief of the Western European division of the Soviet military intelligence (GRU) agency's foreign directorate. A fairly reliable historical source on intelligence operations prior to the Soviet purges of the late thirties. The author was apparently assassinated later in Washington, D.C. Should be read in conjunction with a later memoir by Elisabeth Poretsky, OUR OWN PEOPLE (see below).

Gouzenko, Igor. THE IRON CURTAIN. New York: Dutton, 1948. 279 p.

The memoirs of a former cipher clerk with the GRU who defected from the Soviet embassy in Ottawa in 1945. He provided solid evidence of Soviet espionage conducted to learn the secrets of atomic weaponry.

Granovsky, Anatoli. I WAS AN NKVD AGENT; A TOP SOVIET SPY TELLS HIS STORY. New York: Devin-Adair, 1962. 343 p. Illustrations, no index.

Granovsky's first job in the NKVD was in domestic spying, but he was later trained for espionage work in the United States. He was a captain in the NKVD until he defected to Sweden aboard a Soviet ship in 1946. A popular account, with some insights into the actual workings of the Moscow bureaucracy.

Kaznacheev, Aleksandr. INSIDE A SOVIET EMBASSY; EXPERIENCES OF A RUSSIAN DIPLOMAT IN BURMA. Edited, with an introduction, by Simon Wolin. New York: Lippincott, 1962. 250 p.

A twenty-seven-year-old diplomat and intelligence aide, Kaznacheev describes his experiences in the Soviet embassy in Rangoon, and his defection in June 1959.

Molodiy, Konon Trofimovich [Gordon Lonsdale]. SPY: TWENTY YEARS IN THE SOVIET SECRET SERVICE. THE MEMOIRS OF GORDON LONSDALE. New York: Hawthorn Books, 1965. 220 p. Publisher's afterword.

Lonsdale, a Soviet espionage agent, was taken in Britain in 1961 only to be traded back to the Soviet Union in 1964 for Greville Wynne. This book is probably one of the publications of the cold war espionage game between British and American intelligence and the KGB. Neville Armstrong of the British publishing firm of Neville Spearman, Ltd., is responsible for having brought the Lonsdale memoir from behind the iron curtain. The account of this is provided in the publisher's afterword.

Monat, Pawel, with John Dille. SPY IN THE U.S. New York: Praeger, 1957. 208 p.

The author, a former Polish military attache who defected in Washington, D.C., in the 1950s, reminisces about his intelligence gathering. The work was published as a cold war sensation and should be used with caution.

Newman, Bernard. THE SOSNOWSKI AFFAIR. London: Laurie, 1954. 212 p.

An excellent, detailed account of a Polish spy active in Germany from 1925 to 1934. Juri de Sosnowski was a controversial figure who made effective use of women agents (hence the legend of "the romantic spy"). Sosnowski was exchanged for German agents captured by the Poles, but was later tried and imprisoned in Warsaw.

Page, Bruce; Leitch, David; and Knightley, Phillip. THE PHILBY CONSPIRACY. Introduction by David John Moore Cornwell [John le Carre]. Garden City, N.Y.: Doubleday, 1968. 300 p. Illustrations, no index.

An important account of Soviet espionage agent Kim Philby who worked with British intelligence until his detection and eventual escape to Moscow. Contains details on the British intelligence organization. The authors are a team of journalists from the London SUNDAY TIMES.

Petrov, Vladimir, and Petrov, Evdokia. EMPIRE OF FEAR. New York: Frederick A. Praeger, 1956. 352 p.

An excellent memoir of a husband and wife team who worked in Australia and defected from the Soviet intelligence system. Has a cold war purpose.

Philby, Harold Adrian Russell [Kim]. MY SILENT WAR. New York: Grove Press, 1968. 262 p. No index. Chronological chart, "The British Secret Service and the Men Who Ran It."

This is a brilliantly written, frequently mendacious memoir of a Soviet double agent who penetrated British intelligence and was later stationed in Washington, D.C., where he penetrated both the CIA and the FBI. In 1963 Philby fled to Moscow to become the chief advisor to Soviet intelligence against Britain and the United States. Realization of Philby's thirty-four years as a Soviet double agent created one of the biggest scandals in intelligence history. The book has been skillfully exploited for its political warfare impact by the USSR. Should be read in conjunction with the study by Page, Leitch, and Knightley, THE PHILBY CONSPIRACY (see above).

Poretsky, Elisabeth K. OUR OWN PEOPLE. A MEMOIR OF 'IGNACE REISS' AND HIS FRIENDS. Ann Arbor: University of Michigan Press, 1970. 278 p. Index.

The author was the wife of Ignace Reiss, a Polish Communist who for fifteen years was a Soviet intelligence agent. Reiss was murdered in Switzerland after he broke with the Stalinist regime as a result of the purges in July 1937. An important, detailed account of Soviet and Comintern clandestine operations for the period which should be read in conjunction with Samuel Ginsburg's IN STALIN'S SECRET SERVICE (see above).

Purdy, Anthony, and Sutherland, Douglas. BURGESS & MACLEAN. Garden City, N.Y.: Doubleday, 1963. 182 p.

A popular account of the careers of British diplomats Guy Burgess and Douglas Maclean who defected to the USSR in 1951. A journalistic speculation of what the two defectors might have known and passed on to Soviet intelligence, the indiscretions that might have led to blackmail and recruiting by Soviet intelligence, and the possibilities of their being warned by another Soviet agent that they were under observation by British counterintelligence.

Whiteside, Thomas. AN AGENT IN PLACE. THE WENNERSTROM AFFAIR. New York: Viking, 1966. 150 p. No index.

An excellent, journalistic account of the career of Colonel Stig Wennerstrom, a Soviet double agent from 1948 to 1963 who served as Swedish air attache in both Moscow and Washington, D.C. While in the United States Wennerstrom collected important technical information on the aviation industry and on the Strategic Air Command's targeting of the USSR. He was arrested by the Swedish security police in Sweden in June 1963. A carefully researched account.

E. GREAT BRITAIN

1. General Surveys

Deacon, Richard [pseud.]. A HISTORY OF THE BRITISH SECRET SERVICE. New York and London: Taplinger, 1970. 440 p. Index, notes, illustrations, bibliography.

A narrative about intelligence in England that begins during the reign of Henry VII and carries on through the modern period to 1970. An important work. The bibliography might have been more complete, however.

Read, Conyers. MR. SECRETARY WALSHINGHAM AND THE POLICY OF QUEEN ELIZABETH. 3 vols. Cambridge, Mass.: Harvard University Press, 1925.

This detailed biography of Sir Francis Walshingham provides some information on the espionage network he designed and operated during the Elizabethan period.

Richings, Mildred G. ESPIONAGE: THE STORY OF THE SECRET SERVICE OF THE BRITISH CROWN. London: Hutchinson and Co., 1934. 295 p.

The only other book-length treatment of the British Secret Service besides Deacon's history (see above). An account from the fourteenth century through the reign of Edward VII in 1910.

2. Memoirs and Biographies

Hutton, Bernard J. [pseud.]. FROGMAN SPY: THE INCREDIBLE CASE OF COMMANDER CRABB. New York: McDowell, Obolensky, 1960. 180 p. Illustrations.

The story of Commander Lionel Philip Kenneth Crabb, British naval officer who was killed while attempting to obtain information on a Soviet naval vessel that had brought Khrushchev to Britain on a state visit.

Hyde, H. Montgomery. THE QUIET CANADIAN: THE SECRET SERVICE STORY
OF SIR WILLIAM STEPHENSON. Foreword by David Bruce. London: Hamish
Hamilton, 1962. xii, 255 p. American ed. ROOM 3603: THE STORY OF
THE BRITISH INTELLIGENCE CENTER IN NEW YORK DURING WORLD WAR
II. Foreword by Ian Fleming. New York: Farrar, Straus and Co., 1963.
xiii, 257 p. Index, bibliography, map, illustrations.

Biography of Sir William Stephenson, director of British Security
Coordination (BSC) based in New York City during World War II.
BSC was the center for Anglo-American partnership in the field
of espionage, counterespionage and special operations in the Western Hemisphere. Stephenson was a sponsor to the fledgling OSS
and it was he who opened the doors of British intelligence to
General Donovan, head of OSS. An authentic view into British
intelligence activities in the United States and Latin America.

Lockhart, Robin Bruce. ACE OF SPIES. London: Hodder and Stoughton,
1967. 192 p. Index.

An attempt by the son of the British diplomat Bruce Lockhart to
write a biography of the elusive "master spy," Sidney Reilly.
Reilly was involved in the so-called Lockhart Plot to assassinate
Lenin at the time of the Allied intervention in Russia in the fall
of 1918. A popular, undocumented journalistic account which
must be used with caution since in his zeal to prove Reilly was
"the greatest spy that ever lived," the author, in spite of his
training in British naval intelligence, fails to distinguish between
the historical and the apocryphal. In a preface he writes, "I
make no apologies for a certain lack of completeness in this biography. . . . I have had to contend with the Official Secrets
Act. The records of our Secret Intelligence Service are few and
not easily prised open." Should be read in conjunction with Sidney Reilly's THE ADVENTURES OF SIDNEY REILLY, BRITAIN'S
MASTER SPY, cited below.

Nicholson, Leslie Arthur [John Whitwell]. BRITISH AGENT. London: William Kimber, 1966. 224 p.

The authoritative memoirs of an experienced Secret Intelligence
Service field officer who served SIS from 1929 through the Second
World War. The author's superior and chief-of-station in Mozam-
bique, Malcolm Muggeridge, provides the introduction to the book.
Although it is cynical, this book provides one of the few insights
available into the SIS.

Penkovskiy, Oleg. THE PENKOVSKIY PAPERS. Translated by Peter Deriabin.
Introduction and commentary by Frank Gibney. Foreword by Edward Crankshaw.
Personal comment by Greville Wynne. Garden City, N.Y.: Doubleday, 1965.
xiv, 411 p. Appendices, illustrations. British ed. London: Collins Clear-
Type Press, 1965. With different photographs and chapter arrangement, and
without personal note by Greville Wynne.

Ostensibly the memoirs of Soviet army colonel Oleg Penkovskiy
who for sixteen months provided information to U.S. and British
intelligence on secret troop movements, weapons development, and
political and economic capabilities. Although Penkovskiy was a
bona fide source of information, handled by British agent Greville
Wynne, the book was actually written by personnel of the CIA
(and perhaps British intelligence as well). See chapter 14, section C for main annotation.

Reilly, Sidney George. THE ADVENTURES OF SIDNEY REILLY, BRITAIN'S
MASTER SPY. London: Mathews and Marrot, 1931. xv, 288 p. American
ed. BRITAIN'S MASTER SPY. Edited and compiled by Pepita Reilly. New
York: Harper and Brothers, 1933. 298 p. Illustrations.

Pepita Reilly, who edited the American edition with help from an
unnamed journalist, was Reilly's third wife. This biography must
be used with caution as a source. Nevertheless, it contains photographs of some of Reilly's correspondence and is of value when
used in conjunction with other sources.

Scotland, A.P. THE LONDON CAGE. London: Evans Brothers, 1957. 203 p.
Index.

The author, a British intelligence officer who penetrated the German general staff during World War II, recounts his experiences
in a traditionally low-key British manner. The title derives from
the name given the mansion in Kensington Gardens, London, where
Lieutenant Colonel Scotland had his offices. Includes a thoughtful
final chapter, "The Future of 'The Secret Service'."

Stevenson, William. A MAN CALLED INTREPID: THE SECRET WAR. Preface
by Charles Howard Ellis. Foreword by Sir William Stephenson. New York:
Harcourt Brace Jovanovich, 1976. xxv, 486 p. Index, illustrations, maps,
organization chart of BSC.

A detailed revelation of the many activities of Sir William Stephenson, whose code name was "Intrepid." Canadian-born Stephenson had been in intelligence for years and just before World
War II had provided Churchill, who was out of office, with
figures on German steel production and on the conversion of industry to the manufacture of arms and munitions. Sent to the
United States by Churchill in 1940 as his personal representative
in intelligence matters to President Roosevelt, he established the
British Security Coordination (BSC) in Rockefeller Center. BSC
became, under Stephenson's aegis, the focal point of all the
branches of British intelligence and counterintelligence in the
Western Hemisphere before the United States entered World War
II. The author, a near-namesake but no relation, obtained ap-
proval from Intrepid to write this book, and since the British Official Secrets Act had been loosened by such books as Winter-

botham's THE ULTRA SECRET (see chapter 11, section A) and Masterman's THE DOUBLE-CROSS SYSTEM (see chapter 15, section D), the book contains many interesting revelations not contained in the Hyde book on Stephenson, THE QUIET CANADIAN: THE SECRET SERVICE STORY OF SIR WILLIAM STEPHENSON (see above). Of more than passing interest in this book is the relationship between Stephenson and President Roosevelt before the United States entered World War II. Under Churchill's direction Stephenson disclosed to Roosevelt the secrets of the British success in breaking the German Enigma code (Ultra Operation) while it was withheld from the British Prime Minister Neville Chamberlain. Also described is the influence Stephenson had on both Roosevelt and Donovan in the creation and mission of the OSS. Stephenson also briefed Roosevelt on British intelligence holdings at a time when the United States did not have an intelligence system deployed throughout Europe. The book is a valuable source of material on the political aspects of British-U.S. relations using intelligence as the medium of exchange.

Toyne, John. WIN TIME FOR US. Toronto: Longman's Canada, 1962. 241 p.

An outstanding memoir by a former British intelligence agent who was an engineer in southern Russia before and during the revolution. Eighteen years later, he was sent into Rumania at the beginning of World War II with the mission "to win time for us" by sabotaging Rumanian oil deliveries to Germany, under the cover role of a prosperous British businessman. Interesting vignettes are presented of both revolutionary Russia and the Balkans on the eve of World War II. A number of pertinent observations are made on the difficulties encountered by agents whose reports differ radically from the preconceptions and assessments of their home office.

Walker, David E. LUNCH WITH A STRANGER. London: Allan Wingate, 1957. 195 p. No index. American ed. New York: W.W. Norton, 1957. 223 p.

An excellent memoir by a British journalist who spent seven years in the British secret services under his "cover" as a foreign correspondent for the LONDON DAILY MIRROR, beginning in 1938. An authentic picture of British agent management and the handling of contacts with informants. For additional reports of British agents, see chapter 17, section B.

Wighton, Charles. PIN-STRIPE SABOTEUR. London: Odham's Press, 1959. 256 p.

The story of "Robin," an unusually successful British agent who worked in Switzerland and France between 1940 and 1944. At the beginning of his career Robin was engaged in espionage but later he became important in major sabotage and paramilitary operations. He made substantial contributions of information that helped analysts in London link German rockets to the proving ground at Peenemunde.

Wynne, Greville. CONTACT ON GORKY STREET. New York: Atheneum, 1968. 222 p. Photographs, illustrations, no index.

The memoirs of the British intelligence agent who contacted and handled Soviet army colonel Oleg Penkovskiy. Penkovskiy provided volumes of information on USSR military, political, and economic capabilities and intentions for sixteen months in 1961 and 1962 (see THE PENKOVSKIY PAPERS, cited above). Wynne concludes that it was partially Penkovskiy's information about Soviet missile developments that enabled President Kennedy to penetrate Khruschchev's bluffs during the Cuban missile crisis. Wynne, a World War II counterintelligence operative, was in the postwar period owner of a company that sold electrical equipment; in that capacity he traveled extensively in Europe, the Far East, and India. In 1955 he was selected and trained for developing Penkovskiy as a source of information. In 1963 he was arrested outside a Budapest hotel and taken to Moscow for trial with Penkovskiy who had already been taken by Soviet counterintelligence. Much of the book is taken up with descriptions of Wynne's trial and subsequent eighteen-month jail term until he was traded for Soviet agent Gordon Lonsdale. However, there are also quite a few insights into how the Penkovskiy operations were conceived and carried out, with details describing the method of contact with Penkovskiy. Wynne acknowledges having had the help of a professional writer in preparing these memoirs--which are not without their cold war messages.

Young, Desmond. RUTLAND OF JUTLAND. London: Cassell, 1963. 191 p.

An excellent biography of naval squadron leader, Frederick J. Rutland, awarded the Distinguished Service Cross of Britain, who apparently worked for both the British and American naval intelligence departments from the late 1930s until the Pearl Harbor attack in December 1941. For a summary account of his career, see chapter 8 of Vernon Hinchley's SPIES WHO NEVER WERE, cited in chapter 14, section B.

F. GERMANY

Brissaud, Andre. CANARIS: BIOGRAPHY OF THE HEAD OF GERMAN MILITARY INTELLIGENCE. Translated from the French and edited by Ian Colvin. New York: Grosset & Dunlap, 1974. 347 p. Index, sources.

A well-written and well-documented biography of the one-time head of the German Abwehr by a free-lance French journalist and television director who, since 1945, has devoted his life to investigating intelligence-related aspects of our times. A vivid portrayal of one of Hitler's lesser-known adversaries. The author also wrote a history of the German Nazi party intelligence service, THE NAZI SECRET SERVICE (see chapter 4, section D). Ian Colvin, himself an author of an early book on Canaris, is a British journalist and World War II member of the British foreign office intelligence service.

Gehlen, Reinhard. THE SERVICE: THE MEMOIRS OF GENERAL REINHARD GEHLEN. Translated by David Irving. Introduction by George Bailey. New York: World Publishing, 1972. xxvii, 386 p. Glossary, career milestones, maps, illustrations, no index.

The unreliable and often deliberately misleading memoirs of the former head of German military intelligence on the eastern front during World War II. Because of the files he had accumulated on the Soviet Union, files which he had hidden during the immediate postwar period, he began work for U.S. army intelligence and then for the CIA. He operated an espionage service against the Soviet Union until 1955 when his organization was transferred to the Federal Republic of Germany to operate as its worldwide intelligence establishment. After a series of scandals on leaks of information and infiltration of his organization, he retired in 1968.

Hohne, Heinz, and Zolling, Herman. THE GENERAL WAS A SPY: THE TRUTH ABOUT GENERAL GEHLEN AND HIS SPY RING. Introduction by Hugh Trevor-Roper. Preface by Andrew Tully. New York: Coward, McCann & Geoghegan, 1972. 347 p. Index, bibliography, notes.

Another version of the life and career of General Reinhard Gehlen, one-time head of Wehrmacht intelligence on the eastern front, head of an autonomous intelligence service under the sponsorship of the CIA, and finally head of the West German espionage service-- Bundesnachrichtendienst (BND).

Manvell, Roger, and Fraenkel, Heinrich. THE CANARIS CONSPIRACY: THE SECRET RESISTANCE TO HITLER IN THE GERMAN ARMY. New York: McKay, 1969. xxxv, 268 p. Index, bibliography, notes on sources, chronology.

The authors, who have collaborated on books on Goebbels, Goering, and Himmler, here document the story of the plottings of certain German military intelligence (Abwehr) officers--led by Admiral Wilhelm Canaris--to overthrow Hitler. The authors made contact with every principal survivor of the Abwehr resistance movement, as well as with the families of those leaders who were arrested and executed when the plot was discovered, in order to uncover new material for this book. A generous bibliography is provided along with notes on the sources of information.

Schellenberg, Walter. THE LABYRINTH: THE MEMOIRS OF WALTER SCHEL-
LENBERG. Translated by Louis Hagen. Introduction by Alan Bullock. New
York: Harper, 1956. xx, 423 p. Index, portraits.

> The authentic but sometimes misleading and self-serving memoirs
> of the man who in his twenties became the protege and deputy to
> Reinhard Heydrich, Himmler's chief of intelligence. After Hey-
> drich's assassination, Schellenberg replaced him. Some interesting
> insights into the bureaucratic struggle between Nazi party foreign
> intelligence and the Abwehr, Wehrmacht military intelligence.

Spiro, Edward [Edward H. Cookridge]. GEHLEN: SPY OF THE CENTURY.
New York: Random House, 1972. 402 p. Index, bibliography, notes, illustrations, organization chart.

> Spiro, political journalist, foreign correspondent, and wartime
> British intelligence agent has written extensively on espionage.
> Here he has written an impressive account of the organization of
> Reinhard Gehlen. Should be read in conjunction with Hohne and
> Zolling's THE GENERAL WAS A SPY (see above).

Wighton, Charles, and Peis, Gunter. HITLER'S SPIES AND SABOTEURS:
BASED ON THE GERMAN SECRET SERVICE WAR DIARY OF GENERAL LA-
HOUSEN. New York: Henry Holt and Co., 1958. 285 p.

> An account of seven German military intelligence operations against
> the Allies, including an account of the landing of saboteurs on
> the shores of the United States from a U-boat in June 1942. General
> Erwin von Lahousen was chief of Abwehr II (sabotage) under Admi-
> ral Canaris between 1939 and 1943. During that time he kept a
> diary that was eventually brought to light by the Austrian, Gunter
> Peis. In this book Peis, with British journalist Wighton, recon-
> structs events from the diary and from other sources. See also
> the citation in section G3a of this chapter.

G. THE HISTORY OF ESPIONAGE

1. Before 1914

a. THE AMERICAN REVOLUTION, 1775-83

Bakeless, John. TURNCOATS, TRAITORS, AND HEROS. New York: Lippincott, 1959. 406 p.

> A nearly complete record of secret activities of both sides on the
> American continent during the Revolution. The author was an ex-
> perienced military intelligence officer.

Foley, Rae. FAMOUS AMERICAN SPIES. New York: Dodd, Mead & Co., 1962. 158 p.

> Biographical sketches for young people of American spies in the Revolution and in the Civil War.

Ford, Corey. A PECULIAR SERVICE. Boston: Little, Brown and Co., 1965. xvii, 358 p. Index, bibliography.

> In an introductory note Professor Richard B. Morris of the Department of History, Columbia University, writes: "Corey Ford has given the fullest and most convincing account of the extraordinary operations of Washington's Manhattan agency, known as the Culper Ring. . . . A scrupulously documented and thoroughly researched book." An excellent selected bibliography of books and manuscript sources has been appended.

Lengyel, Cornel. I, BENEDICT ARNOLD: THE ANATOMY OF TREASON. New York: Doubleday, 1960. 237 p.

> Lengyel retells the story of Benedict Arnold in a popular style, using in the main the accepted sources of information.

Pennypacker, Morton. GENERAL WASHINGTON'S SPIES ON LONG ISLAND AND IN NEW YORK. Brooklyn, N.Y.: Long Island Historical Society, 1939. 302 p.

> The author, member of the New York Historical Society, whose hobby is tracing events in Long Island history, has researched available materials in order to identify the men recruited by Washington to act as spies.

Van Doren, Carl Clinton. THE SECRET HISTORY OF THE AMERICAN REVOLUTION. New York: Viking Press, 1941. 534 p.

> An original and enduring work. From previously unavailable papers from the British army headquarters, Van Doren has produced a detailed account of the conspiracy between Benedict Arnold and the British army. The author records the activities of other secret agents as well.

b. THE FRENCH REVOLUTION AND NAPOLEONIC WARS, 1789-1815

Fouche, Joseph. MEMOIRES COMPLETS ET AUTHENTIQUES DE JOSEPH FOUCHE, MINISTRE DE LA POLICE GENERALE. D'APRES L'EDITION ORIGINALE DE 1824. Paris: J. de Bonnot, 1967. 446 p.

> The memoirs of one of the most famous and enduring chiefs of intelligence and counterintelligence of modern times.

Gosselin, Louis Leon Theodore [G. Lenotre]. TWO ROYALIST SPIES OF THE FRENCH REVOLUTION. Translated by Bernard Miall. London: Urwin, 1924. 269 p.

> An account of the activities of Louis Fauche-Borel (1762-1829) and Charles-Frederic Perlet (1759-1828).

Savant, Jean. LES ESPIONS DE NAPOLEON. Paris: Hachette, 1967. 286 p.

> A popular account of the men who spied for Napoleon.

c. THE AMERICAN CIVIL WAR, 1861-65

Bakeless, John. SPIES FOR THE CONFEDERACY. New York: Lippincott, 1970. 456 p.

Baker, LaFayette Charles. HISTORY OF THE UNITED STATES SECRET SERVICE. Philadelphia: King and Baird, 1868. 398 p. Reprinted with a new preface by Herbert C. Friese, Jr. New York: AMS Press, 1973. 704 p. Illustrations.

> An autobiographical account of the secret service activities of the Union forces by the man who rose to become secret service chief over Allan Pinkerton. Good material but tainted with sensationalism and mendacity.

Boyd, Belle. BELLE BOYD IN CAMP AND PRISON, WRITTEN BY HERSELF. New York: Blelock & Co., 1865. 464 p. New edition, same title, prepared from new materials by Curtis Carroll Davis. South Brunswick, N.J.: T. Yoseloff, 1968. 448 p. Bibliography, illustrations.

> The autobiography of a Confederate woman spy who is reputed to have saved Stonewall Jackson's forces with her information.

Bulloch, James Dunwody. THE SECRET SERVICE OF THE CONFEDERATE STATES IN EUROPE. 2 vols. 1884. Reprint. New York: Thomas Yoseloff, 1959. 460 p.; 459 p.

> A detailed record of the intrigue in Europe during the American Civil War. The author spent his time in Europe purchasing ships for the Confederacy and purchasing armament for the ships.

Foster, G. Allen. THE EYES AND EARS OF THE CIVIL WAR. New York: Criterion Books, 1964. 168 p.

Horan, James D. CONFEDERATE AGENT. A DISCOVERY IN HISTORY. New York: Crown, 1954. xxii, 326 p. Bibliography.

> An account of the espionage activities of Captain Thomas Henry Hines.

Kane, Harnett Thomas. SPIES FOR THE BLUE AND GRAY. Garden City, N.Y.: Doubleday, 1954. 311 p. Bibliography, acknowledgments.

A well-written and well-researched history of approximately thirteen episodes of espionage during the Civil War. Excellent bibliography.

Pinkerton, Allan. THE SPY OF THE REBELLION. HISTORY OF THE SPY SYSTEM OF THE UNITED STATES ARMY DURING THE LATE REBELLION. New York: G.W. Carlton, 1883. xxxii, 688 p.

The autobiography of the detective-turned-spy who helped establish espionage for the U.S. Army in the early days of the Civil War. For a time, Pinkerton was chief of the intelligence service of the Union forces under General McClellan.

Stern, Philip van Doren. SECRET MISSIONS OF THE CIVIL WAR: FIRST HAND ACCOUNTS BY MEN AND WOMEN WHO RISKED THEIR LIVES IN UNDERGROUND ACTIVITIES. New York: Rand McNally, 1959. 320 p. Appendix on codes and ciphers of the Civil War.

Annotated anthology of the best accounts, sifted by the author from the mass of material, of dramatic stories of espionage and sabotage on behalf of both the North and the South. Some of the material used had been released from the National Archives in 1953. The author provides interpretations of the effect of espionage and counterespionage activities on the course of the war.

2. World War I and the Interwar Period

Agar, Augustus. BALTIC EPISODE; A CLASSIC OF SECRET SERVICE IN RUSSIAN WATERS. London: Hodder & Stoughton, 1963. 255 p. Illustrations, portraits, maps.

An account of the rescue of "ST 25," that is, Sir Paul Dukes, a British intelligence agent active in Russia before and during the period of Allied intervention.

Asprey, Robert B. THE PANTHER'S FEAST. New York: G.P. Putnam's Sons, 1959. 317 p. Illustrations.

The story of Colonel Alfred Redl, deputy chief of the intelligence bureau of the Austro-Hungarian Imperial Army, and chief of the counterintelligence section, who was exposed as a spy in Russian pay. Upon detection Redl committed suicide in a Vienna hotel in 1913. The author is a former U.S. Army intelligence officer.

Boucard, Robert. THE SECRET SERVICES OF EUROPE. Translated by Ronald Leslie Melville. London: Stanley Paul, 1940. 260 p.

Bywater, Hector C., and Ferraby, H.C. STRANGE INTELLIGENCE. MEM-
OIRS OF NAVAL SECRET SERVICE. London: Constable, 1931. ix, 299 p.
American ed. STRANGE INTELLIGENCE. New York: Long & Smith, 1931.
308 p.

An account of British naval intelligence during World War I.

Dukes, Sir Paul. THE STORY OF "ST 25": ADVENTURE AND ROMANCE IN
THE SECRET INTELLIGENCE SERVICE IN RED RUSSIA. London: Cassell,
1938. 380 p.

The memoir of one of the most talented British agents operative in
Russia in the early days of the Bolshevik seizure of power and the
Allied intervention.

Graves, Armgaard Karl, with Fox, Edward Lyell. THE SECRETS OF THE GER-
MAN WAR OFFICE. New York: McBride, Nast & Co., 1914. 256 p. Illustrations, no index.

Memoirs of a German agent working in England. In 1912 he was
arrested in Glasgow and sent to prison for eighteen months. Upon
release he went to the United States and published this book. Because it was delivered to the publishers just three weeks before the
tragedy of Serajevo, it appeared at the time of the outbreak of
the war and was an instant success. The book, however, contains
no new material.

Hahn, James E. THE INTELLIGENCE SERVICE WITH THE CANADIAN CORPS,
1914-1918. HISTORICAL RESUME BY GENERAL SIR ARTHUR CURRIE. Toronto:
Macmillan, 1930. xxii, 263 p. Maps, illustrations, aerial photographs.

A solid, comprehensive account of Canadian combat intelligence
during the First World War.

Landau, Henry. THE ENEMY WITHIN: THE INSIDE STORY OF GERMAN
SABOTAGE IN AMERICA. New York: G.P. Putnam's Sons, 1937. ix, 323 p.
Index, illustrations, appendix.

The author, then a captain in the British secret service, describes
German sabotage in the United States during the period between
the outbreak of World War I and the entrance of the United States
into the war. He has concentrated principally on the Black Tom
and Kingsland sabotage cases in which he assisted American claim-
ants in their investigations of these cases. To back up his descriptions the author has inserted throughout the book German wireless
and cable messages which the British intercepted and decoded.
The appendix is a detailed chronology of the sabotage events between 7 July 1914 and 6 April 1917, when the United States declared war on Germany.

Nicolai, Walther. THE GERMAN SECRET SERVICE. Translated, with an additional chapter, by George Renwick. London: Stanley Paul, 1924. 299 p. German ed. GEHEIME MACHTE. INTERNATIONALE SPIONAGE UND IHRE BEKAMPFUNG IM WELTKRIEG UND HEUTE. Leipzig: Koehler, 1923. 184 p.

> An important historical source by the chief of intelligence and counterintelligence, or Gruppe IIIb, of the Imperial German General Staff from 1913 throughout World War I. Colonel Nicolai decries the lack of preparedness in the military intelligence service and especially the lack of capability to conduct strategic economic and political intelligence against the Allied states. The German edition of the book was withdrawn from circulation when its author was declared a traitor by the Nazi regime. The extra chapter added by translator George Renwick describes the detection of Colonel Alfred Redl as a Russian spy, and was originally published by Renwick in the SUNDAY NEWS of London.

Rowan, Richard Wilmer. SECRET AGENTS AGAINST AMERICA. New York: Doubleday, Doran & Co., 1939. 267 p. Maps, charts, illustrations.

> In this book the astute chronicler of intelligence history sounds the warning of clandestine infiltration of the United States by foreign powers and the woeful state of U.S. counterintelligence to meet this threat. He elaborates on the organizations of the Germans, Japanese, and Italians that were intruding in the United States and its Latin American neighbors to conduct espionage and sabotage. An excellent review of intelligence against the United States in the immediate pre-World War II period.

Seth, Ronald. THE SPY WHO WASN'T CAUGHT: THE STORY OF JULIUS SILBER. London: Hale, 1966. 189 p. American ed. THE SPY WHO WAS NEVER CAUGHT. New York: Hawthorn Books, 1967. 240 p.

> An account of the activities of Julius Silber, a German expatriate who worked successfully as an espionage agent in the British Postal Censorship Department throughout World War I and returned to Germany after the war.

Steinhauer, Gustav, and Felstead, S.T. STEINHAUER: THE KAISER'S MASTER SPY. London: John Lane, 1930. xii, 356 p. Illustrations. American ed. New York: D. Appleton & Co., 1931. 356 p. Illustrations.

> The memoir of a German espionage agent working in England, a man who had been a private detective and had worked for a time with the Pinkerton Agency in the United States. This mediocre espionage agent turned out to be a better counterspy; he does not deserve the self-ascription of "the Kaiser's master spy."

Sweeney, Walter Campbell. MILITARY INTELLIGENCE: A NEW WEAPON OF WAR. New York: Stokes, 1924. viii, 259 p. Diagrams.

A description of military intelligence during the First World War, with some insight into how the lessons learned from the war were incorporated into military intelligence doctrine in the early 1920s.

Wild, Max. ON THE RUSSIAN FRONT. Translated by Anthony Haigh. London: Geoffery Bles, 1932. 324 p. Maps. American ed. SECRET SERVICE ON THE RUSSIAN FRONT, 1914-1918. New York: G.P. Putnam's Sons, 1932. 324 p. Maps.

An autobiographical account of espionage by one of the better agents of the German secret service.

3. Espionage in World War II

Each war produces a rich harvest of spy stories and semibiographical works of agents employed in various intelligence and counterintelligence services. For example, there have been many books written on German secret services in World War II, probably because Germany lost the war and thus no security limitations have acted to hold down the number of exposes. However, many of the postwar revelations from all countries can be considered partly fictitious. During World War II, nevertheless, there were some outstanding espionage networks, such as the Soviet-controlled Red Orchestra network that operated in Germany itself and in occupied France and Belgium, and the Rado-Rossler ("Lucy") network that operated from Switzerland. There were also several unprecedented counterespionage operations. One was the so-called Double-Cross (XX) System, by which British counterespionage (M.I.5) controlled most German agents sent to England; another was the German counterintelligence-operated North Pole system in which all British agents who parachuted into Holland were controlled or neutralized. Finally, both the British Special Operations Executive (SOE) and its American counterpart the Office of Strategic Services (OSS) engaged in some espionage and counterespionage activities, although the primary mission of both agencies was to "set Europe ablaze" and to organize anti-Nazi resistance movements. These strategic services may best be classed as covert operations and are listed under that category rather than under the history of espionage in World War II.

a. GENERAL WORKS AND MEMOIRS

Books on intelligence in World War II abound throughout this bibliography. Only a few additional titles are added here.

Brown, Anthony Cave. BODYGUARD OF LIES. New York: Harper & Row, 1975. x, 947 p. Index, bibliography, sources and notes, illustrations, glossary, maps.

A single source of information on deception and intelligence operations in World War II. Written by a British journalist after more

than seven years research, it brings together all the deception operations used by the Allies in disguising their military landings, including the Normandy landings. See chapter 21, section B, for
main annotation.

Farago, Ladislas. THE GAME OF FOXES. THE UNTOLD STORY OF GER-
MAN ESPIONAGE IN THE UNITED STATES AND GREAT BRITAIN DURING
WORLD WAR II. New York: David McKay, 1971. xxi, 696 p. Index,
bibliography.

> Farago, student and writer of intelligence, concentrates on describ-
> ing in detail the operations and activities of German intelligence
> against the United States and Great Britain before and during
> World War II. The book covers the period between 1920, when
> German military intelligence was revived, and 1945. Farago
> found a metal footlocker filled with microfilms of the records of
> the Abwehr in the National Archives in 1967, and used this ma-
> terial, supplemented with interviews, to prepare this book. De-
> tailed and adequately documented.

Jordan, George R., and Stokes, R.L. FROM MAJOR JORDAN'S DIARIES.
New York: Harcourt, 1952. 284 p.

> An account of Soviet espionage via Lend-Lease channels by the
> wartime liaison officer at the Great Falls staging base for Lend-
> Lease supplies to Russia.

Piekalkiewicz, Janusz. SECRET AGENTS, SPIES, AND SABOTEURS: FAMOUS
UNDERCOVER MISSIONS OF WORLD WAR II. New York: William Morrow
& Co. Illustrations, photographs; London: Tom Stacey, 1973. 523 p.

> A unique history of intelligence in World War II in pictures. The
> book contains 850 illustrations.

Renault-Roulier, Gilbert [Remy]. MEMOIRS OF A SECRET AGENT OF FREE
FRANCE: Vol. I: THE SILENT COMPANY, JUNE 1940-JUNE 1942. Translated by Lancelot C. Sheppard. New York: McGraw-Hill, 1948. 406 p.
Map, portraits, illustrations. British ed. London: A. Barker, 1948. xx,
406 p. Map, portraits, illustrations.

> The first volume of six describing the author's experiences as an
> intelligence agent of the Free French working in France, and his
> experiences with the French resistance.

> Volume 2 has also been translated, COURAGE AND FEAR. Lon-
> don: Arthur Barker, 1950. Remaining four volumes are: COMMENT
> MEURT UN RESEAU and UNE AFFAIRE DE TRAHISON both by
> Monte Carlo: Raoul Solar, 1947. LES MAINS JOINTES. Monte
> Carlo: Raoul Solar, 1948. MAIS LE TEMPLE EST BATI. Monte
> Carlo: Raoul Solar, 1950.

_____. PORTRAIT OF A SPY. Translated by L[ancelot]. C. Sheppard. London: A. Barker, 1955. 224 p. American ed. New York: Roy Publishers, 1955. 224 p. Illustrations.

A history of the resistance movement in France and especially a history of one network--CONFRERIE NOTRE DAME. "Remy" provides details on how the network was broken by a Belgian working for the German counterintelligence. An excellent chart of the entire Free French resistance is provided.

Trefousse, Hans L. "The Failure of German Intelligence in the United States, 1935-1945." MISSISSIPPI VALLEY HISTORICAL REVIEW 42 (June 1955): 84-100.

An excellent summary of German espionage attempts at U.S targets during the period from 1935 to 1945. Stresses the ineptness and utter failure of these attempts, plus an account of how intelligence was either rejected or misused in decision making by Hitler and the Nazi elite. Based on trial records, diplomatic memoirs, and interrogation reports.

Wighton, Charles, and Peis, Gunter. HITLER'S SPIES AND SABOTEURS: BASED ON THE GERMAN SECRET SERVICE WAR DIARY OF GENERAL LAHOUSEN. New York: Henry Holt and Co., 1958. 285 p. British ed. THEY SPIED ON ENGLAND: BASED ON THE GERMAN SECRET SERVICE DIARY OF GENERAL VON LAHOUSEN. London: Odhams Press, 1958. 320 p.

Early in the postwar period Gunter Peis obtained a copy of the classified (and missing) war diary of General Erwin Lahousen, chief of Abwehr II under Admiral Canaris. Lahousen was probably a coconspirator with Canaris against Hitler. This elaboration gives case histories of German agents in England, Ireland, and South Africa, and of the saboteurs that were landed by submarine on the U.S. coast. Peis and journalist Wighton, author of other books on intelligence, probably elaborated on the short cryptic notes of the diary with information obtained from other sources. Also cited in section F, above.

b. SOVIET-CONTROLLED NETWORKS (RADO—ROSSLER AND THE RED ORCHESTRA)

Accoce, Pierre, and Quet, Pierre. A MAN CALLED LUCY: 1939-1945. Translated by A.M. Sheridan Smith. New York: Coward-McCann, 1967. 250 p. Bibliography, illustrations.

Two French journalists have combined to produce this controversial best seller in France, and a book which caused serious debate in England. It is the story of Rudolf Rossler, code name "Lucy," whose sources of information in Germany the authors attempt to identify. However, the authors admit that their identification of members of the "Lucy" ring in Germany by first names and initial letter of the surname was their own invention. Rossler, a German emigre posing as a Swiss publisher, kept in contact by clandestine radio with ten of his peacetime friends who passed on information direct from the decision level of the German High Command. Unreliable, possibly containing some propaganda messages.

Foote, Alexander. HANDBOOK FOR SPIES. Garden City, N.Y.: Doubleday, 1949. vi, 273 p. British ed. London: Museum Press, 1949. 190 p.

An authentic description of the Rado-Rossler network by one of its senior members and its chief of communications operations. Foote, an Englishman, worked for nine years for Soviet intelligence, escaping from East Berlin in 1947 to return and live in England. In this book he reveals the kinds of information he was coding and radioing to Moscow, plus some details on communications procedures and security practiced by the network. In 1943 he was arrested by the Swiss police and placed in jail for espionage. After his release a year later he returned to Moscow for debriefing and further training.

Hohne, Heinz. CODEWORD: DIREKTOR--THE STORY OF THE RED ORCHESTRA. Translated by Richard Barry. New York: Coward, McCann & Geoghegan, 1971. xxix, 310 p. Index, bibliography, glossary, names of personnel with code names and cover names, organization charts, notes, illustrations.

An account of how a group of ill-prepared Communists in Germany, a few years before World War II, organized themselves into an expionage network to become known as the Rote Kapelle (Red Orchestra). Their self-imposed mission was to infiltrate the German High Command to obtain information which could be relayed to Moscow via clandestine radio circuits. An excellent account, well researched and documented, by a distinguished German journalist who has written other books related to intelligence.

Peyroles, Jacques [Perrault, Gilles]. THE RED ORCHESTRA. Translated by Peter Wiles. New York: Simon & Schuster, 1969. 511 p. Bibliography, illustrations.

The author, a French journalist, gives a detailed description of the members of the Rote Kappelle, with emphasis on the leader Leopold Trepper. The network reported to Soviet military intelligence (GRU) in Moscow and operated in France and Belgium as well as Germany itself. The uncovering of the network was the result of German interception of the network's radio transmissions. There are some inaccuracies.

Trepper, Leopold. THE GREAT GAME. MEMOIRS OF THE SPY HITLER COULDN'T SILENCE. New York: McGraw Hill, 1977. 442 p. Index, appendices, illustrations, photographs.

Trepper, a dedicated militant Communist, established the Red
Orchestra espionage network in 1938, in Brussels, under the aegis
of Soviet military intelligence. Some network operational details
are provided. Trepper emphasizes, however, the role he played
in out-maneuvering the efforts of the special German counterintelligence team created to hunt down the network members, to
play back captured Red Orchestra radios to the Center in Moscow.
The political aim of this "Great Game," directed from Berlin, was
to create conditions for a separate German-Soviet peace arrangement. An important memoir.

H. SELECTED ESPIONAGE FICTION

The best general critique of espionage fiction is "A Short History of the Spy
Story," chapter 16 of Julian Symon's MORTAL CONSEQUENCES: A HIS-
TORY--FROM THE DETECTIVE STORY TO THE CRIME NOVEL (New York:
Harper, 1972). Symons, himself the author of more than a dozen crime novels,
distinguishes between spy stories and "thrillers," and argues that "the spy story
owed its existence to awareness of the threat to national security implied in
professionally organized spying, and also to the slow realization that the spy's
activities may be both intricate and dangerous." He cites James Fenimore
Cooper's novel, THE SPY (1821), as the first example of the genre, followed
by Joseph Conrad's THE SECRET AGENT (1907) and UNDER WESTERN EYES (1911).

A main criterion used for selection here is literary value, and the principal
authority used is Julian Symons. For this reason the twenty-odd expionage
novels of William (Tufnell) Le Queux (1864-1927) have been excluded in spite
of their historical importance since, according to Symons, "the stories are atro-
ciously written and full of padding, although obviously based on considerable
knowledge of military and political affairs." For similar reasons only five of
the forty-odd novels of E. Howard Hunt, ex-CIA officer and a principal figure
in the Watergate break-in, have been included. Here, however, another aspect of spy fiction becomes apparent: How many of the spy stories of the cold
war period were sponsored by intelligence organizations of the United States
or Great Britain in order to keep the business of espionage before the public
eye, or to indicate the "threat" of Soviet intelligence?

However, other criteria for selection have also been used. For example, novels
have been included which provide some additional insight into intelligence
tradecraft. Woodhouse's TREE FROG and BUSH BABY have been written around
the idea of the use of new technological sensors in intelligence surveillance
and collection. Included also are examples of the work of experienced journalists-
turned-spy-novelists, since they show a remarkable knowledge of foreign areas.
For example, a foreign correspondent and Southeast Asia specialist named Collingwood wrote THE DEFECTOR, a provocative account of the Vietnam War,
while ex-war correspondent Tregaskis, author of VIETNAM DIARY and GUADA-
CANAL DIARY, wrote CHINA BOMB, a novel about an intelligence operation
aimed at destroying China's only hydrogen bomb. Leon Uris, successful as a
novelist with a facility ofr blending historical facts with readable fiction,
wrote TOPAZ on the basis of information provided by ex-French intelligence

officer Pierre L. Thyraud de Vosjoli (see de Vosjoli's LAMIA, cited in chapter 4, section E). Added also is the spy novel SAVING THE QUEEN by successful journalist William F. Buckley who drew on his experience in England and the U.S. government, and perhaps on his reported service with the CIA in his earlier years, to describe the activities of a young CIA agent's first mission which leads to extraordinary events at the Court of St. James. Hard to categorize, but interesting nonetheless, is the recent novel THE COMPANY, about CIA-White House scuffling over suppressed reports on political assassination, by President Nixon's former assistant John Ehrlichman.

Then, of course, there are the novels written by experienced intelligence officers themselves. E. Howard Hunt has already been mentioned. Ian Fleming, creator of James Bond, was a British naval intelligence officer during World War II, but not a field operator, as James Bond's exploits might suggest. Victor Marchetti, author of THE ROPE DANCER, was a CIA officer at the agency's headquarters in McLean, Virginia, for fourteen years before he gave it up and began writing (see Marchetti and Marks's THE CIA AND THE CULT OF INTELLIGENCE, cited in chapter 16).

The works of many of the authors are filled with romance, sex, danger, violence, and political intrigue, which is not, on the whole, representative of everyday espionage, although partially indicative of field intelligence during the cold war, which was pointed at covert action rather than information collection. Such fiction has an increasingly large and very loyal reading public. That they are well served is evidenced by the regular appearance of espionage and international intrigue novels on the best seller lists.

The books are listed without annotation, and in the case of authors with two or more titles to their credit, in chronological order.

Ambler, Erich. COFFIN FOR DIMITRIOS. New York: Knopf, 1939. 281 p.

_____. JOURNEY INTO FEAR. New York: Knopf, 1940. 275 p.

_____. EPITAPH FOR A SPY. New York: Knopf, 1952. 259 p.

_____. STATE OF SEIGE. New York: Knopf, 1956. 248 p.

_____. DIRTY STORY. New York: Atheneum, 1967. 269 p.

_____. THE INTERCOM CONSPIRACY. New York: Atheneum, 1969. 211 p.

Behn, Noel. THE KREMLIN LETTER. New York: Simon & Schuster, 1967. 284 p.

_____. THE SHADOW BOXER. New York: Simon & Schuster, 1969. 317 p.

Buchan, John. GREENMANTLE. New York: H. Doran, 1915; Boston: Houghton Mifflin, 1936. 345 p. British ed. London: Hodder & Stoughton, 1916. x, 307 p.

_____. THE THIRTY-NINE STEPS. Edinburgh and London: Blackwood, 1915. 253 p. American ed. New York: G.H. Doran, 1915. 231 p.

Buckley, William F., Jr. SAVING THE QUEEN. New York: Doubleday, 1976. 248 p.

Clark, William. SPECIAL RELATIONSHIP. Boston: Houghton Mifflin, 1969. 223 p.

Clayton, Richard Henry Michael [William Haggard]. SLOW BURNER. Boston: Little, Brown and Co., 1958. 192 p.

Collingwood, Charles. THE DEFECTOR. New York: Harper & Row, 1969. 313 p.

Conrad, Joseph. THE SECRET AGENT: A SIMPLE TALE. London: Methuen, 1907. 442 p. American ed. New York: Harper & Bros., 1907. 372 p.

_____. UNDER WESTERN EYES. New York: Harper, 1911. 377 p.

Cornwell, David John Moore [John le Carre]. CALL FOR THE DEAD. London: Gollancz, 1961. 192 p. American ed. New York: Walker, 1962. 192 p.

_____. THE SPY WHO CAME IN FROM THE COLD. New York: Coward-McCann, 1964. 256 p.

_____. THE LOOKING GLASS WAR. New York: Coward-McCann, 1965. 320 p.

_____. A SMALL TOWN IN GERMANY. New York: Coward-McCann, 1968. 366 p.

_____. TINKER, TAILOR, SOLDIER, SPY. New York: Knopf, 1974. 355 p.

Deighton, Len. THE IPCRESS FILE. New York: Simon & Schuster, 1962. 287 p.

_____. HORSE UNDER WATER. New York: G.P. Putnam's Sons, 1963. 255 p.

_____. FUNERAL IN BERLIN. London: Cape, 1964. 320 p. American ed. New York: G.P. Putnam's Sons, 1965. 312 p.

_____. BILLION-DOLLAR BRAIN. New York: G.P. Putnam's Sons, 1966. 312 p.

_____. SPY STORY. New York: Harcourt Brace Jovanovich, 1974. 224 p.

_____. YESTERDAY'S SPY. New York: Harcourt Brace Jovanovich, 1975. 222 p.

_____. CATCH A FALLING SPY. New York: Harcourt Brace Jovanovich, 1976. 268 p.

Ehrlichman, John. THE COMPANY. New York: Simon & Schuster, 1976. 313 p.

Fleming, Ian. CASINO ROYALE. New York: Macmillan, 1966. 187 p.

_____. FROM RUSSIA WITH LOVE. New York: Macmillan, 1966. 191 p.

Forsyth, Frederick. THE DAY OF THE JACKAL. New York: Viking, 1971. 380 p.

Greene, Graham. THE CONFIDENTIAL AGENT. London: Heinemann, 1939. 286 p.

_____. THE POWER AND THE GLORY. Toronto: Ryerson Press, 1940. 280 p.

_____. THE QUIET AMERICAN. New York: Viking, 1956. 249 p.

_____. OUR MAN IN HAVANA. New York: Viking, 1958. 247 p.

Higgins, Jack. THE EAGLE HAS LANDED. New York: Holt, Rinehart and Winston, 1975. 352 p.

Hunt, Everett Howard. EAST OF FAREWELL. New York: Knopf, 1942. 270 p.

_____. LIMIT OF DARKNESS. New York: Random House, 1944. 227 p.

_____. STRANGER IN TOWN. New York: Random House, 1947. 282 p.

_____. MAELSTROM. New York: Farrar, Straus, 1948. 283 p.

_____. BIMINI RUN. New York: Farrar, Straus, 1949. 229 p.

Lancaster, Bruce. THE SECRET ROAD. Boston: Little, Brown and Co., 1952. ix, 259 p.

Lee, John. THE NINTH MAN. New York: Doubleday, 1976. 306 p.

Littell, Robert. THE DEFECTION OF A.J. LEWINTER. Boston: Houghton Mifflin, 1973. 230 p.

MacInnes, Helen. ABOVE SUSPICION. London: Harrap, 1941. 242 p. American ed. Boston: Little, Brown and Co., 1941. 333 p.

_____. ASSIGNMENT IN BRITTANY. London: Harrap, 1942. 322 p. American ed. Boston: Little, Brown and Co., 1942. 373 p.

_____. THE SALZBURG CONNECTION. New York: Harcourt, 1968. 406 p.

_____. MESSAGE FROM MALAGA. New York: Harcourt, 1971. 367 p.

_____. THE SNARE OF THE HUNTER. New York: Harcourt Brace Jovanovich, 1974. 306 p.

_____. AGENT IN PLACE. New York: Harcourt Brace Jovanovich, 1976. 339 p.

MacLean, Alistair Sturat. THE GUNS OF NAVARONE. Garden City, N.Y.: Doubleday, 1957. 320 p.

_____. ICE STATION ZEBRA. Garden City, N.Y.: Doubleday, 1963. 276 p.

_____. WHERE EAGLES DARE. London: Collins, 1967. 256 p.

_____. PUPPET ON A CHAIN. Garden City, N.Y.: Doubleday, 1969. 281 p.

_____. CIRCUS. New York: Doubleday, 1975. 192 p.

Marchetti, Victor. THE ROPE DANCER. New York: Grosset & Dunlap, 1971. 361 p.

Mason, Francis van Wyck. THE MAN FROM G-2: THREE OF MAJOR NORTH'S MOST IMPORTANT ADVENTURES. New York: Reynal & Hitchcock, 1941. 444 p.

_____. ZANZIBAR INTRIGUE. Garden City, N.Y.: Doubleday, 1963. 231 p.

Maugham, William Somerset. ASHENDEN: THE BRITISH AGENT. London: Heinemann, 1928. 340 p. American eds. Garden City, N.Y.: Doubleday, Doran & Co., 1928. 304 p.; New York: World Publishing Co., 1947. xiii, 304 p.

Oppenheim, E. Phillips. THE SPY MASTER. Boston: Little, Brown and Co., 1938. 300 p.

Sinclair, Upton Beall. PRESIDENTIAL AGENT. New York: Viking, 1944. 655 p.

_____. PRESIDENTIAL MISSION. New York: Viking, 1947. 645 p.

Starnes, Richard. REQUIEM IN UTOPIA. New York: Trident Press, 1967. 213 p.

Stewart, John Innes MacKintosh [Michael Innes]. THE SECRET VANGUARD. London: Red Badge Books, 1940. vi, 236 p. American ed. New York: Dodd, Mead, 1941. 236 p.

_____. THE CASE OF THE JOURNEYING BOY. New York: Dodd, Mead, 1949. 314 p.

_____. THE PAPER THUNDERBOLT. New York: Dodd, Mead, 1951. 333 p.

Tregaskis, Richard. CHINA BOMB. New York: Ives Washburn, 1967. 313 p.

Trevanian [pseud.]. THE EIGER SANCTION. New York: Crown, 1972. 316 p.

_____. THE LOO SANCTION. New York: Crown, 1973. 282 p.

Uris, Leon. TOPAZ. New York: McGraw-Hill, 1967. 341 p.

Woodhouse, Martin. TREE FROG. New York: Coward-McCann, 1966. 252 p.

_____. BUSH BABY. Coward-McCann, 1968. 223 p.

Wylie, Philip. THE SPY WHO SPOKE PORPOISE. New York: Doubleday, 1969. 312 p.

Chapter 15

COUNTERESPIONAGE

Secrecy cloaks the specific activities, techniques, and methods of counterespionage, just as it cloaks the specific activities and techniques of espionage
agents--or what is known in the trade as Humint (clandestine human intelligence collection). Thus there are great gaps in the counterespionage literature, especially in the period of the sixties and seventies. Counterespionage
fiction and movies are misleading in regard to techniques, since they tend to
emphasize the dramatic aspects for audience appeal and entertainment. For
some reason--probably other than secrecy or nonavailability of information--
journalists, scholars, and analysts have not delved into counterespionage as
they have into positive intelligence.

Material in the available literature points up the fundamental doctrine of counterespionage, which is to avoid the speedy apprehension of a spy who has been
detected, allowing him freedom under surveillance until the entire espionage
network is uncovered. An oft-repeated adage of counterintelligence states:
It may be better to keep track of a known spy than to arrest him, since his
replacement will be unknown. Two other basic objectives are to attempt to
gain the consent of detected spies to double against their intelligence organizations, and to use a detected spy as a means to deceive and misinform un-
knowingly.

Two outstanding examples of the turning or doubling of captured spies are
available in the literature; however, they are of the World War II era.
Masterman's THE DOUBLE CROSS SYSTEM which is unique in that it describes
some of the techniques and problems involved in handling numbers of doubled
agents; and Giskes's LONDON CALLING NORTH POLE, a description of
doubling on the weak link of espionage networks--agent communications.

There are also those intelligence agents of one side who have defected to the
other side, but who remain in place as double agents wreaking havoc by uncovering the networks they were once a part of, or deceiving their original
sponsors with fabricated information. In the end they are taken by counterespionage watchfulness. There are stories of the activities of such men in the
literature. For example, Colonel Stig Wennerstrom was a Swedish air force

attache who also did limited intelligence work for the United States but had gone over to Soviet intelligence and had been doubled for fifteen years before his defection was uncovered by Swedish counterespionage (see Ronblom's SPY WITHOUT A COUNTRY). British intelligence agent George Blake was ordered by the British to work for Soviet intelligence as a double agent, but in reality was indeed a Soviet agent. As a double agent he betrayed Western spies working in Germany and in the Warsaw Pact countries. Uncovered by counterespionage and convicted, he escaped from a British prison to the Soviet Union in 1966 (see Spiro's THE MANY SIDES OF GEORGE BLAKE, ESQ.).

A third category to be found in the literature are the stories of those non-intelligence-connected citizens who report attempts at recruitment as agents by a foreign espionage service to their own counterespionage service and then agree to act as counterspies to uncover the foreign espionage net or provide fabricated information. The stories of Herbert Philbrick (I LED THREE LIVES: CITIZEN, "COMMUNIST," COUNTERSPY), Boris Morros (MY TEN YEARS AS A COUNTER SPY), and John Huminik (DOUBLE AGENT) are examples of memoirs written by such men.

Modern espionage agents are greatly assisted by elaborate electronic and photographic devices in securing and recording the information they seek, and in some cases such devices, along with their installation and operating technicians, have replaced the agent altogether. This complicates the job of counterespionage and requires that counterespionage change its methods, keep pace in the technological race, train its own technicians, and develop its own techniques for detection of espionage devices. Only glimpses of this type of electronic counterespionage activity have been disclosed in the literature. For example, in May 1960, UN Ambassador Henry Cabot Lodge, in open session at the United Nations Security Council, exhibited a two-foot, carved wooden replica of the Great Seal of the United States in which counterespionage and security personnel had discovered a wireless device for picking up and transmitting conversations. The seal, a gift from a Soviet official to Ambassador Averell Harriman, had been placed in his office in the American embassy in Moscow. (See Warren Roger's article in the WASHINGTON POST, cited below.)

A. GENERAL BOOKS

Bulloch, John. M.I.5: THE ORIGIN AND HISTORY OF THE BRITISH COUNTERESPIONAGE SERVICE. London: Arthur Barker, 1963. 206 p. Illustrations.

> Unfortunately this history of British counterespionage and security ends when World War II begins. Using material from counterespionage case histories, the journalist author describes M.I.5 from its origin in 1909 to 1940.

Donovan, James B. STRANGERS ON A BRIDGE: THE CASE OF COLONEL ABEL. New York: Atheneum, 1964. xi, 432 p. Index.

This is a journal of the trial of Colonel Rudolf Ivanovich Abel, Soviet intelligence agent in the United States; his imprisonment for nearly five years; and his trade in Berlin for U-2 pilot Gary Powers. It is also an account of the counterespionage operation that led to Abel through the detection of his assistant Reino Hayhanen. The author and attorney Donovan, who was appointed to defend Abel by the Bar Association, was general counsel of the Office of Strategic Services (OSS) and was instrumental in securing the release of more than 9,700 Cubans and Americans taken in the Bay of Pigs operation.

Dulles, Allen Welsh, ed. GREAT TRUE SPY STORIES. New York: Harper & Row, 1968. 393 p.

Of special interest are chapters 3 and 4, "Counterespionage: Spy to Catch a Spy," and "Double Agents: Walking Both Sides of the Street" include a collection of nine accounts of counterespionage taken from the best in this field, with a short introduction to each chapter. Two of the stories are taken from the period of the American Revolution and the remainder from later periods. An account taken from Alexander Foote's HANDBOOK FOR SPIES details the Swiss counterintelligence success in closing down the valuable Soviet Rado-Rossler network through radio direction.

Fuller, Jean Overton. NO. 13, BOB. Boston: Little, Brown and Co., 1954. 240 p. Portrait.

An insight into the operations and successes of German counterespionage in France during World War II. Fuller, a wartime censor in England, tells the story of Captain John Starr, French Section, Special Operations Executive, who was betrayed to German counterespionage. During his interrogations Starr learned that through captured British radios and codes German counterintelligence personnel were operating part of the resistance and underground movements themselves.

Leverkuehn, Paul. "Espionage and Counterespionage." In GERMAN MILITARY INTELLIGENCE, pp. 27-42. New York: Praeger; London: Leidenfeld and Nicolson, 1954. Illustrations, organization chart.

Paul Leverkuehn, a senior member of Germany's wartime military intelligence service, the Abwehr, describes its counterespionage organization and functions and the division of responsibilities between the Abwehr and the political intelligence and security arm of the Gestapo. An organization chart of the Abwehr is included.

Ronblom, H.K. THE SPY WITHOUT A COUNTRY. Translated by Joan Bulman. New York: Coward-McCann, 1965. 222 p. No index.

From reports of official counterespionage investigations and interrogations, personal information, and assistance from experts in military intelligence, author and journalist Ronblom traces the activities of double agent Colonel Stig Wennerstrom, Swedish Air Force.
For nearly fifteen years Wennerstrom remained in place working
for Swedish and American intelligence while he was actually an
agent of Soviet intelligence. Caught by counterespionage, he was
convicted of gross espionage and sentenced to life imprisonment in
June 1964. See also Thomas Whiteside's AN AGENT IN PLACE:
THE WENNERSTROM AFFAIR, cited in chapter 14, section D3.

Spiro, Edward [Edward H. Cookridge]. THE MANY SIDES OF GEORGE BLAKE,
ESQ.: THE COMPLETE DOSSIER. New York and Princeton, N.J.: Vertex
Book, 1970. 254 p.

The full story of George Blake, a double agent who for nine years
disclosed British and American secrets to Soviet intelligence and
counterintelligence. It is written by a prolific author of intelligence literature, himself a one-time British secret agent who knew
George Blake during and after World War II. Spiro traces the
early career of Blake through his experiences in World War II with
Dutch Resistance as well as his experiences as a prisoner of the
Communists during the Korean War.

Turner, William W. HOOVER'S F.B.I.: THE MEN AND THE MYTH. Los
Angeles: Sherbourne Press, 1970. xv, 352 p. Appendix, no index.

This candid study of the FBI by a former special agent includes a
summary chapter, "The FBI as Our Counterspy," which evaluates
the agency's counterespionage role during and after World War II.
Also cited in chapter 8, section A.

B. GENERAL ARTICLES

Blumenthal, Fred. "How We Outsmart Red Spies." PARADE, 11 February
1962, p. 6.

A very interesting article describing some of the specifics of counterespionage against electronic "spies." The author states that between 1952 and 1962, 129 listening devices were discovered in
U.S. embassies abroad and that "spies and counter-spies no longer
are quick-triggered men in slouch hats and belted trench coats.
Rather they are extremely gifted electronics experts, who have
attained pioneering heights in miniaturization and concealment."

Gwynne, Peter, with Friendly, Alfred, Jr. "The Heat Wave Spies." NEWS-
WEEK, 23 February 1976, p. 57. Illustrations.

News of a microwave radiation bombardment of the U.S. Embassy in Moscow leaked through the diplomatic community in Moscow in early February 1976 after the U.S. ambassador warned his staff of the possible danger to health of the radiation. This article explains that the purpose of the radiation was probably to activate electronic eavesdropping devices planted in the embassy by Soviet intelligence.

Rogers, Warren, Jr. "'Bugged' Eagle is Prize Exhibit in Anti-Spy 'Chamber of Horrors'." WASHINGTON POST, 27 May 1960, p. A1. Illustrations.

An account of a replica of the Great Seal of the United States displayed by UN Ambassador Henry Cabot Lodge in the Security Council. The Seal had been bugged by the Soviets to pick up conversations in the U.S. Embassy in Moscow. Rogers goes on to state that the replica was only one item of this nature that had been uncovered by counterespionage and security electronic specialists and were kept in the State Department's "Chamber of Horrors."

Szulc, Tad. "Warsaw Embassy of U.S. Is Bugged." NEW YORK TIMES, 3 November 1964, p. 1. Illustrations.

A report of a State Department announcement that a complete microphone system had been detected in the new building of the U.S. Embassy in Warsaw. The account continues with a description of detection of some forty microphones in the U.S. Embassy in Moscow--partially on the basis of information provided by a KGB defector.

C. MEMOIRS

Huminik, John. DOUBLE AGENT. New York: New American Library, 1967. 181 p. Illustrations, index.

The memoirs of metallurgical specialist John Huminik's six years as a spy for the USSR and counterspy for the FBI. DOUBLE AGENT is written in a low-key manner and is one of the best accounts of agent and double agent handling available. As such it is a valuable supplement to Christopher Felix's A SHORT COURSE IN THE SECRET WAR. For main entry, see chapter 10, section A.

Morros, Boris, as told to Charles Samuels. MY TEN YEARS AS A COUNTER-SPY. New York: Viking Press, 1959. 248 p.

Samuels tells of Morros's recruitment by Soviet espionage in 1936 to provide jobs and fronts for other agents. In 1947 he volunteered as a double agent for the FBI and continued this part until 1957. As a double agent Morros worked with an espionage network which included Jacob Albam, Jack and Myra Soble, Albert and Martha Dodd Stern, and Jane and George Zlatovski--all of whom were indicted for espionage.

Philbrick, Herbert A. I LED THREE LIVES: CITIZEN, "COMMUNIST," COUNTER-SPY. New York: McGraw-Hill, 1952. 323 p. Index, three brief appendices.

The memoirs of a Boston advertising salesman who in 1940 organized a youth group only to find it was secretly controlled by young Communists. After discussions with the FBI, he continued to uncover Communist front organizations and maneuvers until 1949 when he appeared in the open as a government witness to testify against eleven alleged party conspirators, four of whom knew Philbrick as a dedicated member of the Communist inner circle.

Pinto, Oreste. FRIEND OR FOE. New York: G.P. Putnam's Sons, 1953. 245 p. No index. British ed. London: Laurie, 1953. 197 p.

In this second book of his adventures as a counterespionage expert, Pinto has selected for description four cases which best exemplify the difficulties encountered by a counterespionage operative in discerning the truth from a mass of conflicting information, evidence, and theory. Pinto classes two of the four cases as his most difficult in more than thirty years experience in counterespionage; the other two as having unusual qualities that bear on technique and method. An introductory chapter details the methods of escape used by the bulk of the refugees from Occupied Europe. Pinto gathered material for this chapter while he was chief examiner at the refugee center in England at the beginning of World War II. The art of escape forms the background for the four cases selected for exposition and discussion.

_____. SPY CATCHER. New York: Harper & Bros., 1952. 213 p. No index.

A unique first-hand description of the techniques and methods of counterespionage in real-life action during World War II. Pinto, a native of Holland, began his counterespionage career in World War I serving in Belgium, Holland, France, and Italy. When World War II broke out, he was called to duty in England to screen refugees from the continent to detect attempts to bring German espionage agents into England. He was later transferred to the Dutch counterintelligence mission attached to the Supreme Headquarters, Allied Expeditionary Forces, and during the Normandy invasion supervised counterintelligence and security of the armies moving through France and Belgium into Holland. In each of nine chapters Pinto uses an actual case on which he worked to illustrate different aspects of successful counterespionage.

Sansom, Alfred William. I SPIED SPIES. London: Harrap, 1965. 271 p. Illustrated.

The memoirs of a British wartime security officer in Cairo.

Schwarzelder, John. WE CAUGHT SPIES. New York: Duell, Sloan and Pearce, 1946. xii, 296 p.

Following an introduction praising the work of the U.S. Army Counterintelligence Corps (CIC), the author, a former CIC operative himself, devotes twenty-seven chapters to illustrative vignettes and case studies, mainly of counterespionage activity, followed by a chapter on the need for an effective peacetime intelligence agency. "Counterespionage," the author states, "is the art of catching spies," and he proceeds to tell how the army built from scratch to do this job.

D. COUNTERESPIONAGE NETWORKS OR OPERATIONS

Two outstanding counterespionage operations have been selected for inclusion in this section. The Double-Cross System, operated by British counterintelligence, and operation North Pole, a radio deception operation conducted by the counterintelligence arm of German military intelligence (Abwehr).

1. The Double-Cross System

The Double-Cross System was the coordinated use of about 120 German espionage agents who were doubled by British counterespionage (M.I.5) for the purpose of controlling German intelligence in England. They collected information on Germany, and manipulated the information provided to Berlin through these doubled agents. Of the total of 120 Double-Cross System agents, 39 were of great importance in providing planned and coordinated misinformation that helped convince German intelligence that the main thrust of the Allied invasion of Europe would be directed toward the Pas de Calais rather than Normandy. This operation thus stands as one of the most successful strategic deceptions of World War II. The "official" and best version of the operation is given in Sir John C. Masterman's THE DOUBLE-CROSS SYSTEM IN THE WAR OF 1939 TO 1945, but related books which amplify parts of the system are also listed below.

Delmar, Sefton. THE COUNTERFEIT SPY. New York: Harper, 1971. 256 p. British ed. London: Hutchinson, 1973. 256 p. Index.

A well-constructed account of the Double-Cross System by a former British foreign office employee and journalist. The counterfeit spy was a Spaniard who built up several fictitious or "national" networks of German spies against England. The British awarded him the M.B.E. (Member of the British Empire) for his work as a double agent of the Double-Cross System.

Masterman, John C. THE DOUBLE-CROSS SYSTEM IN THE WAR OF 1939 TO 1945. Foreword by Norman Holmes Pearson. New Haven, Conn.: Yale University Press, 1972. xxi, 203 p. Index, appendices.

Almost all German agents of any importance who penetrated Great Britain during World War II were captured, converted into double agents, and worked under the control of M.I.5, sending fictitious reports back to Germany and diverting German attention from Normandy to the Pas de Calais before the invasion of June 1944. The classified report on this operation was written in 1945 by Sir John Masterman, who has since become an Oxford historian, to ensure that the experience and expertise acquired would not be slots. The Official Secrets Act was waived to permit publication of the report as a book in 1971-72. In addition to a description and evaluation of the strategic deception involved, the author makes a number of pertinent observations on the care and handling of double agents, the necessity for planning and coordination, and the potential value of espionage and counterespionage in time of war. In a prepublication interview Masterman stated: "The Secret Service gets blackguarded all over the place. I have wanted this book published to improve what nowadays is called its image. Germany had no spies here during the war who were not under our control. The building up of these people was a matter of years. We started with counterespionage and went on to intelligence and from that to deception" (NEW YORK TIMES, 14 November 1971).

Owen, Frank. THE EDDIE CHAPMAN STORY. New York: Julian Messner, 1954. viii, 245 p.

Eddie Chapman was "Zigzag" of the British Double-Cross System who, as a German agent, was supposed to conduct sabotage of the war industry in England as well as to collect information on anti-U-boat devices and night fighter radio location devices. After selling his services to Germany he was taken to France for training in sabotage, and later parachuted into England with instructions to sabotage the De Haviland bomber plant. Turning himself over to the British, this convicted ex-safecracker became a member of the Double-Cross System and returned to Germany for a hero's reception—and another mission to England. Chapman, with Owen's help, attempted to publish his story, but ran afoul of the British Official Secrets Act. This version, published in America, is a compilation of Chapman and Owen's work plus the research of George Voigt, London correspondent of TIME magazine, commissioned by the publishers to ferret out and fill in the censored portions of the original work. In the foreword to Masterman's book (above), ex-OSS operative and Yale University professor of literature Norman Holmes Pearson states: "The same sort of amplification [of the Double-Cross System] can be done, though less confidently, with Eddie Chapman's own account of himself as 'Zigzag,' the saboteur (he was known as 'Fritzchen' to his German employers), in THE EDDIE CHAPMAN STORY (1954)."

Popov, Dusko. SPY/COUNTERSPY. New York: Grosset & Dunlap, 1974. 339 p. No index.

In this autobiography Dusko Popov describes his double agent activities as "Ivan" for German intelligence and "Tricycle" for the British Double-Cross System. As the son of a wealthy Yugoslav family, educated in France and Germany, he was recruited by German intelligence at the insistence of a former classmate who was himself an anti-Nazi who had joined German intelligence to undermine the war effort. Upon arrival in England Popov went to the British and began work as a double agent for M.I.5 (counterespionage)--but worked for M.I.6 (espionage) as well, and made numerous trips to German intelligence headquarters in Lisbon and Madrid. He also operated in the United States for German intelligence. An appendix in Masterman's book (cited above) contains the intelligence requirements on America which the Germans had furnished Popov in microdot form.

2. Operation Nordpol (North Pole)

In the North Pole operation, the counterespionage element (section 3) of German military intelligence (Abwehr) captured and neutralized all British Special Operations Executive (SOE) operatives dropped into Holland for a two-year period. Beginning with the detection of a radio and the capture of its operator, German counterespionage was successful in turning the link and building the penetration to a point where, at varying times, they controlled as many as fourteen radio links between the Dutch underground and London. Fifty-four agents were intercepted and captured, and quantities of weapons and explosives intended for the Dutch underground were confiscated. The controversy over precisely what happened and who was to blame for the disaster has been the subject of several books and articles. The most important of these are listed below.

Dourlein, Peter. INSIDE NORTH POLE: A SECRET AGENT'S STORY. Translated by F.G. Renier and Anne Cliff. London: Kimber, 1954. 206 p.

The author was one of the SOE operatives parachuted into Holland and captured by North Pole counterespionage agents. The book also contains chapters on the SOE's training of its operatives and on its escape lines.

Ganier-Raymond, Phillipe. THE TANGLED WEB. Translated by Len Ortzen. New York: Pantheon Books; London: Barker, 1968. 203 p. Index.

An interesting account of the controversial North Pole operation in which the author charges the deaths of scores to the ineptness of British SOE officials who never learned, or learned too late, that radio messages from agents in Holland were controlled by German counterespionage. This book raises more questions than it answers.

Giskes, Herman J. LONDON CALLING NORTH POLE. New York: British Book Center, 1953. vi, 208 p. Glossary of terms, no index. British ed. London: Kimber, 1953. 208 p.

The best and most comprehensive account of the North Pole operation by the former chief of German military counterespionage in Holland, Belgium, and northern France and the man who set up the operation and directed it. Interesting expose of techniques of counterespionage and the handling of a large, controlled network. Discusses the lengths to which the Abwehr went to instill British confidence in the controlled network and to allay suspicions by operating "courier routes" through which Allied airmen and unimportant information were allowed to filter into England. Includes an epilogue by the author which touches on the conflicts between the military intelligence (Abwehr) and the political intelligence and police arms of the Nazi operated Reichssicherheitshauptamt. Another epilogue by Lt. H.M.G. Lauwers, a Dutch SOE operative trained in England who was captured and operated a controlled radio link, explains how he came to act under Abwehr direction and the means he took to warn British intelligence that he was controlled. An outstanding book on a model counterespionage operation.

Part IV
COVERT OPERATIONS

No bibliography on intelligence agencies and operations would be complete without a section covering the wide range of clandestine or secret political actions which have come to be called "covert operations" in the post-World War II period. All these interchangeable terms have been used to describe the "strategic services" carried out during World War II by the British Special Operations Executive (SOE) and its American counterpart, the Office of Strategic Services (OSS). Great Britain's wartime leader, Prime Minister Winston Churchill, created the Special Operations Executive not only in order to collect intelligence, but mainly "to set Europe ablaze." Both the SOE and the OSS supported resistance movements in Nazi-occupied Europe which conducted widespread sabotage using guerrilla tactics. Inevitably these operations took on political overtones both in terms of the long-range foreign policy objectives of the sponsoring powers and in the effect they had on domestic political struggles within the occupied countries.

Covert operations may be defined as intervention by any state in the internal affairs of another in order to extend political influence and control, and in time of war to hasten the military defeat of the target state. Since all such operations are hostile by definition, they can only be conducted secretly by agencies which have personnel trained in the use of traditional espionage and counterespionage techniques. For this reason they are usually directed by a clandestine operations division of a national intelligence or security police agency, or by a combination of such agencies. Secret political actions are "sensitive" because if they are exposed or "blown" an international crisis or scandal may easily result, since no government officially admits that it has been intervening in the internal affairs of other states. For example, the United States was deeply embarrassed by the CIA-led Bay of Pigs fiasco in the spring of 1961.

Nevertheless, in addition to being an "intelligence arm of the president," (in the sense that it collects information by clandestine means on a large scale), the CIA has also in practice carried out a wide range of covert operations. It has secretly intervened in a number of trouble spots or crises to extend U.S. influence and control and to thwart real or imaginary Communist seizures of power during the cold war. Its director during this period, the late Allen

Dulles, regarded such operations as an integral part of the "cold war mission" of the agency. In the 1960s American intervention in Vietnam and the rest of Southeast Asia usually began with secret CIA-controlled missions and later escalated above the covert threshold into open intervention and military forms of warfare. It is this role of the CIA which has given rise to much sharp criticism, both at home and abroad, and this criticism is reflected in many of the works listed in this section. In spite of their importance in international relations, there are very few theoretical or even descriptive works dealing with the subject of covert operations as an instrument of foreign policy. These are listed and annotated in chapter 16, "General Works and Surveys." Guerrilla and revolutionary warfare frequently begin as covert operations either directed by clandestine intelligence services or dependent on them for vital information on which to base their operations. However, the enormous literature on guerrilla warfare and insurgency has been excluded from this bibliography, since it is a separate field in itself. For the same reason both Soviet and Western partisan warfare and resistance movements during World War I have also been excluded, although the direction of such movements was clandestine.

Certain political-military deception operations were of strategic importance during World War II. They were mounted by a variety of intelligence agencies, and since they were conducted clandestinely, properly belong to the category of covert operations. A special subsection lists the most important works dealing with these operations as individual cases, such as the strategic deception which accompanied German planning for the attack on the Soviet Union (Barbarossa) or the so-called Double-Cross System by which British intelligence captured and controlled for strategic deception all important German agents infiltrated into Great Britain during the period.

Wartime political-military deception has its counterpart in times of peace. A wide variety of techniques are employed for both domestic and foreign political or "political warfare" purposes, ranging from calculated leaks of false or misleading information to the press to the forging of books and documents which are then exploited through the news media. These operations are usually conducted by the clandestine services divisions of central intelligence agencies by special sections which for convenience are labelled "disinformation" agencies. Although the general field of political warfare and deception is excluded from this bibliography, chapter 21, "Disinformation, Deception, Frauds, and Forgeries," lists some of the more important works dealing with this form of covert operations.

In spite of continuous and in some cases escalating use of covert operations as an instrument of foreign policy by the major powers since World War II, there has been a dearth of scholarly or systematic studies in this area, with the exception of the general works previously listed. Almost everything written on the subject has been confined to books or articles dealing with CIA or Soviet agencies, usually in the form of sensational exposes produced for cold war purposes. In the case of the CIA there have also been a number of books or articles which carry on the self-serving tradition of Allen Dulles's THE CRAFT OF INTELLIGENCE (see chapter 4, section A). In one of these both espionage and covert operations are lumped together under the confusing and dissembling title of "overseas operations." For example, see chapter 4, "Overseas Operations," in Lyman Kirkpatrick's THE U.S. INTELLIGENCE COMMUNITY (cited in chapter 5, section A). The best single source of documentation concerning U.S. covert operations in the Vietnam War remains THE PENTAGON PAPERS (see chapter 5, section A). There are, of course, scattered references through the voluminous secondary literature on the war in Vietnam which is beyond the scope of this specialized bibliography.

Chapter 16

GENERAL WORKS AND SURVEYS

Bailey, Geoffrey [pseud.]. THE CONSPIRATORS. New York: Harper, 1960. 306 p. Notes, glossary, bibliography, index.

Geoffrey Bailey is reportedly the pseudonym of a former Russian-language interpreter at the United Nations. His work is a sensational journalistic account of Soviet covert operations in Western Europe in the period between World War I and II. It deals with the so-called Trust, the kidnappings of Generals Kutyepov and Miller in Paris in the 1930s, and finally with the Tukhachevsky affair. His thesis is that Marshal Tukhachevsky was guilty of a plot to overthrow Stalin in collaboration with certain German generals. The author uses such spurious sources as the well-known forgery attributed to former Soviet foreign minister M. Litvinov, NOTES FOR A DIARY (New York: Morrow, 1955). As a result, THE CONSPIRATORS should be used with extreme caution, since it is basically a political warfare product of the cold war period rather than a historical source.

Blackstock, Paul W. "Covert Military Operations." In HANDBOOK OF MILITARY INSTITUTIONS, edited by Roger W. Little, pp. 455-92. Beverly Hills, Calif.: Sage Publications, 1971. Notes and references. Prepared for the Inter-university Seminar on Armed Forces and Society.

The author extends the theory of covert political action to military operations with particular attention to U.S. intervention in Southeast Asia and Vietnam. Topics discussed include political warfare and foreign policy, the cold war heritage, the post-cold war period, revolution and the third world, covert operations, escalation and deescalation, operational techniques.

. THE SECRET ROAD TO WORLD WAR II: SOVIET VERSUS WESTERN INTELLIGENCE, 1921-1939. Chicago: Quadrangle, 1969. 384 p. Notes, index, dramatis personae.

A detailed historical survey of competing Western and Soviet covert operations for the period, based on primary source materials, in-

terviews with survivors, and some previously untapped archives..
Part 1 deals with the Trust, a counterrevolutionary organization
controlled by Soviet security agencies and used to penetrate Western emigre groups and to disseminate false information to Western
intelligence channels. Part 2 deals with the covert operations of
Western-controlled emigre organizations in the USSR, a series of
penetrations which lent substance to the 1927 war scare. Part 3
concerns Soviet-directed operations against Western targets, including the kidnappings of Generals Kutyepov and Miller in Paris.
Part 4 deals with the Tukhachevsky affair which led to the purge
of Russian generals on the eve of World War II.

_____. THE STRATEGY OF SUBVERSION: MANIPULATING THE POLITICS
OF OTHER NATIONS. Chicago: Quadrangle, 1964. 351 p. Index, notes.

The first scholarly survey of the entire field of secret political
operations abroad including international propaganda or psychological warfare, assassinations, sabotage, intelligence and counterintelligence, insurgency and counterinsurgency. Also an analytical study which reviews the role of the CIA in covert operations
and questions the value of this method in achieving foreign policy
objectives. An important reference; one which tends to separate,
for inspection, the functions of foreign intelligence and covert
operations performed by intelligence agencies.

_____, ed. "Intelligence and Covert Operations: Changing Doctrine and
Practice." Columbia: University of South Carolina, Department of Government and International Studies, December 1973. 125 p. Mimeographed.

Sets forth the results of a "Confidential Intelligence Questionnaire"
circulated among a group of intelligence aides experienced in key
posts at the working level within the U.S. system. Part 2, pages
49-75 deal specifically with covert operations.

Borosage, Robert L., and Marks, John D., eds. THE CIA FILE. New York:
Grossman/Viking, 1976. 236 p.

For two days in the fall of 1974 journalists, scholars, and former
CIA officers met in Washington, D.C., under the auspices of the
Center for National Security Studies, to discuss the way CIA con-
ducts its covert operations. Edited by Borosage, director of the
center, and Marks, coauthor of THE CIA AND THE CULT OF IN-
TELLIGENCE (cited below), the book contains some of the proceedings of the conference in the form of essays. Former CIA Director William E. Colby's rebuttal to the proceedings is included.
In general the essays charge the CIA with damaging the best interests of the nation through its secret political operations.

Copeland, Miles. THE GAME OF NATIONS. New York: Simon & Schuster,
1969. 272 p. Index, appendix, suggested reading list.

A first-hand account by a former CIA official of U.S. intervention in the Middle East from the 1952 Nasser coup d'etat in Egypt
to the Arab-Israeli Six-Day War of June 1967. The author explains the title of his book as follows: "[The] Game of Nations
is what this book is about. . . . It is intended to reveal general
truths about the relations between great powers and those small
powers which, by techniques such as those of Egypt's President
Nasser, are able to gain international influence out of all proportion to their inherent strengths--and even, at times, to win diplomatic victories over one or another of the Great Powers."

Cottam, Richard W. COMPETITIVE INTERFERENCE AND TWENTIETH-CENTURY
DEMOCRACY. Pittsburgh: University of Pittsburgh Press, 1967. 243 p. Index.

An attempt to provide a theoretical base for analyzing foreign intervention short of war during the cold war. The author argues
that the CIA should not be precluded "from direct participation
in the formulation and execution of American foreign policy," and
that "if the CIA is to be effective in the more clandestine aspects
of diplomacy, it must be granted a good deal of freedom to inter-
pret and to improvise upon stated general policy."

Elliot-Bateman, Michael, ed. INTELLIGENCE, SUBVERSION, RESISTANCE.
The Fourth Dimension of Warfare, vol. 1. New York: Praeger Publishers,
1970. 181 p. Bibliography.

The book consists of a series of lectures at the University of Man-
chester in 1967 by practitioners and theoreticians in the special
operations field. The evolution of political war is described where
cultural, social, and economic factors--constituting the fourth dimension of warfare--bear heavily on victory or defeat. The ag-
gressive use of intelligence and subversion is emphasized and explained.

Marchetti, Victor, and Marks, John D. THE CIA AND THE CULT OF INTEL-
LIGENCE. New York: Knopf, 1974. xxi, 398 p. Index, appendix.

Marchetti, a fourteen-year veteran who held various positions in
the CIA including the position of executive assistant to the deputy
director, and Marks, a former State Department intelligence analyst, have combined their experience and knowledge to disclose
familiar and new details of the CIA's operations since the early
1950s. The authors contend that since by the mid-1950s the outlook for successful espionage against the security barriers of the
USSR was somewhat gloomy, and since the U-2 was already on
the drawing boards as a means of high-altitude photographic pene-
tration--a means of collection the authors conclude is expensive
but worthwhile--the CIA changed the priorities of its clandestine
services from espionage to covert political action and paramilitary

operations as a direct weapon of the emerging cold war against the USSR, and an indirect one through operations against the USSR in the Third World countries. Marchetti and Marks provide fresh details on a number of covert operations and especially on the activities essential to the support of such operations. Some espionage operations are also described, plus an analysis of overall intelligence activities by function, organization, and budget. The publication of the book met with substantial opposition from the CIA and was printed before the final legal decisions on censorship were made. It appeared with 168 blanks varying in length from a few words to entire paragraphs. Another annotation for this book emphasizing the unique secrecy aspects is provided in chapter 8, section A.

Rositzke, Harry. "America's Secret Operations: A Perspective." FOREIGN AFFAIRS 53 (January 1975): 334-50.

An authoritative historical review by a former high-level CIA official of the agency's clandestine services from 1947 through the Kennedy-Johnson administrations. Rositzke argues convincingly that psychological warfare operations "not only do not belong in secret service, but . . . should be discontinued," that "a secret intelligence service is not the most suitable vehicle for running paramilitary operations," which should "be transferred to Defense." If this were done, Rositzke favors creation of "a separate truly secret service . . . a small elite professional service devoted exclusively to recruiting high-level agents against carefully selected long-term strategic targets." The present operations Directorate of the CIA "would continue to function abroad on a reduced scale and with a more innocuous mission: to maintain liaison with local security and intelligence services, to protect the agency from hostile penetration, to handle agent or defector walk-ins," with the CIA station chief acting as "the Ambassador's overall assistant in intelligence matters." Following these proposed reforms the CIA "would, above all, continue to focus on its main central function --to give the White House intelligence estimates on situations and trends abroad that are as objective as men can make them." See also the annotation for this article in chapter 7, section B.

Scott, Andrew M. THE REVOLUTION IN STATECRAFT: INFORMAL PENETRATION. New York: Random House, 1965. v, 193 p. Notes, selected readings, index.

An attempt to provide a theoretical base to be used for justifying covert operations. In the chapter "The Revolution in American Statecraft," the author argues that "the interest of the United States dictates the continuation of covert activities as long as the nation is engaged in severe information conflict with the Soviet Union and Communist China. These operations should be screened more closely and perceptively in the future, however, than they have been in the past."

Chapter 17

SOE—THE BRITISH SPECIAL OPERATIONS EXECUTIVE

The British Special Operations Executive (SOE) was a World War II hybrid of various organizations which soon gained its independence and was given the primary mission of "setting Europe ablaze" by means of sabotage, subversion, guerrilla warfare, and the creation and supply of resistance movements in occupied countries. All these activities were to be carried out in a clandestine nature and their success depended in large part on intelligence collection either by the SOE itself or by cooperating intelligence agencies. Thus was forged a war-fighting organization to use all means other than conventional armed forces. Its war fighting and its intelligence activities became very nearly indistinguishable, and the pattern for postwar covert operations by an intelligence-organization was established.

In an unprecedented move the British government in the mid-1960s opened up its archives to a former intelligence staff officer (but not from SOE), M.R.D. Foot, making it possible for him to write a scholarly, definitive history, SOE IN FRANCE. Possibly the reason for this move was that two unofficial histories were being written, one of them critical of SOE. In addition numerous memoirs had already appeared, some of them sketchy and self-serving. By contrast, the archives of the Office of Strategic Services (OSS), the American counterpart of SOE, have remained closed until recently (1976) and only secondary sources have been available. In this chapter the few general works available on the SOE are listed, followed by a section which lists selected memoirs and biographies.

A. GENERAL WORKS

Foot, Michael Richard Daniel. SOE IN FRANCE; AN ACCOUNT OF THE WORK OF THE BRITISH SPECIAL OPERATIONS EXECUTIVE IN FRANCE. 1940-1944. History of the Second World War. London: Her Majesty's Stationery Office, 1966. xxiii, 550 p. Notes, bibliography, index, maps, table of dates, illustrations.

> An astonishing volume of the history of World War II series. This is a definitive work, and the only historical source of its kind in

the area of covert and special operations. It begins with the
story of the origins of SOE, its recruiting and training procedures,
network communications, and field security procedures. Part 2
deals with the various operations of SOE in France. The various
appendices list operational networks or "circuits" which when combined with the index are indispensable for identification of personalities involved and their operational code names. A special
appendix is devoted to the women who served in SOE. The bibliography is especially useful since entries that are memoirs of
SOE agents are rated as to authenticity. The author is an Oxford
historian and was an intelligence staff officer during World War II.

Spiro, Edward [Edward H. Cookridge]. SET EUROPE ABLAZE. New York:
Thomas Y. Crowell, 1967. vii, 410 p. Notes, index, glossary, bibliography,
illustrations.

An unofficial but extensive history of the SOE by a prolific writer
on intelligence activities and a former intelligence officer. Although denied access to official SOE records, the author spent six
years in research for this history and found that most relevant files
on SOE were available for his inspection in the archives of other
nations. The author cites these primary sources in his extensive
bibliography. Especially valuable when used with Foot (see above).
The author was critical of some of the decisions taken in SOE
and as a result met resistance in obtaining clearance from British
security authorities for publication of the book.

Sweet-Escott, Bickham. BAKER STREET IRREGULAR. London: Methuen, 1965.
278 p.

The first general survey of the activities of the SOE to be published. Part general history and part memoir, this book was written by a senior staff officer of the SOE. Provides insights into
the headquarters and policy levels of the organization. Authentic
and interesting; should be used in conjunction with Foot and Spiro
(see above).

B. MEMOIRS AND BIOGRAPHIES

Buckmaster, Maurice James. SPECIALLY EMPLOYED: THE STORY OF BRIT-
ISH AID TO FRENCH PATRIOTS OF THE RESISTANCE. London: Batchworth,
1952. 200 p.

The memoirs of the man who was chief of F Section (French) of
the SOE. Covers aspects of the organization of the resistance
along with some information on resistance tradecraft and on some
individual agents of F Section. The author admits in his preface
that some of the incidents described are not completely factually
accurate.

_____. THEY FOUGHT ALONE: THE STORY OF BRITISH AGENTS IN FRANCE. London: Odhams, 1958. 255 p. American ed. New York: W.W. Norton, 1958. 255 p. Illustrations.

Further memoirs by the one-time chief of F Section of the SOE. No claim to accuracy is claimed in this later book (see also entry for Buckmaster, above). Compilation of case histories with details on resistance tradecraft.

Butler, Ewan. AMATEUR AGENT. London: Harrap, 1963. 240 p. American ed. New York: W.W. Norton, 1964. 240 p. Index, illustrations.

AMATEUR AGENT is the author's account of his six years with the SOE and British intelligence. He was in charge of the SOE's G Section (German), stationed first in Cairo and later in Stockholm. Butler was a journalist before working for the SOE, and his account is useful and interesting. He was responsible for propaganda, harassment, and sabotage operations. His account is especially useful as a source of details on training in the SOE.

Carre, Mathilde-Lily. I WAS THE CAT. Translated by Mervyn Savill. London: Souvenir Press, 1960. 223 p. Illustrations.

Autobiography of the double agent "Victoire." Member of the Interallie network, her efforts provided detailed information on German troop movements and on strategic bombing targets. Outmaneuvered by Abwehr counterespionage.

Churchill, Peter. DUEL OF WITS. London: Hodder, 1957. 368 p.

An account of an SOE agent's mission to France to encourage the resistance movements, and supply them with explosives, arms, and tradecraft.

_____. THE SPIRIT IN THE CAGE. London: Hodder, 1954. 251 p. American ed. New York: G.P. Putnam's Sons, 1955. 312 p. Appendix (dramatis personae), map.

The account of Churchill's mission to France where in 1943 he and his courier Odette were betrayed to Italian authorities by a trusted member of the French resistance. The account describes the two years in various prisons after having been turned over to the Germans.

Cowburn, Benjamin. NO CLOAK, NO DAGGER. London: Jarrolds, 1960. 192 p. Illustrations.

Accurate and detailed descriptions of SOE agent activities in occupied and unoccupied France, including details of air drops, line crossing techniques, network communications, and rendezvous techniques. Cowburn was with the Tinker network.

Fuller, Jean Overton. DOUBLE WEBS, LIGHT ON SECRET AGENT'S WAR IN FRANCE. London: Putnam, 1958. 256 p.

> An investigation into the career of Dericourt of the Farrier network of F Section. The Germans were aware of the activities of this network and questions arose as to loyalties of network members. Dericourt was tried after the war and acquitted. The author, on the basis of evidence obtained from others, affirms the innocence of Dericourt. Some inaccuracies.

_____. THE GERMAN PENETRATION OF SOE: FRANCE 1941-1944. London: Kimber, 1975. 192 p. Index, bibliography, illustrations.

> A compilation of past works, with new information added.

_____. MADELEINE, THE STORY OF NOOR INAYAT KHAN, GEORGE CROSS, M.B.E., CROIX DE GUERRE WITH GOLD STAR. Foreword by Selwyn Jepson. London: Gollancz, 1952. 192 p. Illustrated.

> The biography of Noor Inayat Khan, a member of the Phono network of F Section. Khan was captured by the Germans and was forced to "play back" her radio in a deception game. Money, arms, and men were dropped to this penetrated circuit despite attempts by the operator of the radio to warn London.

Garby-Czerniawski, Roman. THE BIG NETWORK. London: Ronald, 1961. 248 p. Illustrations.

> The author was the chief of the Interallie intelligence-gathering network, and he describes the actual activities of the network. Should be used also as a basis for assessing accuracy of Mathilde Carre's book I WAS THE CAT (see above).

Haukelid, Knut Anders. SKIES AGAINST THE ATOM. Translated by F.H. Lyon. London: Kimber, 1954. 201 p. Illustrations, maps, portraits.

> Recounts the SOE-directed operations against the Norwegian hydrogen electrolysis plant that was providing heavy water to Germany for atomic weapons experiments. See also Sanderson's "The A-Bomb That Never Was" in BEHIND ENEMY LINES (chapter 10, section A). The book contains an introduction describing the nature of SOE activities by Sir Colin Gubbins, early architect of SOE and later its executive director.

Howarth, Patrick, ed. SPECIAL OPERATIONS. London: Routledge and Paul, 1955. 239 p. Biographical notes, illustrations.

> Contains chapters from other books on the SOE and the French resistance.

Marshall, Bruce, from the story told him by F.F.E. Yeo-Thomas. THE WHITE RABBIT. London: Evans, 1952. 262 p. American ed. Boston: Houghton Mifflin, 1953. 262 p. Index, illustrations.

The factual account of the SOE missions of Wing Commander F.F.E. Yeo-Thomas in France. Yeo-Thomas was a member of RF Section of SOE, the French section that worked closely with General de Gaulle's Bureau Central de Renseignements et d'Action (BCRA). The Book provides some details on the operational and political problems experienced in collaborating with the French in London and with the French resistance. The author dwells on some of the gruesome aspects of Yeo-Thomas's capture and imprisonment.

Nicholas, Elizabeth. DEATH BE NOT PROUD. London: Cresset Press, 1958. 294 p. Index, appendices, illustrations.

A painful account of the fate of seven women purportedly executed after being detected by a penetration of the SOE's F Section network PROSPER.

Psychoundakis, George. THE CRETAN RUNNER. Translated, with an introduction by Patrick Leigh Fermor. Notes by Xan Fielding. London: Murray, 1955. xi, 242 p. American ed. New York: Panther Books, 1957. 160 p.

An excellent memoir written by an SOE courier during the German occupation of the Greek island of Crete. Both the translator and Fielding were also SOE agents in Greece.

Seth, Ronald. A SPY HAS NO FRIENDS. London: Deutsch, 1952. 206 p. American ed. New York: Library Publishers, 1954. 206 p.

The recollections of an SOE agent who was captured by the Germans while on a mission to Estonia to sabotage shale oil mines that had been rehabilitated and were producing 300 tons a day to fuel the German armor on the Leningrad front. The author also had intelligence collection missions since it was not expected that he would be able to return to Britain after his sabotage attempt. He made his captors believe he was pro-Nazi and finally was trained in the intelligence branch of the Luftwaffe for espionage missions.

Vomecourt, Phillippe de. WHO LIVED TO SEE THE DAY; FRANCE IN ARMS 1940–45. Foreword by Lord Arthur Tedder. London: Hutchinson, 1961. 288 p. Illustrations. American ed. AN ARM OF AMATEURS. Garden City, N.Y.: Doubleday, 1961. 307 p. Illustrations.

A colorful account of the activities of the de Vomecourt brothers in developing the Autogiro network of F Section and the subsequent capture of brother Pierre. Phillippe details his own later activities in developing the resistance in the unoccupied zone of France and in the areas of Limousin, Berry, and south Normandy.

Chapter 18

OSS—THE U.S. OFFICE OF STRATEGIC SERVICES

Until recently (1976) historians and political scientists have been denied access to the OSS archives so that there is no comprehensive work on the OSS comparable to Foot's book on the British SOE, SOE IN FRANCE (see chapter 17, section A). The CIA is the custodian of the OSS files and recently, under the terms of the Freedom of Information Act, has made some documents available to authors preparing books on the OSS. The CIA declassified, in 1976, the War Report of the Office of Strategic Services (see Anthony Cave Brown's THE SECRET WAR REPORT OF THE OSS, below), and in another case the CIA has released more than 200 documents to an ex-OSS member who is writing about his experiences in Hanoi. Brown's THE SECRET WAR REPORT OF THE OSS and Richard Harris Smith's OSS: THE SECRET HISTORY OF AMERICA'S FIRST CENTRAL INTELLIGENCE AGENCY are the standouts in authoritative and helpful OSS literature. Much of the remainder consists of memoirs or accounts of individual episodes or adventures.

A. GENERAL WORKS

Alsop, Stewart, and Braden, Thomas. SUB ROSA: THE OSS AND AMERICAN ESPIONAGE. New York: Reynal and Hitchcock, 1946. 237 p. Reprint. New York: Harcourt, Brace & World, 1964. 264 p.

> An early book on OSS activities by two journalists who themselves were OSS members who served with the French resistance. The book begins with a description of how the OSS developed; the remainder is divided into two parts: The first is a description of three operations that illustrate the intelligence roles of OSS. The second part describes four operations that illustrate the resistance or paramilitary operations of OSS. The book is replete with characterizations of OSS members. The reprint edition contains a postscript by Alsop in which he describes the evolution of the CIA from the OSS and provides interesting insights into the personalities that guided the CIA in the years 1947 to 1964.

Asprey, Robert B. WAR IN THE SHADOWS; THE GUERRILLA IN HISTORY. Vol. 1. Garden City, N.Y.: Doubleday, 1975. xxxv, 665 p. Bibliography, maps.

This extensively researched and well written work on guerrilla warfare is included because it contains extensive material on the activities of OSS in support of resistance movements in both the European and Pacific theaters of operation in World War II. The book also contains important references to the activities of the British SOE in Europe and the Far East and the relationships of the OSS and SOE. Included are references to the problems that existed between rival intelligence agencies (the French for example) and the SOE and the OSS. See especially chapters 31 through 50.

Brown, Anthony Cave, ed. THE SECRET WAR REPORT OF THE OSS. Introduction by Anthony Cave Brown. New York: Berkley Publishing, 1976. 572 p. Bibliography, glossary, maps, organization chart, illustrations, paperback.

The war report of the Office of Strategic Services was prepared under the direction of Kermit Roosevelt, war-time member of the OSS, during the period 1946-48. The report was retained at a secret security information level within the files of the CIA until its declassification in 1976. Anthony Cave Brown, author of BODYGUARD OF LIES (see chapter 21, section B), edited the report and added additional material, made comments, and provided explanations and names where names were omitted in the report. The first two chapters of the book describe in detail the origins of the OSS and its organization and structure. The remaining nineteen chapters describe the operations of the OSS in various parts of the world. The last chapter describes the activities of OSS in post-war Europe and thus provides an indirect insight into some of the initial movements of the CIA which built on OSS contacts. The introduction includes valuable comments on the OSS-British intelligence relationships during 1941-45, and on some of the best intelligence and counterintelligence literature of the period.

Ford, Corey, and McBain, Alistair. CLOAK AND DAGGER: THE SECRET STORY OF THE OSS. New York: Random House, 1946. 216 p.

A mildly sensationalized early account of the activities of the OSS.

Hymoff, Edward. THE OSS IN WORLD WAR II. New York: Ballantine Books, 1972. 405 p. Paperbound. Index, bibliography, glossary, notes.

A history of OSS activities and operations in Europe and the Far East by a journalist and author of four military unit histories (two marine corps and two army) of the Vietnam War. The author was a member of the OSS during operations in Italy, Greece, and Yugoslavia and supplemented his personal knowledge with interviews with former OSS members. Comprehensive and readable, with good bibliography and notes.

Smith, Richard Harris. OSS: THE SECRET HISTORY OF AMERICA'S FIRST
CENTRAL INTELLIGENCE AGENCY. Berkeley and Los Angeles: University
of California Press, 1972. xii, 458 p. Index, bibliography, illustrations,
notes.

> The author resigned from the CIA after a brief career to join the
> University of California at Berkeley where he undertook to write
> this "political history of the CIA's organizational forebear, the
> wartime Office of Strategic Services." Denied access to OSS
> archives by his former contacts in the CIA, the author worked with
> the extensive memoir literature and supplemented this with more
> than 200 interviews with OSS veterans, named in the bibliography.
> The book is well written, carefully researched, with over 360
> works referenced in the bibliography, and with numerous notes on
> each chapter. This reconstruction covers the OSS from its origins,
> shortly before the entry of the United States into the war, to the
> transitional period when the CIA emerged in the immediate post-
> war period. It vividly portrays the politics and people involved,
> the bureaucratic in-fighting and intrigue, as well as the adven-
> turist spirit of the men in the field. A good insight is provided
> into the organization of the OSS although this aspect is not em-
> phasized. This work is an indispensable guide through the laby-
> rinthine diplomatic complications which arose from the use of com-
> peting covert operational agencies during World War II.

B. MEMOIRS AND BIOGRAPHIES

Ford, Corey. DONOVAN OF OSS. Boston: Little, Brown and Co., 1970.
336 p. Index, bibliography.

> Ford has written this combination biography of William J. ("Wild
> Bill") Donovan and history of the OSS in a popular, uncritical,
> and anecdotal manner. Friend and colleague of Donovan, Ford
> had access to material from his family and his private papers for
> use in the preparation of this book. The book covers Donovan
> from his childhood to his death in 1959, but the important parts
> of his efforts to establish first the Office of the Coordinator of In-
> formation (COI) and then the OSS are retold in interesting detail.
> President Roosevelt wanted a COI to bring together all the intel-
> ligence gathered by all the agencies. However, Donovan envi-
> sioned something additional--an independent agency that not only
> did the intelligence clearinghouse job, but also acted as an of-
> fensive weapon, complementing the armed forces by fighting through
> sabotage, resistance, subversion, and propaganda. Donovan estab-
> lished the Research and Analysis (R&A) branch made up of histo-
> rians, economists, geographers, psychologists, and scholars to do
> the intelligence analysis mission. It is in the area of unorthodox
> warfare that Donovan spent his time and in relating Donovan's
> efforts; there the author combines personal characterizations of
> Donovan and anecdotes of the OSS. See also the annotation in
> chapter 14, section C.

Hall, Roger. YOU'RE STEPPING ON MY CLOAK AND DAGGER. New York: W.W. Norton, 1957. 219 p.

A humorous account of the experiences of a member of the OSS. There is, however, some information on the details of training in the OSS and of field activities.

Icardi, Aldo. ALDO ICARDI: AMERICAN MASTER SPY. New York: University Books, 1956. 275 p.

Lieutenant Icardi was the Italian-American interpreter with an OSS team operating near German-occupied Milan in December 1944. The team was headed by Major William V. Holohan, who disappeared under mysterious circumstances. An Italian court later found Icardi guilty in absentia of Holohan's murder. Following an extradition hearing, a congressional investigation (a report of which was published), and a perjury trial, Icardi won a technical acquittal in 1956. This memoir was his defense and he relates everything that happened the night Major Holohan disappeared. There is also quite a bit of detailed information on OSS operations and on the training he underwent upon joining the OSS.

Kaufman, Louis; Fitzgerald, Barbara; and Sewell, Tom. MOE BERG: ATHLETE, SCHOLAR, SPY. Boston: Little, Brown and Co., 1975. 274 p. Index, illustrations.

The biography of Morris ("Moe") Berg, linguist, lawyer, for fifteen years a catcher in big league baseball, and a successful American intelligence field agent. Recruited into the OSS in 1943, Berg soon specialized in gathering information overseas on the progress in Germany in the development and assembly of an atomic weapon. At one point Berg attended a lecture by one of Germany's leading physicists and experimenter in atomic research. The physicist, Werner Heisenberg, was lured through Berg's efforts to Switzerland to lecture at the Federal Institute of Technology. The authors traced Berg's life in intelligence through factual research and interviews.

Phillips, William. VENTURES IN DIPLOMACY. Beacon Press, 1952. 477 p.

The recollections of the man who, for a time, was chief of the large London office of the OSS. Prior to that Phillips was U.S. ambassador to Italy from 1936 to 1941.

Taylor, Edmond. AWAKENING FROM HISTORY. Boston: Gambit, 1969. xxi, 522 p.

An excellent memoir by an OSS officer who first led the Psychological Warfare Branch in North Africa and in late 1943 served as deputy to Admiral Louis Mountbatten, head of the combined Anglo-American South East Asia Command (SEAC). This was the

organization that allowed OSS operations in the Far East when
General MacArthur would not. After the war Taylor served on
the U.S. Psychological Strategy Board and later became a staff
writer for REPORTER magazine.

C. NETWORKS AND OPERATIONS

Alcorn, Robert Hayden. NO BANNERS, NO BANDS: MORE TALES OF THE
OSS. New York: McKay, 1965. 275 p.

The sequel to NO BUGLES FOR SPIES (see below). A series of
interesting vignettes based on authentic OSS operations, including
excellent examples of agent handling and cover.

_____. NO BUGLES FOR SPIES: TALES OF THE OSS. New York: David
McKay, 1962. 209 p.

A series of true stories of OSS activities in occupied Europe, North
Africa, and the Far East by a man who first joined OSS as a civilian employee and later was commissioned captain in the army
and assigned to the London OSS office as administrative-executive
officer. Alcorn was also in charge of special funds of the OSS
for the entire European theater of operations and thus was aware
of the various money exchange activities required to finance operations in foreign countries. One episode of his book describes
these activities.

Booth, Walter B. MISSION MARCEL PROUST. New York: Dorrance & Co.,
1972. 168 p.

The rich memoir of Colonel Booth who describes two OSS operations he commanded, Marcel and Proust. The operations were with
the French Maquisards. The book presents a clear and interesting
picture of operations with the French resistance, almost a documentary rather than a memoir.

Downes, Donald. THE SCARLET THREAD: ADVENTURES IN WARTIME ES-
PIONAGE. London: Derek Verschoyle, 1953. 207 p. Maps.

The recollections of a New England school teacher who in 1939
turned to espionage for the British in the Near East, and after
Pearl Harbor joined the OSS. His activities in North Africa and
in Italy are described along with his duties as a trainer of agents.
While with the OSS in Washington he successfully entered neutral
embassies in order to secure information and codes. He is se-
verely critical of the FBI regarding its policy to retain intelligence and counterintelligence in the Western Hemisphere as its
own private hunting preserve and to bring pressure to bear on the
other American intelligence agencies to refrain from poaching.
The book was first accepted and then turned down by three Ameri-

can publishers because of these criticisms and other revelations.
It is possibly the first "politically sensitive" book on intelligence
--something that became quite ordinary by the 1970s.

Dulles, Allen Welsh. GERMANY'S UNDERGROUND. New York: Macmillan,
1947. xiii, 207 p.

This book deals directly with the events leading up to the Hitler
assassination attempt of 1944. It deals only indirectly with OSS
operations in Europe, although the author was chief of the OSS
mission in Switzerland during that period.

_____. THE SECRET SURRENDER. New York: Harper & Row, 1966. 268 p.
Index, bibliography, maps, illustrations.

The authentic account of the OSS-directed operation Sunrise which
brought about the surrender of a million German and Italian troops
in April 1945 at Caserta, Italy. Dulles guided the delicate negotiations from his OSS station in Switzerland. In this dramatic
narrative Dulles describes the activities necessary to keep channels of communications open with an SS general across the Swiss-
Italian boundaries. The author acknowledges the contributions of
Gero von S. Gaevernitz who conducted some of the negotiations
and contributed material for the book.

Klein, Alexander. THE COUNTERFEIT TRAITOR. New York: Holt, Rinehart,
1958. 301 p. Appendices.

The account of the activities of Brooklyn-born Texas oil salesman
Eric Erickson in Germany, locating oil refineries for strategic targeting and gathering information on German synthetic oil production. Erickson worked out of Sweden under the sponsorship of
Prince Carl Bernadotte in this remarkable British-OSS combined
operation. Some episodes are slightly disguised, and the author
uses fictional techniques of re-creation of dialogue. Some of
Klein's factual errors are corrected in the article "Master Spy"
by journalist Lloyd Shearer in PARADE, 21 August 1960, pages
6-8.

Morgan, William J. SPIES AND SABOTEURS. London: Victor Gollancz,
1955. 183 p. American ed. THE OSS AND I. New York: W.W. Norton,
1957. 281 p. Illustrations.

The author, a professional psychologist, recounts his activities in
the OSS first as a psychologist selecting spies, saboteurs, and resistance leaders and then as an agent himself, working with the
French underground, the Maquis. In the British edition Morgan
describes his enlistment in the army in 1942 and his assignment to
the OSS. He was assigned to the staff of the British spy school
at Pemberley. He was the only American on the staff which selected SOE agents for field training and later deployment. The

author relates how tests were developed. After more than a year at Pemberley, Morgan volunteered for service in France and was then sent through the same school he had seen so many candidates go to. The British edition ends with the completion of his own training. In the American edition the author repeats all this and then goes on to describe his activities in occupied France as a resistance leader named "Marceau," and his organization and training of a band of 550 guerrilla fighters.

Murray, Henry A., et al. ASSESSMENT OF MEN. SELECTION OF PERSONNEL FOR THE OFFICE OF STRATEGIC SERVICES. New York: Rinehart, 1948. xv, 541 p. Index, appendices. Also published as ASSESSMENT OF MEN (SELECTION OF PERSONNEL FOR THE OFFICE OF STRATEGIC SERVICES). Washington, D.C.: Government Printing Office, 1948.

A detailed report prepared by the OSS Psychological Assessment Staff on the testing of qualifications of men and women recruited by the OSS for tasks to be performed under severe stress in enemy-occupied country. The report provides valuable information on the OSS itself plus insights into the types of jobs to be performed to acquire intelligence information and to conduct sabotage and other special operations.

Tompkins, Peter. ITALY BETRAYED. New York: Simon & Schuster, 1966. 352 p.

_____. THE MURDER OF ADMIRAL DARLAN. New York: Simon & Schuster, 1965. 287 p.

Written by Tompkins from material he collected while deputy to the director for psychological warfare of the Allied forces which landed in North Africa.

_____. A SPY IN ROME. Preface by Donald Downes. New York: Simon & Schuster, 1962. 347 p. Map.

This book is the edited and expanded notes and diary of OSS agent Peter Tompkins, written in enemy-held country in all violation of strict security measures. In November 1942 the author was deputy to the director of psychological warfare in Algiers; however, he disassociated himself from this type of activity to become an active OSS field officer. He went from recruiting Italians for espionage behind German lines after the landings at Salerno to an assignment in Rome during the last months of the German occupation. There he developed a Socialist-based espionage network. His book reflects the intricate political intrigues which took place during the Italian campaign, and much of the bitterness which they engendered.

D. OSS IN THE FAR EAST AND SOUTHEAST ASIA

The OSS operated in the China–Burma–India theater of operations and in Ceylon, Thailand, and Indochina. In China there was some controversy when the OSS started up activities after other organizations had already organized for intelligence and guerrilla operations. Some insight into these problems is provided in Milton Miles's A DIFFERENT KIND OF WAR (cited in chapter 6) and in Roy O. Stratton's SACO: THE RICE PADDY NAVY (Pleasantville, N.Y.: C.S. Palmer, 1950). In the part of the Pacific theater of operations commanded by MacArthur, the OSS was virtually excluded from setting up detachments. Supposedly MacArthur already had his espionage and sabotage and guerrilla operations well in hand in his Allied Intelligence Bureau, and in any case MacArthur resisted in his area organizations that reported directly to Washington and not to him. The best single source of material on the tangled webs of controversy and the best expose of OSS activity in China, India, Indochina, Burma, Ceylon, and Thailand is Richard Harris Smith's OSS: THE SECRET HISTORY OF AMERICA'S FIRST CENTRAL INTELLIGENCE AGENCY, especially chapters 8 through 10 (see section A, this chapter).

Barrett, David. DIXIE MISSION: THE UNITED STATES ARMY OBSERVER GROUP IN YENAN. Berkeley, Calif.: Center for Chinese Studies, 1970. 96 p.

> Colonel Barrett, an army G-2 China specialist, headed a joint army–OSS intelligence mission which visited Chou En-lai in Yenan during July 1944.

Peers, William R., and Brelis, Dean. BEHIND THE BURMA ROAD: THE STORY OF AMERICA'S MOST SUCCESSFUL GUERRILLA FORCE. Boston: Little, Brown and Co., 1963. 246 p. Index, maps, appendix.

> While the Allied Intelligence Bureau (AIB) was MacArthur's answer to long-range intelligence and guerrilla operations in the Pacific island chain, OSS Detachment 101 was Stilwell's answer to long-range reconnaissance and harrassment of the Japanese lifeline in the Burma area. BEHIND THE BURMA ROAD is the story of Detachment 101 written by its commander (Peers) from 1943 to 1945. Peers went on to fame as an unconventional warfare expert of the postwar period and was promoted to the rank of lieutenant general. Coauthor Brelis was a field agent of Detachment 101, first as a sergeant, then a lieutenant, and is now a successful novelist and journalist. The chief of intelligence of Burma's Northern Area Command estimated that Detachment 101 provided from 85 to 95 percent of the usable intelligence available on Japanese movements, and the Tenth Air Force estimated that 85 percent of the targets it struck in the area were designated by Detachment 101.

Chapter 19
CIA: COVERT OPERATIONS

Agee, Philip. INSIDE THE COMPANY: CIA DIARY. New York: Stonehill, 1975. 640 p. Appendices, acknowledgments, organization charts, no index.

> An account of the CIA operations in Latin America in the fields of political action and propaganda. Provides a useful categorization system for covert operations as used in the CIA school. For main entry, see chapter 14, section C.

Ayers, Bradley Earl. THE WAR THAT NEVER WAS. Indianapolis, Ind.: Bobbs-Merrill, 1976. 235 p. No index.

> An account of how CIA trained and led anti-Castro guerrilla fighters at bases in Florida and the Bahamas. The author, one-time U.S. Army captain, was assigned to the CIA and assisted in the training of the guerrillas.

Cooper, Chester L. THE LOST CRUSADE. Foreword by W. Averell Harriman. New York: Dodd, Mead & Co., 1970. ix, 559 p. Index, bibliography, chronology of events, notes.

> Written by a CIA intelligence analyst and member of the White House staff in the Johnson administration. This is one of the best-informed and most authoritative, comprehensive accounts of the American activities in Vietnam and Southeast Asia from the beginning through the Cambodian border crossing in the spring of 1970. A dispassionate account of policy making which touches indirectly on covert operations in such key cases as the Tonkin Gulf incidents and other stages in the escalation of the conflict.

Corson, William R. THE BETRAYAL. New York: W.W. Norton, 1968. 317 p. No index.

> From the position of a Combined Action Platoon leader, the author, a former marine colonel, ridicules and attacks American policy and operations in Vietnam. He argues that the scope of covert operations was not as wide as is generally believed.

Cox, Arthur M. MYTHS OF NATIONAL SECURITY--THE PERIL OF SECRET GOVERNMENT. Boston: Beacon Press, 1975. 231 p. Index, bibliography.

The author, lecturer on foreign affairs and former member of the State Department and the CIA, describes CIA and Soviet KGB operations.

Fitzgerald, Frances. FIRE IN THE LAKE. Boston: Little, Brown and Co., 1972. 491 p. Index, bibliography, notes.

An outstanding study of the American pacification policy and the progress of the Viet Cong National Liberation Front. It gives the reader an understanding of Vietnamese politics in the light of such environmental factors as the traditional peasant society, French colonial rule, and modernization. There are numerous references to intelligence and covert operations, including the covert bombing of Laos in 1964, the counterinsurgency program, the impact of intelligence estimates, and the Phoenix program, which centralized certain counterespionage and counterterror operations.

Gravel, Michael, ed. THE SENATOR GRAVEL EDITION--THE PENTAGON PAPERS. 5 vols. Boston: Beacon Press, 1971. Vols. 1-4, documents; vol. 5, index and critical essays edited by Norm Chomsky and Howard Zinn. 4,100 p.

With the release of the Pentagon Papers came perhaps the most comprehensive study tracing American involvement in the Vietnam War. The Gravel edition represents the bulk of material turned over to Congress at the height of the controversy surrounding publication by the NEW YORK TIMES. Volumes 1 through 4 are commentary and analysis by Pentagon researchers; volume 5 contains fifteen essays by leading critics of the war effort on the implications of the papers, as well as name and subject indexing for the bulk of the papers contained in the first four volumes. The assembled papers indicate that in spite of the relatively accurate intelligence assessments of deteriorating conditions in Vietnam, the official optimism in Washington dictated that such pessimistic reports be altered, overlooked, or discounted. Covert operations sponsored and funded by the United States in support of South Vietnam (34 A operations and Desoto patrols) are shown to be directly responsible for events leading to the Tonkin Gulf incidents; inaccurate and incomplete reporting of these activities resulted in U.S. policy shift to war footing. See also the annotation for this work in chapter 5, section D.

Halberstam, David. THE BEST AND THE BRIGHTEST. New York: Random House, 1972. 688 p. Index of proper names, bibliography.

A trenchant analysis by a Pulitzer Prize-winning journalist of decision making in the Vietnam War, combined with extensive character sketches of the principal policy makers during the Kennedy and Johnson administrations. Scattered throughout the book are revealing descriptions of the mishandling of strategic intelligence, especially estimates, as well as discussions of covert operations, including the 34 A operations which led to the Gulf of Tonkin incidents. A valuable source, but one which is difficult to use since the index is confined to proper names. Should be used in conjunction with Gravel's edition of THE PENTAGON PAPERS (see above).

Hilsman, Roger. TO MOVE A NATION: THE POLITICS OF FOREIGN POL-ICY IN THE ADMINISTRATION OF JOHN F. KENNEDY. Garden City, N.Y.: Doubleday, 1967. xxii, 602 p. Index, notes, maps.

The author, who was head of the Bureau of Intelligence and Re-search in the State Department, discusses intelligence during the Kennedy administration in addition to covert operations in Laos, Cuba, the Congo, China, Indonesia, Malaysia, and Vietnam. Hilsman argues that covert operations were both oversold and over-used during the cold war period. See also the annotation for this book in chapter 5, section A.

Hunt, E. Howard. GIVE US THIS DAY. New Rochelle, N.Y.: Arlington House, 1973. 235 p. Index, organization chart, illustrations.

In this memoir Watergate figure E. Howard Hunt provides a per-sonal account of his nineteen months on the Bay of Pigs operation as an officer of the CIA. The author writes from memory having had no access to official files or documents. Names of CIA per-sonnel are used and an organization chart of the "Cuba Project" in the CIA is included.

Phillips, David Atlee. THE NIGHT WATCH. 25 YEARS OF PECULIAR SER-VICE. New York: Atheneum, 1977. 309 p. Index, epilogue.

A well-written memoir of the author's experiences in the CIA's Clandestine Services, first as a field operations specialist in Latin America and finally as chief of the Western Hemisphere Division of the Directorate of Operations. Phillips describes his role in the Bay of Pigs operation. Upon retirement from CIA he founded the Retired Intelligence Officers Association through which forum he, and others who have joined, are able to speak freely as pri-vate citizens in support of intelligence and the CIA.

Prouty, Leroy Fletcher. THE SECRET TEAM: THE CIA AND ITS ALLIES IN CONTROL OF THE UNITED STATES AND THE WORLD. Englewood Cliffs, N.J.: Prentice-Hall, 1973. xiv, 496 p. Index, bibliography, appendices.

The author, a retired air force colonel, was for nine years, from 1955 to 1963, the focal point officer for contacts between the CIA operational directorate and the various agencies of the De-partment of Defense. Assigned to the Joint Staff of the office of the Joint Chiefs of Staff, Prouty was charged with briefing Department of Defense officials on CIA covert operations, and with the solicitation of assistance from the air force to support CIA's covert operations. The author provides key insights into the detrils of covert operations as they were planned and carried out; he relates these insights in terms of the CIA's official mission.

"The Report on the CIA that President Ford Doesn't Want You to Read." THE VILLAGE VOICE, 11 February 1976. Pp. 1-21; and in a supplement to THE VILLAGE VOICE, 16 February 1976. Pp. 1-24. Reprinted in a SPECIAL SUPPLEMENT TO THE VILLAGE VOICE under the title, "The Pike Papers: House Select Committee on Intelligence CIA Report." October 1976. 36 p.

THE VILLAGE VOICE, a weekly New York newspaper, published excerpts of the secret final report of the investigations into the U.S. intelligence community of the House of Representatives Select Committee on Intelligence (Rep. Otis G. Pike of New York chairman). The 338-page secret report was provided to THE VILLAGE VOICE editor by Daniel Schorr, veteran CBS correspondent, who has repeatedly refused to name his source of the report--even under Congressional pressure. The excerpts printed by THE VILLAGE VOICE detail performance of the intelligence community during crisis periods such as the Tet Offensive of the Vietnam War, the Mid-East wars, the invasion of Czechoslovakia by the Soviets, and Indian-Pakistan War. Also reprinted are accounts of the financial activities of the community and the covert action activities of the CIA.

Rositzke, Harry. THE CIA'S SECRET OPERATIONS. ESPIONAGE, COUNTER-ESPIONAGE, AND COVERT ACTION. Introd. by Arthur M. Schlesinger, Jr. Pleasantville, N.Y.: Reader's Digest Press, 1977. Distributed by T.Y. Crowell. 286 p.

An important memoir based on the author's 25 years of CIA experience in a variety of assignments in the Clandestine Services. The book contains a mixture of autobiographical descriptions and textbook-like, trade craft insights designed, as the author states, to "replace ignorance and distortion (about covert action) with fact." Rositzke devotes three chapters to covert action dealing with black propaganda, paramilitary operations, and political action operations. The book is not without its pro-CIA, pro-covert action messages.

Smith, Joseph Burkholder. PORTRAIT OF A COLD WARRIOR. New York: G.P. Putnam's Sons, 1976. 448 p.

An engaging account of the author's career during twenty-two years as a covert action specialist in the CIA's Clandestine Services in Asia and Latin America. A handbook of covert action techniques, adequately supplied with autobiographical descriptions of the constant battle between the CIA and the Soviet KGB. Describes black propaganda operations during the Bay of Pigs.

U.S. Congress. House. Committee on Foreign Affairs. Subcommittee on Inter-American Affairs. UNITED STATES AND CHILE DURING THE ALLENDE YEARS, 1970-1973: HEARINGS. 1975. 677 p. Chronology of events in Chile, bibliography.

A record of the testimony of witnesses on events in Chile and on Chile-U.S. relationships during the period 1970-73. The hearings were held during the period between July 1971 and mid-September 1973. The report includes eight appendices which are reprints of articles that appeared in the press concerning the activities of the CIA in Chile. A bibliography of Chile during the Allende years, prepared by the Library of Congress, is included as an appendix. The report is not specifically pointed toward covert activities, but represents a valuable source when used with the Senate report COVERT ACTION IN CHILE 1963-1973 (see below).

U.S. Congress. Senate. Select Committee to Study Governmental Operations with Respect to Intelligence Activities. ALLEGED ASSASSINATION PLOTS INVOLVING FOREIGN LEADERS: INTERIM REPORT. 94th Cong., 1st sess., 20 November 1975. xiii, 349 p.

A preliminary report of the Church Committee investigating intelligence activities of the alleged U.S. and CIA involvement in assassination plots of five foreign leaders: Fidel Castro of Cuba, Patrice Lumumba of Congo (Zaire), Rafael Trujillo of the Dominican Republic, General Rene Schneider of Chile, and President Ngo Dinh Diem of the Republic of South Vietnam. Covert action as a vehicle for foreign policy implementation is examined, with details on the assassination plots provided. A summary of findings and conclusions is also provided. Additional, supplemental, and separate views of some of the members of the committee are included at the end of the report. Remarkable detail is provided as to the covert operations in the five countries.

———. COVERT ACTION IN CHILE 1963-1973: STAFF REPORT. 94th Cong., 1st sess., 1975. 62 p. Tables, chronology of events in Chile 1962-1975.

A report of the committee chaired by Senator Frank Church into the activities of the CIA in Chile. The range of covert actions is investigated from review of extensive documents of the CIA, the Departments of State and Defense, and the National Security Council; and from the testimony of officials and former officials. The effects of the covert actions are analyzed, and the authorization, assessment, and oversight process are reviewed. Conclusions of a preliminary nature are made.

———. FOREIGN AND MILITARY INTELLIGENCE. Book I. 94th Cong., 2d sess., 26 April 1976. Rept. no. 94-755. 651 p. Glossary, organization charts, appendices, footnotes with bibliographic references.

This final report of the Senate committee chaired by Senator Frank Church of Idaho contains much information on the scope and origin of covert operations as conducted worldwide by the CIA. See chapter 4, section A for main annotation.

———— . SUPPLEMENTARY DETAILED STAFF REPORTS ON FOREIGN AND MILITARY INTELLIGENCE. Book IV. 94th Cong., 2d sess., April 1976. Rept. no. 94-755, 175 p. Appendix, organization charts.

A staff report of the Church Committee of the Senate on the history of the Central Intelligence Agency. The history, the most detailed yet to be published in the open literature, provides information on the early activities of the CIA, its organization and operating policies, and the changes in direction implemented by each of the directors of the CIA. Separate chapters are accorded descriptions of the clandestine services and the organization for intelligence production. An invaluable source of official information on the organization and functions of the CIA from 1946 through 1975. The staff report also includes an addenda to the interim report on ALLEGED ASSASSINATION PLOTS (see above).

Wise, David. THE POLITICS OF LYING: GOVERNMENT DECEPTION, SECRECY AND POWER. New York: Random House, 1973. 415 p. Index, bibliography, notes.

Part 2, "Secrecy," includes brief descriptions of certain CIA covert operations. Chapter 8 is devoted to "The Case of the Colorado Tibetans," who were trained by the CIA at Camp Hale, Colorado, during the period 1958-61. See also the annotation for this work in chapter 8, section A.

———— . "The Secret Committee Called '40.'" NEW YORK TIMES, 19 January 1975, p. E4.

Wise, author of several books on U.S. intelligence and government deception, describes the role of the 40 Committee of the National Security Council in approving covert actions to be taken by the CIA's clandestine services. He names the membership of the committee and also traces some of its history from 1948.

Chapter 20

THE SOVIET UNION: PARTISAN WARFARE AND
POLITICAL WARFARE

Armstrong, John A., ed. SOVIET PARTISANS IN WORLD WAR II. Foreword
by Philip E. Moseley. Madison: University of Wisconsin Press, 1964. xi,
810 p. Index, glossary, selected Soviet sources, selected bibliography.

> A monumental group of studies were prepared by the War Docu-
> mentation Project (Project Alexander) for the U.S. Air Force,
> based on captured German and Soviet documents, in 1954. Pro-
> fessor Armstrong, a member of the project staff, has adapted ten
> of these studies for publication as a book. Chapter 5 by Kurt
> DeWitt deals specifically with "The Partisans in Soviet Intelli-
> gence." Other contributing scholars such as Alexander Dallin
> and Gerhard Weinberg have since become distinguished historians
> in the area of German-Soviet affairs. There are 100 pages of
> selected source documents listed.

Kirkpatrick, Lyman B., and Sargeant, Howland H. SOVIET POLITICAL WAR-
FARE TECHNIQUES: ESPIONAGE AND PROPAGANDA IN THE 1970S. New
York: National Strategy Information Center, 1972. 82 p. Paperbound. Bib-
liographical notes.

> Lyman Kirkpatrick, one-time executive director in the CIA, here
> portrays Soviet espionage, the largest in history, as an important
> offensive weapon in the Soviet arsenal dedicated to achieving
> control and domination wherever possible. Howland Sargeant,
> leading authority on government information programs and Soviet
> propaganda, and one-time assistant secretary of state for public
> affairs, convincingly argues that Soviet propaganda is another of-
> fensive weapon of the Soviet arsenal striving to expand and to
> increase the strength of the Soviet bloc of nations.

U.S. Congress. Senate. Committee on the Judiciary. Subcommittee to Investigate the Administration of the Internal Security Act and Other Internal
Security Laws. Study prepared by Suzanne Labin. THE TECHNIQUES OF
SOVIET PROPAGANDA. 90th Cong., 1st sess., 1967. 63 p. Index, appendix, footnotes.

A pamphlet prepared by Suzanne Labin, journalist and graduate of the Sorbonne, and published by the Senate for wide dissemination, describes the political warfare objectives and techniques of the USSR.

Chapter 21

DISINFORMATION, DECEPTION, FRAUDS, AND FORGERIES

The clandestine services divisions of intelligence agencies of the great powers have sections which specialize in the production and dissemination of misinformation (usually called disinformation) for political warfare purposes. To the extent that such covert operations are successful, the fraud involved is not exposed, so that the literature in the field consists mainly of periodic exposes by one intelligence service of the alleged frauds and forgeries of its rivals, or occasional scholarly articles or books which discuss disinformation as part of the broad spectrum of political warfare and covert operations. Accordingly, material on disinformation is scattered throughout the general works of both the Soviet and American intelligence agencies which are annotated elsewhere in this bibliography. Only books and articles dealing specifically with the subject are listed below.

A. DISINFORMATION

Bittman, Ladislav [Lawrence M. Martin]. THE DECEPTION GAME: CZECHO-SLOVAK INTELLIGENCE IN SOVIET POLITICAL WARFARE. Syracuse, N.Y.: Syracuse University Research Corp., 1972. ix, 246 p. Index.

> The author of this curious political warfare hybrid is a Czech defector who served "as a former Czechoslovak disinformation officer" for his country's intelligence service. Under a 1970 copyright the original manuscript by Lawrence M. Martin was entitled "Department D: The Disinformation Center of Soviet Bloc Intelligence." Content analysis of the "Department D" text indicated that it was partly original material and in part a team product, and the manuscript was rejected for publication by the Syracuse University Press and other publishers. The new version contains a lengthy autobiographical preface in which the author indicates the political warfare motivation behind the publication and predicts "without hesitation" that Prague and Moscow "will call it a fraud and literary espionage written at the direction of the CIA." The use of such barbarisms as "literary espionage" for disinformation indicates the kind of confusing cold war terminology which characterizes the entire book.

B. DECEPTION IN WORLD WAR II

The use of rumor and so-called "black propaganda," and the deliberate spreading of false information (disinformation) for political warfare purposes properly belongs under a catch-all category of "psychological warfare" which is excluded from this bibliography. However, the secret or clandestine use of disinformation is usually handled by the covert operational elements of intelligence agencies for either political or mixed political-military objectives, such as strategic deception as to location or timing of a military operation or campaign. All sides made extensive use of such deception in World War II, frequently with important strategic consequences. Books dealing with the most important of these operations are listed in this bibliography according to the cases themselves. However, one history of deception operations used in World War II stands out and the title and annotation of this extraordinary book follows.

Brown, Anthony Cave. BODYGUARD OF LIES. New York: Harper & Row, 1975. x, 947 p. Index; bibliography; sources and notes; illustrations; glossary; maps; list of interviews; list of archivists, historians, and librarians consulted.

An extraordinary history of intelligence and deception in World War II. Heretofore it has been necessary to research numerous sources for fragments of the total World War II deception operations, but Brown has pulled it all together after more than seven years of research into British and American military archives, using documents declassified as late as 1975, and interviews with knowledgeable persons. The author, a former foreign correspondent and British journalist, reveals the entire scope of deception operations conducted to disguise Allied military movements, especially the Normandy landings. Considerable attention is given to the British code breakers of the German coding machine, the Ultra operation, and how deception operations were planned and tuned according to feedback obtained from Ultra. Another branch of the deception game investigated by the author was that practiced by anti-Hitler officers of the German armed forces in seeking to obtain a separate peace with the Allies. This is the best single source of information on intelligence and deception operations, expertly researched, with generous bibliography and source material.

1. Gleiwitz and Related Border Provocations

On August 22, 1939 (one day before the signing of the German-Soviet peace pact), Hitler made a speech in which he stated that he would "give a propagandistic cause for starting a war," referring to a series of staged Polish border incidents, of which the best known is the fake attack on the German radio station Gleiwitz. On a much larger scale, months before the German invasion of the Soviet Union in June 1941, a massive campaign of deception and disinformation successfully confused not only Stalin but also Soviet intelligence as to how the build-up for Barbarossa (the German code word for the invasion) should be interpreted. A selection of the growing literature on both these cases is listed below.

Best, Sigismund Payne. THE VENLO INCIDENT. London and New York: Hutchinson, 1950. 260 p. Illustrations, maps, portraits.

> An account of a deception operation conducted by Nazi party intelligence (SD) across the German-Dutch border in November 1939. Walter Schellenberg of the SD entered into a deception operation with two British intelligence officers, Captain S. Payne Best, the author of this account, and Major R.H. Stevens. Schellenberg persuaded them that German generals were determined to overthrow Hitler and they needed assurances from England that a new anti-Nazi regime would be accepted. The negotiations were conducted at Venlo, near the border on the Dutch side. Best and Stevens were eventually captured and taken across the border to captivity for the rest of the war. For more on the Venlo incident see Schellenberg's memoirs THE LABYRINTH, cited in chapter 14, section F, and Brissaud's THE NAZI SECRET SERVICE in chapter 4, section D.

Blackstock, Paul W. "Covert Operations and Policy Sabotage." In THE STRATEGY OF SUBVERSION: MANIPULATING THE POLITICS OF OTHER NATIONS, pp. 208-13. Chicago: Quadrangle, 1964.

> An analysis of the political-military setting of the Gleiwitz incident based on all available documentary and related research materials.

Peis, Gunther. THE MAN WHO STARTED THE WAR. London: Odhams, 1960. 233 p.

> A melodramatic and inaccurate account of the Gleiwitz incident by Alfred Naujocks, the major of the Nazi party intelligence service Sicherheitsdienst (SD), who led the attack on radio station Gleiwitz, as told to German journalist Gunther Peis. For more on the incident and on Naujocks see Andre Brissaud's THE NAZI SECRET SERVICE, cited in chapter 4, section D.

Runzheimer, Juergen. "Der Ueberfall auf den Sender Gleiwitz im Jahre 1939." VIERTELJAHRESHEFTE FUER ZEITGESHCICHTE 10 (1962): 408-26.

> An excellent, authoritative article, based on exhaustive research, on the Gleiwitz incident.

Shirer, William L. THE RISE AND FALL OF THE THIRD REICH: A HISTORY OF NAZI GERMANY. New York: Simon & Schuster, 1960. 1,245 p. Index, bibliography, notes.

> On the Gleiwitz incident see pages 518-20, 595, 599, and 601. Based primarily on Naujock's Nuremberg trial evidence which is

partly misleading. On the Venlo incident see pages 864–66 and the footnote on page 692.

2. Barbarossa: German Deception and the Invasion of the USSR

Whaley, Barton. CODEWORD BARBAROSSA. Cambridge, Mass.: M.I.T. Press, 1973. x, 376 p. Index, bibliography, notes, illustrations, map, appendices.

A monumental, detailed study of German strategic deception in connection with the planning and launching of the campaign against the USSR (Barbarossa). For the main annotation see chapter 5, section A.

3. Operation "North Pole": Radio (Funkspiel) Deception in Holland

Germany's military intelligence organization (Abwehr) successfully neutralized British SOE activities in Holland during World War II by capturing agents and then controlling their radio communications for deception purposes. Three of the books dealing with this operation are listed below; for annotations see the crosslistings in chapter 15, section D2.

Dourlein, Peter. INSIDE NORTH POLE: A SECRET AGENT'S STORY. Translated by F.G. Renier and Anne Cliff. London: Kimber, 1954. 206 p.

Ganier-Raymond, Phillipe. THE TANGLED WEB. Translated by Len Ortzen. New York: Pantheon Books; London: Barker, 1968. 203 p. Index.

Giskes, Herman J. LONDON CALLING NORTH POLE. New York: British Book Center, 1953. vi, 208 p. Glossary of terms. British ed. London: Kimber, 1953. 208 p.

4. Operation "Mincemeat": Deception before the Allied Invasion of Sicily

Montagu, Ewen. THE MAN WHO NEVER WAS. Foreword by Lord Hastings L. Ismay. New York and Philadelphia: Lippincott, 1954. xii, 160 p. Appendices, map, illustrations.

An all-too-brief account of operation Mincemeat, a successful deception operation by Royal Navy intelligence to mislead German intelligence as to the exact location of the invasion of southern Europe. The deception consisted of dressing an anonymous corpse as a major in the Royal Marines, planting proper identity papers

on him as well as false secret documents indicating that the invasion would occur in Greece rather than Sicily, and casting him
adrift from a submarine to float to the shores of neutral Spain
where it was known numerous German intelligence agents operated.
The author planned and directed this operation and he provides
excellent insights into deception planning, documentation, and
estimation of German reactions to the acquired information.

5. The "Double-Cross System": Deception prior to the Normandy Invasion

Masterman, John C. THE DOUBLE-CROSS SYSTEM IN THE WAR OF 1939 TO
1945. Foreword by Norman Holmes Pearson. New Haven, Conn.: Yale University Press, 1972. xxi, 203 p. Index, appendices, list of abbreviations.

Describes in detail the highly successful counterespionage and deception operations conducted by British counterintelligence in which
they controlled most of the German agents in Great Britain during
World War II. Through this control the British were able to plant
false information (subsequently reported to Berlin) as to where the
main thrust of the Allied invasion would take place. For another
annotation, see chapter 15, section D1.

C. FRAUDS AND FORGERIES

Blackstock, Paul W. AGENTS OF DECEIT: FRAUDS, FORGERIES AND POLITI-
CAL INTRIGUE AMONG NATIONS. Chicago: Quadrangle, 1966. 315 p.
Notes, index, appendix by George F. Kennan.

A scholarly analysis of such historical forgeries as the Testament
of Peter the Great, and the Protocols of Zion and the Zinoviev
letters, an examination of the use of disinformation for political
warfare purposes in the 1920s and the cold war period. The appendices include an article on the Sisson Documents by George
F. Kennan and an official briefing, "The Soviet and Communist
Bloc Defamation Campaign," originally introduced into the CON-
GRESSIONAL RECORD (September 28, 1965). Among the cold
war forgeries discussed are Protocol M, the Bluebird Papers, false
Soviet memoirs (such as Maxim Litvinov's NOTES FOR A JOUR-
NAL), and the Penkovskiy Papers.

Harrison, Wilson R. SUSPECT DOCUMENTS: THEIR SCIENTIFIC EXAMINA-
TION. New York: Praeger, 1958. vii, 583 p. Index, glossary, suggested
readings, illustrations.

This is the definitive study of the subject written by an expert
who holds both M.Sc. and Ph.D. degrees. It is based on twenty-
four years experience and more than 7,000 cases examined while

the author was head of the Forensic Science Laboratory of the British Home Office. An indispensable reference in the case of all suspected frauds or forgeries.

U.S. Congress. Senate. Committee on the Judiciary. Subcommittee to Investigate the Administration of the Internal Security Act and Other Internal Security Laws. COMMUNIST FORGERIES: HEARING. 87th Cong., 1st sess., 2 June 1961. 121 p. Index, appendices, illustrations, maps.

This committee report contains the testimony of Richard Helms, then assistant director of the CIA on Communist forgeries of all types, plus twenty-two appendices each illustrating a specific forgery and tracing its dissemination. Excellent illustrations and reprints of forgeries.

_____. COMMUNIST PASSPORT FRAUDS. 85th Cong., 2d sess., 11 July 1958. 98 p.

A committee report on the use of American passports by Soviet Communists and Soviet intelligence for fraudulent purposes. Deals also with the obtaining of U.S. passports from American volunteers in the Spanish Civil War. The report provides details on specific cases.

SELECTED BIBLIOGRAPHY OF FIFTY TITLES

The following titles are suggested for personal collections of essential books in the field and for small libraries which must limit their selections to representative works.

Agee, Philip. INSIDE THE COMPANY: CIA DIARY. New York: Stonehill, 1975. 639 p. Appendices, acknowledgments.

Bakeless, John. TURNCOATS, TRAITORS AND HEROS. Philadelphia: Lippincott, 1959. 406 p.

Barron, John. KGB: THE SECRET WORK OF SOVIET SECRET AGENTS. Pleasantville, N.Y.: Reader's Digest Press, distributed by E.P. Dutton Co., New York, 1974. xiv, 462 p. Index, notes, bibliography, appendices, illustrations.

Blackstock, Paul W. THE SECRET ROAD TO WORLD WAR II: SOVIET VERSUS WESTERN INTELLIGENCE, 1921-1939. Chicago: Quadrangle, 1969. 384 p. Index, notes, dramatis personae.

_____. THE STRATEGY OF SUBVERSION: MANIPULATING THE POLITICS OF OTHER NATIONS. Chicago: Quadrangle, 1964. 351 p. Index, notes.

Brissaud, Andre. THE NAZI SECRET SERVICE. Translated by Milton Waldman. New York: W.W. Norton, 1974. 320 p. Index, bibliography, appendices, organization charts, illustrations.

Brown, Anthony Cave. BODYGUARD OF LIES. New York: Harper & Row, 1975. x, 947 p. Index, bibliography, notes and sources, maps, glossary, illustrations.

Selected Bibliography

Cline, Ray S. SECRETS, SPIES AND SCHOLARS. Washington, D.C.: Acropolis Books, 1976. 294 p. Index, notes, glossary of terms, illustrations, organization charts.

Collier, Richard. TEN THOUSAND EYES. New York: E.P. Dutton, 1958. 320 p. Appendix, organization chart, maps, illustrations.

Copeland, Miles. WITHOUT CLOAK AND DAGGER: THE TRUTH ABOUT THE NEW ESPIONAGE. New York: Simon & Schuster, 1974. 351 p. Index, appendices.

Dallin, David J. SOVIET ESPIONAGE. New Haven, Conn.: Yale University Press, 1955. xi, 558 p. Index, notes.

Deacon, Richard [pseud.]. HISTORY OF THE RUSSIAN SECRET SERVICE. New York: Taplinger, 1972. viii, 568 p. Index, bibliography, notes, illustrations.

Donovan, James B. STRANGERS ON A BRIDGE: THE CASE OF COLONEL ABEL. New York: Atheneum, 1964. xi, 432 p. Index.

Dulles, Allen Welsh. THE CRAFT OF INTELLIGENCE. New York: Harper & Row, 1963. 277 p. Index, bibliography, photographs.

Farago, Ladislas. THE BROKEN SEAL: THE STORY OF "OPERATION MAGIC" AND THE PEARL HARBOR DISASTER. New York: Random House, 1967. 439 p. Index, bibliography, notes.

Felix, Christopher [pseud.]. A SHORT COURSE IN THE SECRET WAR. New York: E.P. Dutton, 1963. 314 p.

Foot, Michael Richard Daniel. SOE IN FRANCE: AN ACCOUNT OF THE WORK OF THE BRITISH SPECIAL OPERATIONS EXECUTIVE IN FRANCE, 1940-1944. History of the Second World War Series. London: Her Majesty's Stationery Office, 1966. xxiii, 550 p. Index, bibliography, appendices, maps, illustrations.

Giskes, Herman J. LONDON CALLING NORTH POLE. New York: British Book Centre, 1953. vi, 208 p. Glossary of terms.

Gravel, Michael, ed. THE SENATOR GRAVEL EDITION--THE PENTAGON PAPERS. Boston: Beacon Press, 1971. 5 vols. Index to all vols. in vol. 5. 4,100 p.

Hagen, Louis. THE SECRET WAR FOR EUROPE: A DOSSIER OF ESPIONAGE. New York: Stein & Day, 1969. 287 p. Index, appendix, illustrations.

Hilsman, Roger. STRATEGIC INTELLIGENCE AND NATIONAL DECISIONS. Glencoe, Ill.: Free Press, 1956. 187 p. Index, footnotes with some bibliographic references.

Hingley, Ronald. THE RUSSIAN SECRET POLICE: MUSCOVITE, IMPERIAL RUSSIAN, AND SOVIET SECURITY OPERATIONS. New York: Simon & Schuster, 1970. xiii, 313 p. Index, bibliography, notes.

Irving, David. THE MARE'S NEST. Boston: Little, Brown and Co., 1965. 314 p. Index, appendix, illustrations, maps.

Kahn, David. THE CODEBREAKERS: THE STORY OF SECRET WRITING. New York: Macmillan, 1967. xvi, 1,164 p. Index, bibliography, notes, chart, photographs, illustrations, maps.

Kent, Sherman. STRATEGIC INTELLIGENCE FOR AMERICAN WORLD POLICY. 3d ed. Hamden, Conn.: Archon Books, 1965. 226 p. Index, appendix, illustrations.

Kirkpatrick, Lyman B., Jr. THE U.S. INTELLIGENCE COMMUNITY: FOREIGN POLICY AND DOMESTIC ACTIVITIES. New York: Hill & Wang, 1973. ix, 212 p. Index, selective bibliography.

Klass, Philip J. SECRET SENTRIES IN SPACE. New York: Random House, 1971. xvi, 236 p. Index, illustrations.

McLachlan, Donald. ROOM 39: A STUDY IN NAVAL INTELLIGENCE. New York: Atheneum, 1968. xvii, 438 p. Index of names, appendix, notes, organization chart, tables.

Marchetti, Victor, and Marks, John D. THE CIA AND THE CULT OF INTELLIGENCE. New York: Knopf, 1974. xxvi, 398, xxi p. Index, appendix.

Masterman, John C. THE DOUBLE-CROSS SYSTEM IN THE WAR OF 1939 TO 1945. New Haven, Conn.: Yale University Press, 1972. xxi, 203 p. Index, appendices.

Orlov, Alexander. HANDBOOK OF INTELLIGENCE AND GUERRILLA WARFARE. Ann Arbor: University of Michigan Press, 1963. 187 p.

Page, Bruce; Leitch, David; and Knightley, Phillip. THE PHILBY CONSPIRACY. Garden City, N.Y.: Doubleday, 1968. 300 p.

Selected Bibliography

Peyroles, Jacques [Gilles Perrault]. THE RED ORCHESTRA. Translated by Peter Wiles. New York: Simon & Schuster, 1969. xi, 511 p. Bibliography, photographs, illustrations.

Pinto, Oreste. SPY CATCHER. New York: Harper & Bros., 1952. 213 p.

Ransom, Harry Howe. THE INTELLIGENCE ESTABLISHMENT. Cambridge, Mass.: Harvard University Press, 1970. 309 p. Index, selective bibliography, notes.

Rositzke, Harry. THE CIA'S SECRET OPERATIONS. ESPIONAGE, COUNTER-ESPIONAGE, AND COVERT ACTION. Introduction by Arthur M. Schlesinger, Jr. Pleasantville, N.Y.: Reader's Digest Press, 1977. 286 p. Index.

Rowan, Richard Wilmer, with Deindorfer, Robert G. SECRET SERVICE: THIRTY-THREE CENTURIES OF ESPIONAGE. New York: Hawthorn Books, 1967. xi, 786 p. Index, notes.

Smith, Richard Harris. OSS: THE SECRET HISTORY OF AMERICA'S FIRST CENTRAL INTELLIGENCE AGENCY. Berkeley and Los Angeles: University of California Press, 1972. xii, 458 p. Index, bibliography, notes, illustrations.

Spiro, Edward [Edward H. Cookridge]. GEHLEN: SPY OF THE CENTURY. New York: Random House, 1972. 402 p. Index of names, bibliography, organization chart, illustrations.

Stevenson, William. A MAN CALLED INTREPID: THE SECRET WAR. New York: Harcourt Brace Jovanovich, 1976. xxv, 486 p. Index, maps, organization chart, illustrations.

Strong, Sir Kenneth. MEN OF INTELLIGENCE: A STUDY OF THE ROLES AND DECISIONS OF CHIEFS OF INTELLIGENCE FROM WORLD WAR I TO THE PRESENT DAY. New York: St. Martin's Press, 1971. 183 p.

Tuchman, Barbara W. THE ZIMMERMANN TELEGRAM. New York: Viking Press, 1958. 244 p. Index, bibliography, notes.

Ungar, Sanford J. FBI: AN UNCENSORED LOOK BEHIND THE WALLS. Boston: Little, Brown and Co., 1976. 682 p. Index, bibliography, organization chart, appendix, illustrations.

Whaley, Barton. CODEWORD BARBAROSSA. Cambridge, Mass.: M.I.T. Press, 1973. x, 376 p. Index, bibliography, notes, appendices, glossary, maps, illustrations.

Whitehead, Don. THE FBI STORY. New York: Random House, 1956. 368 p. Index, notes.

Wilensky, Harold L. ORGANIZATIONAL INTELLIGENCE: KNOWLEDGE AND POLICY IN GOVERNMENT AND INDUSTRY. New York: Basic Books, 1967. 226 p. Index, bibliography, charts.

Winterbotham, Frederick W. THE ULTRA SECRET. New York: Harper & Row, 1974. xiii, 199 p. Index.

Wise, David. THE AMERICAN POLICE STATE: THE GOVERNMENT AGAINST THE PEOPLE. New York: Random House, 1976. 437 p. Index, author's notes.

Wohlstetter, Roberta. PEARL HARBOR: WARNING AND DECISION. Stanford, Calif.: Stanford University Press, 1962. 426 p. Index, bibliography, illustrations.

Wynne, Greville. CONTACT ON GORKY STREET. New York: Atheneum, 1968. 222 p. Portraits, illustrations.

AUTHOR INDEX

This index is primarily a reference list of the authors of the works cited in the text. Also indexed are the names of editors, translators, and those credited with authorship of an introduction or forward. Often these persons have been experienced intelligence officials and their names will be known to American readers. The names of figures important to the history and development of intelligence, and about whom the authors have written, are also recorded. Alphabetization is letter by letter. Underlined numbers refer to main areas of emphasis within the entry subject.

Author Index

Author Index

Ford, Corey 147, 162, 204, 205
Ford, President Gerald 87, 89, 90, 91
Forsyth, Frederick 174
Foster, G. Allen 163
Fouche, Joseph 162
Fourcade, Marie Madeleine 145
Fow, Matthew H. 85
Fox, Edward Lyell 165
Fraenkel, Heinrich 160
Freedman, Larry 32
Friendly, Alfred, Jr. 182-83
Frisbee, John L. 116
Froehlke, Secretary Robert F. 82
Fuchs, Klaus 88, 113
Fulbright, Sen. William J. 92
Fuller, Jean Overton 181, 200
Furash, Edward E. 135

G

Galland, Joseph Stanislaus 5
Galloway, Alec 116
Ganier-Raymond, Phillipe 187-88, 222
Garby-Czerniawski, Roman 200
Garthoff, Raymond L. 23, 62
Garwin, Richard L. 116
Gatewood, R.D. 42
Gee, Winifred 88
Gehlen, Gen. Reinhard 160, 161
Gentry, Curt 113
Germain, Jean Rene 116
Gibney, Frank 99, 148, 150
Gillers, Stephen 85, 86
Ginsburg, Samuel 152
Giskes, H.J. 73, 179, 188, 222, 226
Glass, Gen. Robert R. 62
Goddard, George W. 108
Godfrey, E. Drexel, Jr. 76
Goldberg, David M. 80
Gosselin, Louis Leon Theodore 163
Goudsmit, Samuel 105, 108, 109
Goulden, Joseph C. 32
Goulding, Phil G. 76
Gouzenko, Igor 152
Graham, Gen. Daniel O. 43
Gramont, Sanche de. See Morgan, Ted
Granovsky, Anatoli 153
Grant, Robert M. 62

Gravel, Sen. Michael 56, 212, 226
Graves, Armgaard Karl 165
Green, Constantine M. 109
Greene, Graham 174
Greene, Richard 133, 135
Greenwood, Ted 116-17
Groth, Alexander 43
Gubbins, Sir Colin 200
Guisan, General Henri 28
Gunzenhauser, Max 3, 20, 25, 133
Gwynne, Peter 182-83

H

Hagen, Louis 140, 161, 227
Hagen, Walter 25-26
Haggard, William. See Clayton, Richard Henry Michael
Hahn, James E. 27, 165
Haigh, Anthony 167
Halberstam, David 212-13
Hall, Roger 206
Hall, Adm. Sir William 124-25
Halloran, Richard 90
Halperin, Morton H. 38, 86
Hamilton, Andrew 43
Hamilton, Peter 133, 135-36
Hari, Mata 143-44, 146
Harkness, Gladys 43-44
Harkness, Richard 43-44
Harriman, Ambassador Averell 180, 211
Harris, Dixie R. 125
Harris, Don R. 76
Harris, William R. 3
Harrison, Wilson R. 223-24
Hart, B.H. Liddell 23
Haukelid, Knut Anders 113, 200
Haven, Violet S. 5
Hay, John H., Jr. 63
Hays, Robert G. 63-64
Heiman, Grover 72, 109
Heiman, Leo 151
Helms, Richard M. 44, 47, 48, 49, 50
Hersh, Seymour M. 44, 87, 90-91, 117
Heymont, Colonel Irving 63
Higgins, Jack 174
Hilsman, Roger 32-33, 44, 213, 227

Author Index

Author Index

Rogers, Warren, Jr. 183
Ronblom, H.K, 181-82
Roosevelt, Kermit 204
Roots, Peter C. 109
Rosenberg, Ethel and Julius 144
Rosenthal, Jack 49
Rositzke, Harry 81, 196, 214, 228
Roskill, S.W. 66
Ross, Thomas B. 24, 36, 142
Rossler, Rudolf 169-70
Rothchild, John 71
Rowan, Richard Wilmer 9, 141-42, 166, 228
Ruggles, Richard 118
Runzheimer, Juergen 221
Rutland, Frederick J. 159

S

Samuels, Charles 183-84
Sanderson, James Dean 113
Sansom, Alfred W. 185
Sapin, Burton M. 49
Sargeant, Howland H. 217
Savant, Jean 163
Savinkov, Boris 22
Schaf, Col. Frank L., Jr. 18
Schellenberg, Walter 25, 64, 161, 221
Schemmer, Benjamin F. 67
Schlesinger, Arthur M., Jr. 214, 228
Schlesinger, James R. 49
Schwarzelder, John 185
Scotland, A.P. 157
Scott, Andrew M. 196
Scoville, Herbert, Jr. 45
Seegar, Murray 103
Senate. Committee on Aeronautical and Space Programs 120
Senate. Committee on Armed Services 54, 120
Senate. Committee on Foreign Relations 69, 94-95
Senate. Committee on Government Operations 54
Senate. Committee on Naval Affairs 54
Senate. Committee on Rules and Regulations 55

Senate. Committee on the Judiciary 21-22, 54, 83, 95, 151, 217-218, 224
Senate. Select Committee to Study Government Operations with Respect to Intelligence Activities 18, 95, 215-16
Sergeyev, F. 21
Seth, Ronald 9-10, 29, 142, 143, 150-51, 166, 201
Sewell, Tom 206
Shabad, Theodore 103
Shearer, Lloyd 92, 208
Sheehan, Neil 56
Sheldon, Dr. Charles S. II 120, 123
Sheppard, Lancelot C. 168-69
Shirer, William L. 221
Shloss, Leon 82
Silber, Julius 166
Simons, Howard 119
Sinclair, Upton Beall 176
Singer, Kurt D. 142, 146
Sinkov, Abraham 125
Slade, Barbara 145
Slater, Leonard 113-14
Slessor, Air Force Marshall Sir John 126
Slusser, Robert M. 101, 151
Smith, A.M. Sheridan 169-70
Smith, Edward E. 100
Smith, John T. 114
Smith, Joseph Burkholder 214
Smith, Mark E. 49
Smith, Richard Harris 203, 205, 210, 228
Soble, Jack and Myra 183
Solzhenitsyn, Alexander 104
Sorge, Richard 104, 151, 152
Sosnowski, Juri de 153
Special Supplement to Village Voice 48
Spiro, Edward 146, 151, 161, 182, 198, 228
Stagg, J.M. 67
Stahl, Lydia Von 146
Starnes, Richard 176
Starr, Capt. John 181
State, Department of. See U.S. Department of State
Stead, Philip John 27, 67
Steele, Congressman Robert H. 38

238

TITLE INDEX

In this index the titles of scholarly and general works, reports, monographs, memoirs and biographies are capitalized and underlined. The titles of articles from journals, newspapers, news magazines, and periodicals are in lower case print and placed within quotation marks. Titles of espionage fiction are capitalized, but not underlined. Subtitles of nonfiction works are not included except where the main title provides no clear indication of the substance or subject. Additional information on substance or subject is sometimes added, in brackets, when the title and subtitle lack this assistance to the reader. Alphabetization is letter by letter. In some cases titles have been shortened.

A

ABEL 152
"A-Bomb That Never Was, The" 113
ABOVE SUSPICION 175
"Access by [Capital] Hill to CIA Data Recommended" 45
ACCOUNTABILITY, A MATTER OF THE TRUE STORY OF THE PUEBLO AFFAIR 123
ACE OF SPIES 155
ACROSS TO NORWAY 132
Act to Provide for the Administration of the CIA 53
ADMIRAL DARLAN, THE MURDER OF 209
"AEC Chief to Replace Helms as CIA Director" 49
AERIAL PHOTOGRAPHY, MANUAL OF 114
AERIAL PHOTOGRAPHY: THE STORY OF AERIAL MAPPING RECONNAISSANCE 109
AGENT IN PLACE 175

AGENT IN PLACE, AN. THE WENNERSTROM AFFAIR 155
AGENTS OF DECEIT: FRAUDS, FORGERIES AND POLITICAL INTRIGUE AMONG NATIONS 223
AIR SPY 107, 144
ALDO, ICARDI: AMERICAN MASTER SPY 206
ALLEGED ASSASSINATION PLOTS INVOLVING FOREIGN LEADERS [CIA] 215
ALLIED INTELLIGENCE BUREAU 59, 63
ALLOCATION OF RESOURCES IN THE SOVIET UNION AND CHINA-- 1975: HEARINGS 55-56
ALSOS 105, 108-9
ALSOS MISSION, THE 105, 113
AMATEUR AGENT 199
AMBASSADORS AND SECRET AGENTS 139
AMERICA, SECRET AGENTS AGAINST 166
AMERICAN BLACK CHAMBER, THE 127

Title Index

Title Index

Title Index